Learning Race and Ethnicity

Youth and Digital Media

Edited by Anna Everett

The MIT Press
Cambridge, Massachusetts
London, England

For information about special quantity discounts, please email special_sales@mitpress.mit.edu.

This book was set in Stone sans and Stone serif by Aptara, Inc.

Printed and bound in the United States of America.

Library of Congress Cataloging-in-Publication Data

Learning race and ethnicity : youth and digital media / edited by Anna Everett.
     p.   cm.—(The John D. and Catherine T. Macarthur Foundation series on digital media and learning)
Includes bibliographical references.
ISBN 978-0-262-05091-3 (hardcover : alk. paper)—ISBN 978-0-262-55067-3 (pbk. : alk. paper)
1. Race relations.   2. Ethnic relations.   3. Internet—Social aspects.
4. Technology—Social aspects.   I. Everett, Anna, 1954–
HT1521.R23519   2008
305.8—dc22   2007029780

10 9 8 7 6 5 4 3 2 1

CONTENTS

Foreword

In recent years, digital media and networks have become embedded in our everyday lives, and are part of broad-based changes to how we engage in knowledge production, communication, and creative expression. Unlike the early years in the development of computers and computer-based media, digital media are now *commonplace* and *pervasive*, having been taken up by a wide range of individuals and institutions in all walks of life. Digital media have escaped the boundaries of professional and formal practice, and the academic, governmental, and industry homes that initially fostered their development. Now they have been taken up by diverse populations and non-institutionalized practices, including the peer activities of youth. Although specific forms of technology uptake are highly diverse, a generation is growing up in an era where digital media are part of the taken-for-granted social and cultural fabric of learning, play, and social communication.

In 2005, The John D. and Catherine T. MacArthur Foundation began a new grant-making initiative in the area of digital media and learning. An initial set of exploratory grants in the study of youth practices and the development of digital literacy programs has expanded into a major initiative spanning research, educational reform, and technology development. One component of this effort is the support of this book series. As part of the broader MacArthur Foundation initiative, this series is aimed at timely dissemination of new scholarship, fostering an interdisciplinary conversation, and archiving the best research in this emerging field. Through the course of producing the six initial volumes, the foundation convened a set of meetings to discuss the framing issues for this book series. As a result of these discussions we identified a set of shared commitments and areas of focus. Although we recognize that the terrain is being reshaped even as we seek to identify it, we see these as initial frames for the ongoing work to be put forward by this series.

This book series is founded upon the working hypothesis that those immersed in new digital tools and networks are engaged in an unprecedented exploration of language, games, social interaction, problem solving, and self-directed activity that leads to diverse forms of learning. These diverse forms of learning are reflected in expressions of identity, how individuals express independence and creativity, and in their ability to learn, exercise judgment, and think systematically.

The defining frame for this series is not a particular theoretical or disciplinary approach, nor is it a fixed set of topics. Rather, the series revolves around a constellation of topics investigated from multiple disciplinary and practical frames. The series as a whole looks at the relation between youth, learning, and digital media, but each book or essay might deal with only a subset of this constellation. Erecting strict topical boundaries can exclude some of the most important work in the field. For example, restricting the content of the series only to people of a certain age means artificially reifying an age boundary when the phenomenon demands otherwise. This becomes particularly problematic with new forms of online participation where one important outcome is the mixing of participants of different ages. The same goes for digital media, which are increasingly inseparable from analog and earlier media forms.

In the case of learning, digital media are part of the redefinition and broadening of existing boundaries of practice and our understanding of what learning means. The term *learning* was chosen rather than *education* in order to flag an interest in settings both within and outside the classroom. Many of the more radical challenges to existing learning agendas are happening in domains such as gaming, online networks, and amateur production that usually occur in informal and non-institutional settings. This does not mean we are prejudiced against learning as it happens in the classroom or other formal educational settings. Rather, we hope to initiate a dialog about learning as it spans settings that are more explicitly educational and those that are not.

The series and the MacArthur Foundation initiative respond to certain changes in our media ecology that have important implications for learning. Specifically, these are new forms of media *literacy* and changes in the modes of media *participation*. Digital media are part of a convergence between interactive media (most notably gaming), online networks, and existing media forms. Navigating this media ecology involves a palette of literacies that are being defined through practice but require more scholarly scrutiny before they can be fully incorporated pervasively into educational initiatives. Media literacy involves not only ways of understanding, interpreting, and critiquing media, but also the means for creative and social expression, online search and navigation, and a host of new technical skills. The potential gap in literacies and participation skills creates new challenges for educators who struggle to bridge media engagement inside and outside the classroom.

The shift toward interactive media, peer-to-peer forms of media communication, and many-to-many forms of distribution relate to types of participation that are more bottom-up and driven by the "user" or "consumer" of media. Audiences have always had the opportunity to "talk back" to corporate media or to create their own local media forms. However, the growing dominance of gaming as a media format, the advent of low-cost digital production tools, and online distribution means a much more dynamic range in who participates and how they participate in the production and distribution of media. Gamers expect that media are subject to player control. Add to this the fact that all forms of media are increasingly being contextualized in an online communication ecology where creative production and expression is inseparable from social communication. Finally, new low-cost digital production tools mean that amateur and casual media creators can author, edit, and distribute video and other rich media forms that were once prohibitively expensive to produce and share with others.

We value the term *participation* for the ways in which it draws attention to situated learning theory, social media literacies, and mobilized forms of media engagement. Digital media networks support existing forms of mass media distribution as well as smaller publics and collectivities that might center on peer groups or specialized niche interests. The presence of social communication, professional media, and amateur niche media in shared online spaces introduces a kind of leveling effect, where small media players gain new visibility and the position of previously authoritative media is challenged. The clash between more socially driven or niche publics and the publics defined by professional forms of media is playing out in high-profile battles in domains such as intellectual property law, journalism, entertainment, and government. For our purposes, the questions surrounding knowledge and credibility and young people's use of digital media to circumvent adult authority are particularly salient.

The emerging power shift, where smaller and edge players are gaining more visibility and voice, is particularly important to children and youth. If we look at children and youth through the lens of digital media, we have a population that has been historically subject to a high degree of systematic and institutional control in the kinds of information and social communication to which they have access. This is one reason why the alchemy between youth and digital media has been distinctive; it disrupts the existing set of power relations between adult authority and youth voice. While many studies of children, youth, and media have for decades stressed the status of young people as competent and full social subjects, digital media increasingly insist that we acknowledge this viewpoint. Not only must we see youth as legitimate social and political actors, but we must also recognize them as potential innovators and drivers of new media change.

This does not mean that we are uncritical of youth practices or that we believe that digital media necessarily hold the key to empowerment. Rather, we argue against technological determinism, stressing the need for balanced scholarship that recognizes the importance of our current moment within the context of existing structures and unfolding histories. This means placing contemporary changes within a historical context as well as working to highlight the diversity in the landscape of media and media uptake. Neither youth nor digital media are monolithic categories; documenting how specific youth take up particular forms of media with diverse learning outcomes is critical to this series as a whole. Digital media take the form they do because they are created by existing social and cultural contexts, contexts that are diverse and stratified.

As with earlier shifts in media environments, this current turn toward digital media and networks has been accompanied by fear and panic as well as elevated hopes. This is particularly true of adult perception of children and youth who are at the forefront of experimentation with new media forms, and who mobilize digital media to push back at existing structures of power and authority. While some see "digital kids" as our best hope for the future, others worry that new media are part of a generational rift and a dangerous turn away from existing standards for knowledge, literacy, and civic engagement. Careful, socially engaged, and accessible scholarship is crucial to informing this public debate and related policy decisions. Our need to understand the relation between digital media and learning is urgent because of the scale and the speed of the changes that are afoot. The shape and uses of digital media are still very much in flux, and this book series seeks to be part of the definition of our sociotechnical future.

Mizuko Ito
Cathy Davidson
Henry Jenkins
Carol Lee
Michael Eisenberg
Joanne Weiss
Series Advisors

Introduction

Anna Everett

University of California, Santa Barbara, Department of Film and Media Studies

Children are at the epicenter of the information revolution, ground zero of the digital world . . . Children can for the first time reach past the suffocating boundaries of social convention, past their elders' rigid notions of what is good for them. —John Katz[1]

The Digital Divide is not just about putting free PCs in the hands of the underserved. It's about helping people empower themselves using technology. —Nettrice Gaskins[2]

People can be hurtful on the Internet to women, calling them names and saying they have no opinion on important topics. The racist people on the Internet may send mean messages calling black or foreign people names or sending pictures of racist events. People are hurtful because they will never see the others they are being racist or sexist against. —Adam S.[3]

This volume appears at an auspicious moment in the development and pervasive spread of digital media technologies into all realms of American society and culture. Our usage of the term *auspicious* in this context is quite deliberate and apropos for this investigation of digital media at the interface of race and ethnicity because it denotes a promising, fortunate, and propitious outcome.[4] Given the increasing affordability of computers and other digital technologies, and especially their ubiquity in the lives of American youth across racial and ethnic divides, this is precisely the right timing for this volume and its contribution to the MacArthur Foundation's visionary Digital Media and Learning (DMAL) initiative launched in 2006. In fact, it will become apparent that, upon reflection, issues surrounding the rates of digital media diffusion among youths of color are at once very complex and rather simple, as the chapters comprising this volume readily attest. Thus, it becomes important to note that our optimism about the nexus of race and ethnicity, youth cultures, and digital media technologies at this historical juncture is not a contemporary retread of earlier utopian notions that tended to posit information technologies (IT) as a panacea for what ails contemporary humankind.

As the chapters collected here demonstrate, our guarded enthusiasm for digital media technologies as beneficial in the lives of minority youths is not a case of positive technological determinism. But rather is tempered by our recognition of, but not resignation to, the undeniable consequences of a persistent inequality in the deep structures of our nation's IT economy. At the same time, it is difficult not to be optimistic about the myriad ways minority youths today successfully appropriate digital media tools to speak truth to power, to enliven the promises of a digital democracy, and to retrofit what I have been calling "the digital public sphere" to suit their own generational concerns and agendas. Exemplary in this regard are: (1) the 2001 use of the Web by "conscious" hip-hop artist KRS-One to promote and organize his 4th annual Hip Hop Appreciation Week in New York City, with a theme of "Charity," and the overarching goal of "decriminalizing" hip-hop's public image;[5] (2) the massive 2006 protests against U.S. congressman Jim Sensenbrenner's Immigration Reform Bill HR4437, organized largely by Latino/a, Chicana/o youths using cell phones and the social networking site MySpace, among other media tools, to mobilize hundreds of thousands of people to boycott school and work to take their grievances to the streets of such cities as Los Angeles, Washington, DC, and Detroit, to name a few;[6] (3) the efforts of activist youths from the Global Kids organization (which has an enormous minority youth constituency) to amplify their voices and concerns online, and to preserve a dedicated teen space in the popular 3-D virtual community called *Second Life*,[7] from the encroachments of adults, among other critically conscious uses.

Of course the three exemplars above represent a microcosm of the much larger, and more far-reaching, phenomenon of youth engagement with digital media, for both good and ill. This notion of a benefit/threat dialectic is at the crux of our concern with digital media learning as a double-edged sword cutting through the life experiences of youths of color. And whether or not we subscribe to the accepting, technophilic, view or its negating, technophobic, counterview, there is no going back to a nostalgic, predigital existence. This is certainly the case for youth today who, as Don Tapscott puts it, "are growing up digital."[8] With this reality in full view, the authors in this volume have identified some important aspects of our emergent digital culture and their consequences for young people of color and our society at large. They also raise some necessary and provocative questions, and ultimately they proffer some significant new directions for future work and play as we race to tame cyberspace.

What's Race and Ethnicity Got to Do With It?

In the early to mid-1990s, the national discourse on race matters and technological progress was defined by the now very familiar and persistent trope of the "digital divide." At issue here is the power of this discourse to construct and naturalize an IT insider/outsider binary opposition that easily casts underrepresented racial minority groups, in general, and youths, in particular, literally as poster children for what I argue is too often the disabling rhetoric of the digital divide. As I argue elsewhere:

The overwhelming characterizations of the brave new world of cyberspace as primarily a racialized sphere of whiteness inhere in popular constructions of high-tech and low-tech spheres that too often consign black [and other minority] bodies to the latter with the latter being insignificant if not absent altogether.[9]

For those of us working in the area of digital media technologies and society, the National Telecommunications and Information Administration's 1995 study "Falling Through the Net: A Survey of the 'Have-Nots' in Rural and Urban America"[10] is a crucial document, a statistical touchstone. This 1995 report, and its subsequent "Falling Through the Net" follow-up studies, are often the point of departure for most serious discussion of inequities in technology access found in America during these early years, and still persisting today. See especially Tyrone Taborn's critique (in this volume) of how the report has been used as an alibi for costly failures in several ill-conceived attempts to redress disparities between the information haves and have-nots among underserved groups on the basis of race and class locations. It is interesting that this notion of a technology gap, signified by communities of information haves and have-nots, and the phrase "digital divide," got traction among proponents of universal access and the public at large at roughly the same time. For me, the suspicion has been with the unanticipated consequence or function of the digital divide rhetoric to become a self-fulfilling prophecy, an alibi for the precipitous de-funding of universal access programs and community technology centers in impoverished rural and urban spaces in the post-Clinton and post–September 11 eras. Still, I was surprised by the etymology of the digital divide as the metaphor of choice for race and technology matters in the nation's popular imaginary.

In January 2000, Steve Cisler wrote the article "Hot Button: Online Haves vs. Have-Nots: Subtract the 'Digital Divide'" for the *San Jose Mercury News*. He was quite wrong in predicting that the phrase *digital divide* would have a short shelf-life and thereby "last no longer than the buzz words 'infobahn' and 'techno-realism' did." But his tracing of the phrase to its first appearance in print and its later uptake by certain IT sectors is revealing. Writing about the 1999 *ah-ha* moment when policy experts, high-tech executives, and nonprofit organizations discovered the phrase *digital divide*, Cisler reminds us that, although "it has a nice ring to it," we should be wary because

it's simplistic [and] insulting to some. . . . Even those who embrace the term now may not realize the meaning has shifted over the past four years. In 1996, Amy Harmon, then a journalist at the *Los Angeles Times*, wrote a story about the split between a husband who spent a great deal of time online and the wife who felt alienated from him because of his obsession with computers. Harmon called this a "digital divide." In another article a writer characterized the battle of the digital television standard as a "digital divide."

Of particular saliency for our purpose, Cisler continues:

The roots of the current meaning arose about the same time. Allen Hammond, a law professor at New York Law School and Larry Irving, a political appointee at the Department of Commerce who headed up the National Telecommunications and Information Administration, began using the term in public speeches to characterize the split between those who owned computers and were online and various classes of Americans, including women, blacks, American Indians, the disabled, rural and low-income Americans, who were not. Irving's use of the phrase has become a kind of alliterative shorthand that some groups, especially non-profits serving the disadvantaged have found helpful in raising money and calling attention to the lack of equity in access to digital tools and resources. . . . Masking the complexity of both online users and the Americans offline by using such a simplistic phrase will not help solve the problems of inequity.[11]

This lengthy quotation encapsulates quite clearly the power and resilience of this term to bridge several divides—historical, ideological, fiscal, and so forth; hence its cultural longevity, contrary to Cisler's miscalculation. It is impossible to address matters of race, technology, and society without confronting Irving's remediation of Harmon's digital divide concept along gender lines. "Perhaps," as Cisler observes, "this term is fitting for the digital age."[12]

Our aim, however, is to intervene in this crucial issue outside of the usual or familiar binary rhetorics of information haves and have-nots, technophiles and technophobes, information rich and poor, etc., and certainly beyond the problematics of the race- and class-based digital divide rhetoric of limits discussed above. To this end, Dara N. Byrne, Tyrone D. Taborn, and Antonio López turn the traditional digital divide logic on its head, with their specific case studies, discourse analyses, critical ethnographies, and historical revisions that explode essentialist constructions of minority youth as low-tech, IT outsiders. Raiford Guins, and coauthors Chela Sandoval and Guisela Latorre give us an exciting glimpse into the realm of digital art practices and entrepreneurial fervor rarely considered in connection with youth of color.

Understand, though, that no disavowal of the very real structural inequalities and disparities undermining our society is proffered here as we keep in view what Jan A. G. M. van Dijk calls "the deepening divide"[13] in our present-day information society. In fact, Jessie Daniels, Douglas Thomas, and coauthors Mohan Dutta, Graham Bodie, and Ambar Basu recalibrate our technophilic visions by demonstrating that digital media have not failed to eradicate familiar racial fault lines in our information age, but have introduced new racial divides and novel strategies for preserving what George Lipsitz has termed "the possessive investment in whiteness."[14] Although the rhetoric of the digital divide survives as a twenty-first-century master narrative, this book makes the case unequivocally that it is not the only narrative of significance where race and ethnicity, youth, and the information economy converge.

This returns us to the question posed earlier: What's race and ethnicity got to do with it? While some might think it is easy to dismiss Global Kids' Jackson K, and his sentiment that "there is little discrimination in the digital world,"[15] those of us who are scholars, skeptics, and enthusiasts for digital media learning and youth are advised to heed Jan A. G. M. van Dijk's warning that, indeed, *deepening* "divides are byproducts of old inequalities, digital technology is intensifying inequalities, and new inequalities are appearing."[16] Still, Alexander G. Weheliye observes that "while gender and sexuality have been crucial to theories of both cyberspace and the posthuman, the absence of race is perfunctorily remarked and of little consequence to these analyses."[17] Weheliye's remarks in the context of black music practices echoed my own longstanding concern that "From 1995 to the present . . . the structured absences of black [and by extension other minority] bodies that have marked most popular imaginings of the brave new world order were in danger of reifying [or naturalizing] an updated myth of black intellectual lag, or black Technophobia."[18]

This *Learning Race and Ethnicity* volume answers a more important question about what race has to do with IT. Our survey of youth and digital media technology addresses one of the most persistent, and difficult topics to engage honestly, clearly, empathetically, and with an informed understanding of the multivalent race and ethnicity issues that form, deform, and reform twenty-first-century American culture. That said, it should hardly be surprising that our volume revolves around a range of questions and issues pertaining to race and ethnicity. For example, how are race and ethnicity presented, represented, known, and understood generally in digital media interactions and transactions, such as in game-play, online databases, friendship/social networks, blogs, grassroots community organizing, listservs, IMs, and SMS (short message service), and so forth? Similarly, the authors in this volume raise questions about how race and ethnicity still influence specific contours of online and other digital activities that are too often obfuscated or marginalized in the mainstream public sphere, for example, the prevalence of hate speech online and cyberbullying on social network sites. The nation's penchant for disavowing its "possessive investment in whiteness" is supported by mainstream media discourses of exceptionalism where societal racism is concerned. By sensationalizing a recent spate of high-profile celebrity utterances of racist hate speech, the mainstream media perpetuate attitudes about racism as unfortunate, exceptional blights that occasionally erupt on America's presumed postracist, color-blind, and racially tolerant body politic. Here, I include the well-publicized cases of film star Mel Gibson's anti-Semitic tirade directed at a California police officer in July 2006; Michael

Richards's (of *Seinfeld* TV show fame) racist rant against black hecklers at a Los Angles comedy club in November 2006 (he calls the hecklers "niggers," among other shocking remarks); actor Isaiah Washington's homophobic slur against a fellow actor on the hit TV show *Grey's Anatomy* in 2006 (he calls a coworker a "faggot"); and the "shock jock" Don Imus's infamous racist and sexist diatribes in April 2007 against Rutgers University's predominately black women's basketball team (he calls the young women "nappy-headed hos"). It is significant, for our purposes, that all but one of these stories came to light after appearing first on the Internet, not in the traditional mainstream media.[19] This fact is important for our volume because it is the case that youths get their news and information primarily from the Internet and other digital media forms, not from newspapers or television. More important is our concern that rarely does the problem of endemic, institutional racism that still defines key aspects of our civil society get a hearing, whether through traditional or digital media outlets. These are some of the questions and concerns guiding the essays in this book.

More immediately, our current focus on issues of race and ethnicity, youth cultures, and demographics is rightfully juxtaposed to recent histories of mainstream digital technologies and discourses during the early years of technological expansion. For example, in the early years of the Internet's massification, there was a popular cartoon depicting a dog typing on a personal computer with a caption reading, "Nobody knows you're a dog on the Internet." Around this same time, in the early to mid-1990s, the telecom giant MCI produced a compelling TV commercial claiming that there are no races, no genders, and no infirmities in the new world of the Internet because here "people can communicate mind to mind." These popular examples were clearly symptomatic of the nation's desire to imagine and construct colorblind or hypertolerant virtual communities and digital public spheres through the Internet's text-driven digital environments during the late 1980s and early 1990s.

Today, however, the popularity and pervasiveness of static and moving visual images in digital media produced by ubiquitous digital cameras, cell phone and mobile cams, Web cams, streaming video, audio, and so on mean that now everyone knows if you're a dog on MySpace and elsewhere in the digital domain. And the color of the dog counts. This innovation of the graphical user interface (GUI) has served to reinstate the raced human body at the center of academic and popular debates about posthumanism, cyberculture, technoculture, gaming culture, and now even post-cyberpunk culture, where some important theorizing and research have begun in earnest to reconsider matters of race and ethnicity in the information age. We offer this volume as an important next step in pushing still further from margin to center this important and vexing topic.

Structure and Organization

There are a total of eight essays in this volume, and they are organized along three specific lines of inquiry. Under the first rubric, entitled, "Future Visions and Excavated Pasts," are the chapters of Dara N. Bryne and Tyrone D. Taborn, whose investigations offer compelling discourses indicative of present and future directions for minority youth, who are transforming the rules of virtual and online identity politics. An important historical dimension is foregrounded here as well to provide a necessary corrective to a systemic erasure of the rightful claim youths and larger communities of color have on today's information society and economy. For mainstream youths and youths of color, it is essential that their "situated knowledges" of our society's current digital media environment include their underrepresented groups' historical legacies of contribution and participation as they steel themselves for the challenges of the global information society.

Key features in the two leading chapters are formulations of new strategies for e-racing familiar aspects of the digital divide and identity politics. Byrne and Taborn address in their own ways the continuing failure of our society to achieve universal access to and partic- ipation in our information economy for all racial and ethnic groups, in what many view as our post–Civil Rights era. At the same time, each one stresses the amazing strides made historically by underserved minority youth and their larger community groups to bridge the technology gap despite formidable structural obstacles (e.g., governmental de-funding, IT industry employment outsourcing and indifference, and other barriers to full participation in the information economy). Their work enables us to assess the current state of minority in- clusion/exclusion in a complex digital culture and a concomitant networked society. A major aspect of their research involves historicizing racial and ethnic minority populations' inno- vative uses of information technologies and their scientific contributions to the technology revolution as a necessary precondition for ensuring a strategy of community sustainability through digital media learning for present and future generations of underserved groups.

Byrne's chapter, entitled "The Future of (the) Race: Identity, Discourse, and the Rise of Computer-mediated Public Spheres," looks at minority youths' proto–social networking sites prior to the advent of MySpace, Facebook, and others. What is particularly revealing about this chapter is its unexpected honesty concerning racially dedicated Web sites. For, despite the hype of and hope for colorblind digital spaces, Byrne reveals the fact of renewed interest in and practices of community building specifically dedicated to racial and ethnic identity positions, particularly after September 11. Using case studies such as AsianAvenue.com, BlackPlanet.com, and MiGente.com, this chapter follows these sites' respective discussion threads to understand the persistence of such racialized online communities.

Where Byrne addresses the current, and likely future, contours of minority youths' en- gagement with digital media in terms of identity formation and preservation, Tyrone D. Taborn's chapter, "Separating Race from Technology: Finding Tomorrow's IT Progress in the Past," provides a needed historical overview of key technology leaders and innovators from underrepresented groups. It also considers the importance of excavating and incorporating these often ignored histories into educational programs targeting our nation's so-called at- risk youth and those underserved young people from ethnic and racial minority groups. For Taborn there is an obvious flaw in the digital divide rhetoric that authorizes short-sighted approaches to bridging the technology gap in schools located in underserved and underrep- resented communities, urban and rural alike. He argues convincingly that "the prevailing views rely on the notion that closing the digital divide is primarily about providing techno- logical artifacts, not creating technological literates."

The next section of the book focuses on "Oppositional Art Practices in the Digital Do- main." Raiford Guins, Chela Sandoval and Guisela Latorre, and Antonio López facilitate our encounter with youth artists from African American, Chicano/a, and Native American com- munities and their creative processes involving digitizing youth cultural practices both on- and offline. That youth, as a result of being "born digital," are very technology savvy is not news to anyone. However, the extent to which minority youths are not merely consumers of IT but also talented producers of digital media (what some dub "prosumers," combining the terms *producer* and *consumer*, with a distinct privileging of the former) may be surprising to many. Their discussions consider how youths from various racial and ethnic backgrounds create music, art, and political networks and communities, both online and in the real world. From socially and politically conscious African American hip-hop music culture to "rock the vote," so to speak, the community mural projects and the Latino/a, Chicano/a anti-immigration protests, this chapter will explore how youths themselves express their varied experiences and talents to productive ends with digital media technologies.

Raiford Guins introduces us to this culture of entrepreneurial prosumers in his chapter, "Hip-Hop 2.0." Guins explores how contemporary youth culture, particularly hip-hop music entrepreneurs, and hip-hop artists (such as KRS-One, for instance), increasingly use the Internet to circulate politically conscious rap music beyond the profit motive. They galvanize their fan bases for progressive grassroots community benefits and organizing, political activism, and other modes of counter-hegemonic activities. Hip-hop artists, Guins shows, are now masterful in their deployment of digital media to send and receive messages and images beyond the legal, economic, and social restrictions governing big, powerful mainstream media conglomerates, and the Big Box distribution chains like Wal-Mart.

From the digitized performing arts to the fine arts of drawing and painting, Chela Sandoval and Guisela Latorre guide us through a theoretical and practical admixture of virtual and material cultural borderlands. Their chapter, "Chicana/o Artivism: Judy Baca's Digital Work with Youth of Color," is an amazing ethnographic journey through intergenerational Chicano/a oppositional cultural production. They track an important shift in the history of Chicano/a community muralism in California as the popular art practice migrates from the real community spaces to the digital realm. Through what I want to describe as an ethnoanalysis of Chicana mural artists, Judy Baca's work with Chicano/a youth from the 1970s to the present day, Sandoval and Latorre consider how under Baca's tutelage, Chicana girls are empowered to participate in virtual and real-life community art and activism usually dominated by Chicano boys and men as popular muralists and taggers. Framed by Chela Sandoval's influential works on "methodologies of the oppressed," and decolonizing cyberspace pedagogy, the chapter combines digital media theory and praxis as manifest in contemporary Chicano/a communities.

Antonio López shares his years of community organizing as a technology worker with several Native American nations and their unique approaches to and engagements with digital media literacy. His chapter, entitled "Circling the Cross: Bridging Native America, Education, and Digital Media Literacy," is insightful and revealing along several lines. In the main, López considers how digital media education is being practiced in First Nation or Native American communities at the moment that the War on Terror functions to redirect funding away from community tech centers among the nation's underserved minority populations. Of particular interest here is how digital learning occurs not in school but in untraditional and informal environments, outside of what might be considered the U.S. government's panopticon, or historical surveillance apparatus. As a fitting complement to Taborn's chapter, López's ethnoanalysis is similarly historical in scope and future-oriented in its particular counterhegemonic, indigenous logic.

In this third and final grouping of chapters, a more sober reality check is provided by Jessie Daniels, Douglas Thomas, and coauthors Mohan J. Dutta, Graham Bodie, and Ambar Basu, where the fact of cyber hate and the myth of colorblindness are brought into disturbing relief. Despite idealistic rhetorics purporting that the Internet, and other digital technologies, would help to usher in a new millennial ethos of tolerance, of digital democracy, and of colorblind social interactions, this lofty goal has yet to materialize. There has been an interesting turn on the colorblindness front as the emergence of covert hate sites are replacing many overt ones of the recent past. In this discussion, we want to look at the new face of hate online, and how youths are simultaneously lured by perpetrators of regimes of hate and intolerance in digital spaces, including in massively multiplayer online gaming. Among the pressing issues here are interventionist efforts to increase critical literacy skills for youths encountering "cloaked Web sites" and race-baiting gaming networks, and developments of strategies to motivate youths of color toward sustainable behavioral practices in online health seeking.

Jessie Daniels initiates us into digital media culture's dark side, to draw on a *Star Wars* cinematic referent. In "Race, Civil Rights, and Hate Speech in the Digital Era," Daniels investigates how what she calls "cloaked Web sites" published by hate groups appropriate discourses and images of racial, ethnic, and religious minorities to spread virulent anti-Semitism, antiblack, and other hate propaganda. Among the key concerns at work here is the development of educational strategies designed to impart twenty-first-century critical thinking skills for adolescents who are often unprepared for these new modes of recruitment into regimes of hate. She illustrates how the digital era has shifted the terrain of race, civil rights, and hate speech. Daniels divulges key encoding/decoding features unique to online, Web-based mechanisms of undermining decades of civil rights gains in these emergent and overt hate speech environs. She argues convincingly that what is at stake in this shifting digital terrain is how youth make and evaluate knowledge claims and cultivate a vision for social justice.

Douglas Thomas's chapter, "KPK, Inc.: Race, Nation, and Emergent Culture in Online Games," is in dialog with the mendacity of online hate that Daniels studies. Thomas examines the unintended effects of transnational adoption of an online game, *Diablo II*, focusing on a series of events following the introduction of highly skilled Korean players into a popular U.S. game, examining the emergence of player cultures that negotiate issues of space, nation, and identity in complex, and oftentimes violent, ways. Thomas considers the resurgence of destructive nationalist sentiments in the increasingly popular and influential digital games segment known as massively multiplayer online gaming (MMOG), even in this age of global media culture and putative colorblind virtual communities. At issue in this chapter centering on the MMOG, *Diablo II*, is how racial bigotry becomes the motivating force behind American gamers who craft strategies to thwart Korean gamers' abilities to continue gameplay because the American youths blame the Korean youths for destabilizing the server and generally disrupting the games' pleasure principles.

The final chapter in this volume takes up the little-known issue of youths from racial and ethnic minorities becoming increasingly aware of the advantages of health seeking online. In their chapter, "Health Disparity and the Racial Divide among the Nation's Youth: Internet as a Site for Change?" coauthors Mohan Dutta, Graham Bodie, and Ambar Basu look at the intersection of technology access and use among minority youth and the pervasiveness of Internet health information. Of particular concern for them is how online health seeking among the nation's young adults from underrepresented or minority groups mirror general patterns of health disparities within the national health care system. Their chapter seeks to build a model of online health seeking that incorporates both general and social divisions, and individual uses and expectations of e-health. They have discovered that although these communities do not avail themselves of the breadth and depth of this increasingly important augmentation to traditional health care options, these youths have begun to use health Web sites to educate themselves about communicable diseases, teen pregnancy, and sexuality matters, along with other health and medical information. Their chapter represents one obvious voice for broadening this volume's scope in terms of next steps for prompting beneficial digital learning by youth, who can be encouraged to seek out other life-skills information online beyond the usual entertainment motivations for spending time online.

Conclusion

As we developed these interdisciplinary works from several critical, theoretical, methodological, and paradigmatic approaches, we discovered and enjoyed an important experience of collaboration that was not simply a matter of mutual interest in the topic of race and digital media technologies. Indeed, we genuinely embraced the notion of creating a volume in the wikification model of collaboration and scholarly networking, which the MacArthur Foundation's DMAL group devised and cultivated. It is fair to say that we have only scratched the surface of this hefty topic, and in the future we look forward to exploring new threads and linkages that transect our individual chapters.

It is not often that scholars (university-based and independent), technology workers, grassroots activists, technology entrepreneurs, and others, are invited to become partners and cocreators in a bold field-building endeavor of groundbreaking and paradigm-shifting significance as is represented by this current MacArthur Foundation DMAL initiative. This has been a productive and creative experience. We hope you find reading this book as engrossing, exhilarating, inspiring, and even dismaying as we did writing it.

Some Key Concepts and Terms

We want to prime your reading of the chapters with a list of key words and concepts that the authors developed during the course of exchanges. Please look for them and their contextual meanings as you delve into the eight chapters that comprise this volume. We wanted to keep the list relatively brief. Please look at how some of these familiar words and concepts become redefined as a result of their situatedness within these new digital media learning frameworks.

1 White supremacy
2 Hate speech
3 Epistemology
4 Nonneutral literacy
5 Colonial legacy
6 Tribal perspectives
7 Digital technology
8 Alternative epistemology
9 Native America
10 Access
11 Untraditional learning environments
12 Artivism/artivist
13 Digital mural
14 Conciencia de la mestiza
15 Chicana/o muralism
16 Alma López
17 Counterhistories

Acknowledgments

There has been a particularly significant element to the production of this work that I want to mention in conclusion. An integral component of what I have described above as the *wikification* of this book were the Race and Ethnicity Online Forum and the Spotlight Blog, also produced for the DMAL project. These online discussions have contributed much to the discursive logics and critical perspectives of the essays in this volume including this introductory chapter. Both the online forum and the blog consisted of several discussion threads about race and ethnicity in digital media and youth cultures. The online forum, for example, featured invited experts working in these areas who agreed to respond to a set of questions, including How can young people of color balance or incorporate new media technology within traditional, urban, and rural community contexts? I also asked, In what ways, if any, are new media redefining notions of race and ethnicity? And what about hate speech, racist video games, and disparities in health care affecting minority youth?

   The invited experts responded to the discussion questions based upon their individual research interests, scholarship, activist practices, and creative experiences. The expert participants in the DMAL initiative's online forum were Jacques La Grange, Helen H. Park, Teresa Foley, Alexander G. Weheliye, Kali Tal, Legand (Lee) Burge, Victor Masayesva, Robert Logan, Thomasandthetrainyard, Joshua Kun, Anna Beatrice Scott, Tricia Rose, S. Craig Watkins, George Lipsitz, Jillana Enteen, Ellen Seiter, Joe Feagin, Beverly Ray, Linda Neuhauser, Gary Kreps, Catherine Smith, Brit Svoen, Amie Breeze Harper, Nettrice Gaskins, Mechelle De Craene, Sandy Alvarez, Moony, Mary Joe Deegan, and all the volumes' authors. We gratefully acknowledge the important contribution these individuals have made to this book and to the larger DMAL project.

   Now, it is extremely important that I take this opportunity to thank my many collaborators on this important work. I am especially grateful to Michael Carter for inviting me to participate in this exciting project and for his guidance and strong support during all stages of this book. I learned so much from him. Ruth Rominger's genial touch and technical acumen proved invaluable in the facilitation of our numerous virtual and actual meetings, and teleconferences. I also want to acknowledge Henry Jenkins and Carol Lee, who were excellent advisors on the manuscript. They provided beneficial input and careful attention to early drafts of this work. Connie Yowell's leadership and commitment to the DMAL project and particularly to our volume was inspirational and greatly appreciated. Without her vision and authority, this amazing program would have remained simply a great idea unrealized. It was a pleasure to work with all the talented authors on this project, Jessie Daniels, Tyrone Taborn, Chela Sandoval, Antonio López, Douglas Thomas, Raiford Guins, Mohan Dutta, Dara Byrne, Ambar Basu, Graham Bodie, and Guisela Latorre. Working with all the other editors (Tara McPherson, Katie Salen, Lance Bennett, David Buckingham, Miriam Metzger, and Andrew Flanagin) and members of the DMAL project has been a tremendously rewarding experience. I must thank Aldon Nielsen for his unwavering support and sincere concern throughout this effort, which have meant more than I can express in this space. Finally, I thank Eric Witz, Daniel Bouchard, and the MIT Press editorial team for their kind and capable assistance with this book.

Notes

1. See, e.g., Jon Katz's fuller quote in his "Introduction" to *The Children's Culture Reader*, ed. Henry Jenkins (New York and London: New York University Press, 1998), 30.

2. Nettrice Gaskins, Response: Do We Need to be Concerned about How Young People Encounter and Interact with Race and Ethnicity Issues Online and in Other Digital Media Technologies, in *Stakeholders in Digital Media/Rethinking the Digital Divide,* MacArthur Foundation Open Forum, 2006, http://community.macfound.org/openforum. Retrieved April 14, 2007. Gaskins made these remarks as part of the MacArthur Foundation Online Forum in the DML project. She was an invited expert included because of her own expertise and background as a technology worker. Her fuller comments can be found on the MacArthur Online Forum. See all the expert discussions at http://community.macfound.org/openforum. Retrieved April 14, 2007. Follow the Discussion button to the Race and Ethnicity folders, and for this particular post, see the Race and Ethnicity folder entitled "Stakeholders."

3. Adam S., Global Kids, *DMEC. In/Tolerance*, 2006, http://www.holymeatballs.org/2006/03/dmec_essay_quotes_intolerance.html. Retrieved April 14, 2007. This quotation is excerpted from Adam S., one of the youth participants in the Global Kids organization, a New York City–based educational organization that works with the MacArthur Foundation's Digital Media and Learning initiative. Global Kids sponsored the winter-spring 2006 Digital Media Essay Contest (DMEC) to assist and encourage youths to think critically about the role of digital media in their lives.

4. See the *Random House Webster's College Dictionary* (New York: Random House, 2000), 90.

5. For details on the Hip-hop Appreciation Week, see http://www.sohh.com/articles/article.php/2273/1. Retrieved May 9, 2007. On the site, KRS is quoted as, "Our theme this year is 'Charity.' The purpose of Hip-hop Appreciation Week is to decriminalize Hip-hop's public image and promote the nine elements of Hip-hop Kulture so that Hip-hoppas may form a 'Common Spirit' amongst each other. This, we believe, is the beginning of Hip-hop's preservation and further development."

6. Among more than 1,300 Google hits for the key word string "students" and "HR4437," see the Web site entitled "Students' Responses to HR4437" for representative coverage and photos of the 2006 boycott at http://www.studentsresponseshr4437.com/. Retrieved August 20, 2006.

7. *Second Life* is described on its Web site as "a 3-D virtual world entirely built and owned by its residents. Since opening to the public in 2003, it has grown explosively, and today is inhabited by a total of 6,030,223 people from around the globe." See http://secondlife.com/whatis/.

8. Don Tapscott, *Growing Up Digital: The Rise of the Net Generation* (New York: McGraw-Hill, 1998).

9. Anna Everett, The Revolution Will Be Digitized: Afrocentricity and the Digital Public Sphere, *Social Text* 71 (2002): 133.

10. Larry Irving et al., Falling Through the Net: A Survey of the 'Have Nots' in Rural and Urban America, 1995, Report of National Telecommunications and Information Administration, http://www.ntia.doc.gov/ntiahome/fallingthru.html. Retrieved April 14, 2007.

11. This article by Steve Cisler was originally published in the *San Jose Mercury News* newspaper on January 16, 2000. See Cisler's "Hot Button: Online Haves vs. Have-Nots," http://www.athenaalliance.org/rpapers/cisler.html. Retrieved April 14, 2007.

12. Ibid.

13. *The Deepening Divide* is Jan A. G. M. van Dijk's useful book calling attention to the complexity of what we understand as the digital divide. See Jan A. G. M. Van Dijk, *The Deepening Divide: Inequality in the Information Society* (Thousand Oaks, London, New Delhi: Sage Publications, 2005), 4.

14. George Lipsitz, *The Possessive Investment in Whiteness: How White People Profit from Identity Politics* (Philadelphia: Temple University Press, 1998).

15. Jackson K., of Global Kids, and *Second Life*. See the entry at this Global Kids related blog: http://www.holymeatballs.org/2006/03/dmec_essay_quotes_intolerance.html. Retrieved April 14, 2007.

16. Van Dijk, *The Deepening Divide*, 6.

17. Alexander G. Weheliye, 'Feenin': Posthuman Voices in Contemporary Black Popular Music, *Social Text* 71 (2002): 22.

18. Everett, The Revolution Will Be Digitized, 133.

19. See, e.g., the Web sites iTribe.biz, TMZ.com, and YouTube.com. Using these stars' names and the terms *racism* and *homophobia* as key words or search terms, the Web sites display their archives of these high-profile stories.

PART I: FUTURE VISIONS AND EXCAVATED PASTS

The Future of (the) "Race": Identity, Discourse, and the Rise of Computer-mediated Public Spheres

Dara N. Byrne

John Jay College of Criminal Justice, Department of Speech, Theater & Media Studies

Pretend you are a white person. Hmmm . . . Yahoo chat sites, Excite, Globe, noooo . . . I think I'll go to Asian Avenue. Why? Because I want to learn Asian culture, of course. . . . How about the forums? The only thing a white person will contribute is a posting that will defend their position or undermine anything that would not be in their best interests, whether it helps Asians or not. Often they will appeal to an idealistic logic that has no basis in the real world. I think the minds and opinions of Asians are diverse enough to provide opposing views in all forums. So why are white people here? What do you think? My personal view is to let them hit on the girls. However, they should not be in the forums because they contribute NOTHING to the forum, except to taint the forums with their own self-serving ideas. Hell, they already got control of the media, is there any way for an Asian to express their [sic] ideas to other Asians without a white person corrupting the exchange of ideas?
—Delpi[1]

The quotation above was taken from an April 2000 discussion thread on AsianAvenue.com, an Asian American Web site that serves as one of the most popular online social networks for the Asian diaspora. This polemical posting, contributed under the pseudonym "Delpi,"[2] though not unique in its subject matter, articulates Delpi's sense that AsianAvenue represents an Asian public sphere—an imaginary borderless place superimposed on "real" Web space. By questioning the motives of white participants, who are perceived as "corrupting the exchange of ideas," Delpi appeals to members of his community who, by virtue of being racial citizens, would likely share in the notion that this immaterial territory should be marked and defended. In fact, Delpi expresses a desire to ensure that the exchange of ideas remains pure, or at least racially honest and "authentic," by virtue of limiting the dialogue to its "real" citizens. Delpi's protective impulse is rather common in such discussion forums, where participation by racial others—particularly whites—is often viewed as an effort to thwart "nation" (and movement) building, identity formation, belonging, and ownership.

The forum is a locus of community vitality on such racially dedicated sites. Their discussion threads serve as relatively permanent recorded instances of discourse production, and they are central to public life as they offer members the unique opportunity to react and respond to a myriad of globally relevant and racially specific topics. Despite the popular claim that the Internet presents the possibility of a raceless space, participation on dedicated sites is growing exponentially. That just three of the most trafficked—AsianAvenue.com, BlackPlanet.com, and MiGente.com—are home to more than 16 million subscribers[3] suggests that the dissolution of racial identification in cyberspace is neither possible nor *desirable*.

Theorizing about the ways in which dedicated sites serve as informal learning environments makes the case for studying them even more compelling, especially for minority youths. To understand more about what participants learn and teach each other about race and ethnicity online, this chapter focuses on the exchange of ideas, and public Discourse,[4] on dedicated Web sites. I explore prevailing views about race by analyzing the rhetorical dynamics of more than 3,000 discussion threads in the Heritage and Identity forums on AsianAvenue, BlackPlanet, and MiGente. Drawn from data accumulated over a seven-year period (August 1999 to August 2006), the analysis shows (1) how online communities are giving rise to new collective subjectivities unfolding across local, national, and international lines; (2) how real-world forces, such as the shift in racial tensions post-9/11, contribute to renewed commitments to racial identification and anti-imperialism; and (3) how these discourses accept and reject racial typologies. There are three parts to this chapter. The first part addresses the current impact of computer-mediated networks and new media on the development of dedicated public spheres online and youth participation therein. The second part presents an analysis of race-related discussion threads and is guided by a Critical Language Studies[5] framework, one that helps to illustrate the often hidden connections between language, power, and ideology.[6] The third part considers the role ongoing participation plays in the ways young people teach–learn about race and ethnicity.

When we consider the significant role played by online forums, listservs, and other computer-mediated social networks in the lives of minority youths, this phenomenon of dedicated sites takes on new meaning. This is especially pertinent given the desirability of youths as target markets for these Internet companies. Community Connect, Inc. (CCI), is the parent company of AsianAvenue, BlackPlanet, and MiGente. CCI's first site, AsianAvenue, was introduced in 1997, and in less than two years it became the leading Asian American Web site, garnering more than 2.2 million members by March 2002.[7] As a result of this success, BlackPlanet was launched in September 1999. In the first year, more than 1 million members joined BlackPlanet, and by April 2002 its community expanded to 5.3 million users.[8] Both AsianAvenue and BlackPlanet have consistently ranked among the highest trafficked sites for their respective ethnic markets. The third site, MiGente, was launched in October 2000, and is considered the most popular English-language community for Latinos. More than 500,000 members registered within the first two years.[9]

At the time of this writing, AsianAvenue had about 1.4 million members, BlackPlanet about 14.9 million, and MiGente about 2.5 million. Though the company does not release any statistics about its users, changes to platform design, special features, and advertisers over the years suggests that their interest is in appealing to a primarily sixteen- to twenty-four-year-old ethnic base. Advertisements and sponsorships have come from JCrew, Disney, Sony, Miramax Films, college preparation resource the Princeton Review, and the U.S. Army. Features have included dating subscription services, early career job searches in partnership with Monster.com, modeling discovery opportunities with Ford Models, and exclusive music content from singers like Janet Jackson, Mario Vasquez, and Enrique Iglesias, as well as rappers P. Diddy and Ludacris. Taking the largest share of the e-commerce pie among ethnic social networking companies, CCI expected to net about $20 million in revenues across all three sites in 2006, of which 15 percent was expected to come from its dating services, 50 percent from advertising, and 35 percent from job notices.[10]

As impressive as CCI's stake is in the young online ethnic market, some might consider participation in any one of the organization's sites a bit passé, given the current media and critical attention focused on the more recent crop of mainstream sites such MySpace, Friendster, and Facebook. Noted for their innovations in attracting mainstream youth, these more popular social networks have been so successful that any one of them has a membership base that is at least double the size of the three CCI sites combined. So marginalized is CCI from discussions on the impact of social networking on our youth, even on minority youth, that in a September 2006 BusinessWeek.com article, one media expert erroneously pegged CCI (launched in 1997) as at the forefront of the "second wave" of social networking sites, while naming Friendster (launched in 2002) as an example of a "first wave" site.[11] Admittedly, popularity and participation on the three CCI sites seemed to have peaked back in 2002. At that time, its largest site, BlackPlanet, had daily participation averaging in the millions. Today its figures are somewhere in the thousands of daily users. Likewise, the $20 million in revenues that places Community Connect in the top three of the social networking companies (based on sales) is all but a blip on NewsCorp/MySpace's $327-million radar. But when it comes to longevity, sustaining an interactive community, and the ability to continue recruiting younger participants over a seven-plus-year span, CCI seems to have figured out what some critics see as the real challenge facing those popular "first wave" sites.[12]

The ongoing Web presence in the lives of more than 16 million young Asian, black, and Latino users means that the CCI sites have become established pillars of their respective communities rather than the latest fads with unpredictable futures. These sites represent relatively stable homes for their target users; whether they are long-time members or are newly emerging voices, holding membership on at least one of the CCI sites is likely. This ongoing Web presence also means that these dedicated sites can serve as valuable resources for understanding the ways in which ethnic communities construct, stabilize, modify, and challenge individual and community senses of identity over a relatively long period of time. It must be noted that there are few other Web communities out there that can provide researchers with opportunities for exploring the ways in which sustained online interaction impacts a community's ideas about nation, culture, race, and ethnicity, much less those that are organized around youth expressions of these issues. In this sense, CCI sites bear as much relevance on these *au courant* discussions about youth participation on social networking sites as do MySpace and the others. Given that race and ethnicity are the principal features around which public life is organized on AsianAvenue, BlackPlanet, and MiGente, it is critical that scholarship begins to pay attention to the variety of ways young people publicly engage with concepts like these, especially with respect to the diasporic interconnectedness that such sites offer.

Ironically, the relative anonymity of dedicated sites like CCI's may be one of the key reasons they continue to thrive. Recent work by Vorris Nunley posits that unmonitored and unrestricted quasi-public places like African American barbershops and beauty salons, sites of what he calls African American hush harbor rhetoric, serve as important spaces for the production and exchange of community-centered knowledges.[13] Historically, the term *hush harbor* refers to the places where slaves gathered to participate in various aspects of public life, hidden, unnoticed, and especially inaudible to their white masters. As Nunley argues, the hushedness ensured the survival of this form of African American publicness and the rhetorical practices that serviced it.[14] Drawing loose parallels with Nunley's notion of hush harbor rhetoric, these little theorized dedicated sites that fly well below the mainstream radar have also, for years, been developing a sense of group cohesion and rhetorical practices that members perceive as being very valuable to their online lives because they are relatively free of *mass* participation by ethnic outsiders.

The importance of racially "pure" public spaces is an aspect of community life that CCI participants are especially not afraid to talk about. As Delpi so aptly describes in the posting quoted at the beginning of this chapter, the site is premised on an exchange of ideas in a specialized public sphere where racial identity serves as common ground for participants and as a primary determinant of one's right to participate. In this way, dedicated Web sites can be thought of as imaginary public spheres that overcome the complexities of real-world distancing by using computer-mediated technologies to cultivate critical spaces for discursive exchange.

Because this chapter proceeds from the perspective that discourse is governed by social practice, the primary concern of this study is analyzing the relationship between texts, processes, and social conditions as reflective of "both the immediate conditions of the situational context and the more remote conditions of institutional and social structures."[15] I believe that the application of a critical language theory is an essential tool for investigating the intersection between race, representation, and the production of social knowledge. Of equal importance are the ways in which online discourses intersect with young users, and addressing the dearth of research and critical analyses of the ways in which participants, the majority of whom are likely to be 16–24, articulate race and social interaction. The goal is to provide valuable insights into the disjunctures between local, national, and international identifications, which are essential for new thinking about intersections between globalization and diaspora cultures, and their relevance for youths of color.

Part I: New Media Publicness

Latino, contrary to popular belief, is not a racial group. But yet, when referred to it is always put in comparison to racial groups such as whites, blacks, or asians [sic]. But Latinos come in all racial groups, from the average Negra in Santiago de Cuba to the indigenous peoples of Peru to its former Japanese President Fujimori. It seems every other day I get that annoying question: "What are you?" Well, human of course. My nationality? Well, American, born and raised. "No, I mean, really, what are you?" What question is really being asked here? Does the spanish [sic] I speak change who I am? Does the cinnamon skin determine my personality or my capacity to learn and achieve? I am a mixture of many things, but I will always be me. So tell me, what are you really???? —labellalatina1001[16]

For MiGente's labellalatina1001 (name changed), the fundamental question, "What are you?" is as personal as it is communal. The seemingly individual and self-reflective question, one that considers the relevance of race to her personality, also addresses the tensions between history, culture, nationhood, and identity formation. Notice that even though she is frustrated with the limitations of race as a means of grouping and categorizing others, she still begins her question by asserting its naturalness. As she explores the layers of her identity, labellalatina1001 offers potential respondents an outline of the methodological implications of the question. In fact, by wondering about the connection between country and culture or skin color, personality and intelligence, labellalatina1001 articulates not only the richness of her racial identification but also its potential inadequateness. By structuring the question in this manner, the series of responses is inclined to engage with the history of (their) "race" and the interplay of dominant ideologies.

From the ongoing reverberations of Trujillo's reign in the Dominican Republic to the destructiveness of intraracial hate, respondents also present several theories about how the members of the community should conceptualize their race. Interestingly, most users' initial posts contextualize their personal experiences—signifying their degree of authenticity and authority—by describing their skin color, their bloodline, or their familiarity with back home (food, music, visiting every summer). In so doing, users rarely questioned another's right to contribute to the dialogue, whether or not they agreed with the one who thought "we are all African cuz [sic] we got the African blood," or whether they applauded the one who proclaimed, in all caps, "WE ARE [OUR] OWN RACE!!!!!"[17] In integrating various aspects of personal and community history, participants construct a framework for engaging with their Latinoness.[18] That this dialogue generated some forty-seven pages of threaded discussion and was sustained for more than a year, with members continually revising their definitions, indicates that their sense of Latinoness is neither bound to group consensus nor is it completely independent of it.

This dialogue is but one example of how online community forums serve as vital public spaces[19] for (re)thinking and (re)producing social knowledge and why new theorizing about new media publicness is necessary. Remarking on the relevance of poststructuralist theorists like Foucault, Lacan, Deleuze, and Guattari to digital media analysis, noted scholar Sherry Turkle observed that, as online interactions increasingly move us away from the computer's information-gathering purpose, the boundaries between real and virtual have become blurred, if not irrelevant.[20] Her study of Internet identity exemplifies what the French scholars named above meant when they argued that the self and other—fluid, unstable, and reflexive—are constituted in language. According to this position, language affects the character of human consciousness and conditions as it is conditioned by users' experiences.

So even when free to make up any identity online as Turkle discusses, the discourse that makes the characters real or "authentic" is inevitably structured by an interplay of sociocultural forces. As Lisa Nakamura shows, when white users play Asian characters in online games, they engage in a form of cyber tourism that is often guided by centuries-long Western fantasies of the exotic Oriental other.[21] In terms of poststructuralist theory, racial identity (or any form of identity, for that matter) is not a universal reality; rather, it is a sequence of intersecting rhetorics, each articulating some existing social knowledge. Like scripts, or what Stuart Hall describes as a "common sense" within culture, the ideologies undergirding such knowledge prescribe how users think, act, and function, the roles they play, the assumptions they make, and the ways in which they interpret and understand lived experiences.[22]

For more than fifteen years, a small group of academics has been writing about the intricacies of identity formation and community building online.[23] From Howard Rheingold's notion of the Internet as a virtual community to Anna Everett's early attention to the role networked connectivity might play for the black public sphere, this emerging discourse about race and ethnicity in online discourse questions how offline realities condition users online. But with the Internet and cyberlife now well into their teenage years, scholarship is increasingly faced with the implications of online realities conditioning users in the world offline. Waning in popularity is Sherry Turkle's view that users' online worlds are parallel with their offline worlds.[24] Some scholars, like Emily Noelle Ignacio, contend that Turkle's use of the term *parallel* gives the false impression that users engage in community and communication practices that are completely apart from their "real" lives, much like the way parallel lines in a diagram never touch one another.[25] Preferring the term *perpendicular* instead, Ignacio suggests that, because many Internet communities are also home to "real" offline communities[26]—as would clearly be the case for Asian-, black-, and Latino-targeted sites—these worlds are more likely to connect with each other than they are to be absolutely distinct. Serving as extensions of and intersections with each other, social and community-based interaction in both worlds play significant roles in shaping the identities of their users.

As we know well, the social and community-based dimension of the Internet has been flourishing for quite some time. From classmates.com (founded in 1995) to the MySpace boom in 2005, belonging to a social networking community has characterized much of the online experience, so much so that MySpace is known as "one of the major destinations on the Web" and has become a real competitor for the likes of MSN, Yahoo! and AOL.[27] When the site received more page views in 2005 than search engine giant Google, some bloggers humorously quipped that MySpace should launch its own record label and vie for world—aka media—domination.[28] In an almost prophetic turn later that year, MySpace, with Rupert Murdoch at the helm, announced its partnership with Interscope Records and the launch of a record label.[29] As MySpace CEO Chris Wolfe stated, "It's become a lot more than just a website. It's become a lifestyle brand."[30] Indeed, MySpace has become a lifestyle, with more than 80 million registered users and the resources to impact consumer and market interests alike. Further indicative of MySpace eclipsing a *mere* Web presence is its August 2006 partnership with Google. As Fox executives report, the typical reason users leave MySpace is to use a search engine, so by providing onsite googling capabilities, MySpace would be able to retain participation for longer periods of time and, of course, increase marketing potential. Evidently, there is immense value in sustaining online communities, as news of this deal drove both Google and NewsCorps market price up.[31]

In many ways, social networking sites like these straddle the debate between a viable youth-centered public sphere and a calculated corporate venture.[32] On the one hand, the popularity of these sites translates into vibrant communities with strong communications networks, especially through the use of tools such as instant messengers, chatrooms, Weblogs, and discussion boards that, among other things, increase the rapidity of discursive exchange. On the other hand, there are the commercial interests and the efforts to appeal to the broadest base of participants. When MySpace's Wolfe remarked that "radio has become less and less important,"[33] perhaps the only truism behind such a statement is that the decline in radio listenership is indicative of the audience's taste for real-time dialoguing and consumer-controlled content.

On social networking sites, community members serve both as producers and consumers, and have an equal ability to influence and to be heard. As Kollock notes, online participants are generally motivated by the anticipation of reciprocity, the opportunity to build their reputations and the reputations of the sites, and the sense that their contributions directly affect the pulse of the community.[34] Drawing on Rheingold's notion that the Internet is a gift economy,[35] Kollock explains that, in addition to the gratification of helping to build the site's culture, users are rewarded with full rights of access.[36] In this way, pride of membership is also about being an active producer as opposed to a passive or irrelevant consumer. But filling out demographic profiles, providing e-mail addresses, accepting cookies, and, in some cases, selecting from a list of potential advertisers (as is the case for joining BlackPlanet and MiGente), has become part and parcel of the gift exchange of this social experience. As the commercial stakes in online communities rise, so too will the interest in directing the attention of participants, or controlling the format of interaction, to suit the profit-making agendas of corporate partners. Nonetheless, the promise of new media publicness is compelling.

Functioning as vibrant public spaces—imagined territories developed by CCI made real in typed discursive exchanges—participants, who are stripped of their local exigencies, shape online communities to sometimes reflect, refine, reject, and reproduce social knowledge as informed by their offline experiences.[37] But new media publics also proffer well-defined discourse communities based around the sensibility of a purely online aesthetic with grammars of communication that dictate much more than when to use ROFL or LOL.[38] With the expectation of civic engagement and the de-centering of an absolute information source, the traditional sense of consensus is eroded, and is certainly not a prerequisite to community development. Aside from the obvious trend in establishing social communities, there is an additional effort toward sustaining them. First, sustaining refers to the effort to keep participants logged on and active for longer periods of time; this, in turn, increases the rate and quality of fresh content. Second, sustaining also refers to the longevity of the community on the whole. As noted before, some communities have maintained Web presences for more than ten years. While it may be too early to predict the material impact of these long-term Web cultures, the desire to carve out online niches, to territorialize Web space, and to commit to preserving them, speaks to the most basic need to stake out turf and plant roots.

More than a decade ago, some scholars were declaring that increasing trends toward globalization have dissolved territories,[39] that national borders have become immaterial, superfluous, or superseded;[40] that nationally organized politico-cultural identities are being "deterritorialised";[41] and that "supraterritorial" spaces based upon "distanceless, borderless interactions"[42] are de-centering the role of territorial and place-based socio-institutional forms. But this new media publicness and the overwhelming popularity of online communities is unequivocally tied to creating and defining borders, if only symbolically, and publicly laying claims to distinct identities. Signs of territory, and the accompanying rhetorics of "nation building," are more visible than ever.

My own recent experience lurking in a black chatroom on Yahoo! made it clear just how territorialized certain Web spheres have become. When a participant posted messages in Arabic, several members "shouted" (using a big font) to either stop or leave the chatroom because he had "no business speaking where you don't belong." Another remarked, "Why come online if no one can't understand you. Makes no since [sic]."[43] Angered over a breakdown in the exchange of ideas—the centerpiece of social networking—English-speaking members readily identified the poster as an outsider who likely had no real right to participate in that dialogue, and perhaps even on the English-language–dominated "World" Wide Web. That the poster could very well have been black did not seem to be important enough to grant him access, since—for these participants—a "real" community is clearly forged out of a common tongue. Though not deliberately intending to refer to a historically racialized term, the "tribal" impulse and the subsequent territorial responses exhibited here are difficult to ignore. As will be explored later in this chapter, instances where Asian, black, or Latino members vilify a common enemy—particularly white participants, as representatives of white power structures—are fairly prevalent on dedicated sites.

Though it can be tempting to reduce these discourses to reverse racism or to make the claim that participants on dedicated sites tend to be racist (as is sometimes the position held by outsiders), more careful analysis shows that participants are much more concerned with the ways outside voices can affect public dialogues than they are about these individuals having access to the sites. In fact, it is the outsider's motivation for contributing to this aspect of community life that is most scrutinized—treated with suspicion—because many see these discussions as intimately connected with the future of (the) race. As the analysis in Part II of this chapter shows, public life is organized around rich dialogues about the myriad of ways racial identity guides community life online. The effect of whiteness, ideologically and materially, is but a small part of it.

Everett's postulations about black public life online shows that, among other things, dedicated sites are being used to strengthen ties across national borders (as is exemplified in the Nigerian diaspora site Naijanet), and to support activist interests (as is demonstrated by the ways black women used the Internet to share information about the 1997 Million Woman's March within their on- and offline communities).[44] In this sense, black publics online are borne out of desires to deepen interconnectivity and to use new media, whether strategic or not, for their own community-building purposes. It is important to underscore Everett's examples here because they show that, while marginalized communities are creating spaces for interaction online, raced publics are not responses to that marginalization.

In fact, the connection between Internet technologies and diasporan interconnectivity, as can be evidenced by the popularity and ongoing presence of dedicated sites, lays challenge to the centrality of generalized publicness that philosophers like John Rawls tend to privilege. Rawls argues that, in order to participate in *the* public sphere, participants must strip themselves of their private interests so that they can come to some form of consensus about issues of general concern to all.[45] According to him, "comprehensive doctrines" (like race or religion, for instance), are private matters that impede upon our ability to have "overlapping consensus," because such doctrines inevitably influence our ability to think or act "rationally" about collective interests.[46] But, as shown in the examples offered by Everett, Naijanet, and the Million Woman March, in particular, participants' raced and ethnic identities are the common ground out of which a vibrant online public life emerges. Although these participants may very well be engaged in other publics, as in the case of some MiGente members who hold memberships on MySpace, their comprehensive doctrines are neither secondary nor completely separated.[47] Even though participants are not drawing clear lines between "public" and "private" in the way for which Rawls has argued, the strengthening of communication networks has nonetheless created new pathways for translating such public discourse into meaningful social action.

There are some indications that one of the consequences of an online race-centered public life—activism particularly around issues of social justice—is just on the horizon. Consider that in July 2006 a coalition of black gay bloggers launched a worldwide online campaign to protest the scheduled performances by Jamaican dancehall artists Beenie Man and TOK at LIFEbeat's annual HIV/AIDS fundraising conference in New York to benefit infected people in the Caribbean.[48] The concert was sponsored by music powerhouses Black Entertainment Television, *Vibe Magazine*, Music Choice, and New York–based radio station Power 105.1 FM. Outraged at scheduled performances by artists who have been criticized for lyrics that call for violence against gays, the coalition posted a series of blogs on the subject and e-mailed organizers, activists, media, loyal readers, and concert organizers. Within twenty-four hours, there was intense media coverage. A few days later, efforts included a news conference at LIFEbeat headquarters, protests by leading black LGBT figures in New York, and e-mails from black gay activists in London voicing their support. By July 12, LIFEbeat canceled the concert, citing fear of violence stemming from the pressures of "a select group of activists."[49]

LIFEbeat's response—canceling the concert, rather than canceling those particular performances—was an unintended, albeit serious, consequence of an effort aimed at addressing what protesters truly saw as the perpetuation of intracommunity intolerance of its gay members. LIFEbeat's decision to cancel the concert must be understood as an attempt to cast blame deliberately on these activists for speaking out and as evidence of the organization's refusal to enter into (perhaps be a catalyst for) serious community dialogue about these matters. That the outcome of LIFEbeat's discursive gatekeeping was a canceled benefit concert does not negate the significance of the coalition's using its online social networks to incite civic action and bring about community change. Likewise, this example shows how strategic organizing online, coupled with diasporic interconnectedness, can potentially translate into meaningful grassroots action in just a few days. After all, the protest came from the black American and British GLBT communities in response to performances by Jamaican dancehall artists at a benefit concert in New York for persons in the Caribbean living with HIV/AIDS.

Part II: Heritage, Identity, and Discourses of Racial Authenticity

I don't believe that the brother was implying that anyone "smiled" as the Towers came down. If he was thinking in the same sense as I was, he probably had "raised brows" that the "chickens had come home to roost." Our government doesn't have clean hands in [foreign] policies whatsoever. We have been playing the "dozens" for quite sometime now. And now, it's ironic, that the shoe is on the other foot. It's sad that when a black man or woman gets pulled over by a police officer, he or she doesn't know [whether] or not they are going to make it home alive. Depending on what city you live in, this is a reality. In Americas [sic] silent war against "the boyz in the hood," we all became victims. The movie Crash covered this magnificently. So to see that [the] script had been flipped, and know that the white male was now the "target" of profiling, the target of his own conception, was almost like poetic justice.
—MinorityReporter[50]

This admission from BlackPlanet's pseudonymous MinorityReporter that he has very little sympathy for (white) Americans over the 9/11 attacks sparks a rather interesting debate about the community's place in American public life. His response, and the originating question "How do you feel about another black person who had no feelings about 9/11?" also represents a rather noticeable shift in discussions around this topic.[51] In 2001, participants on BlackPlanet (and all three CCI sites) expressed sympathy, fear, and a sense of allegiance with the United States. But today those expressions tend to ebb and flow between suspicion and disinterest. (In 2005, no threads on MiGente or BlackPlanet acknowledged 9/11.) When participants talk about 9/11, it is frequently the source of intense debate as to whether this really is "family business." Although some participants support the troops and were saddened by 9/11, many note that their empathy was heightened only as a result of being made aware of the deaths of "innocent black people." When ShugaSuga is incensed by the feeling that blacks are siding with "the terrorists" who "hate white America," she reminds them that "anyone of us could have died in that [terrorist] attack," and that mourning with the nation does not detract from "the knowledge of 'self' and the hardships in this society."[52] Her response is a useful counter to MinorityReporter's view that (black) family business is distinct from American business. ShugaSuga offers participants a way of intertwining them, especially given the longstanding contributions that African Americans have made. Furthermore, she cautions her family to be wary of siding with those who:

don't care about what happened to us [during] slavery and [Jim Crow] . . . they don't care about Black [people] at all . . . they hate America . . . and as far as they are concerned we are part of America . . . they didn't send out a memo for all the Black people to stay home so that only whites got killed . . . they attacked our country and they are the enemy . . . period.[53]

Noting that there is a significant difference between being allies in the fight against social and economic problems blacks face and the killing of thousands of Americans who likely played no role in the injustice they suffer, ShugaSuga's post inevitably alters the tone of the discussion from one that was previously unsympathetic to one that encourages patriotism and sympathy, even in spite of the injustices done unto black people.

In the example above and the ones at the beginning of each section of this chapter, my analyses and observations are informed by critical theory, to underscore the intersection between the creation and dispersion of social knowledge about race and ethnicity online. In an environment where a fundamental component of online life for these young people is discourse about race, new knowledge is constituted both by individual and by institutional interpretations of these notions. In light of this complex discursive context, my recourse to Critical Discourse Analysis (CDA), a methodological tool in Critical Language Studies, is used to call attention to some of the often hidden connections between language, power, and ideology. In this way, the application of CDA allows us to interrogate further the intersection between online discursive events (or conversations) and participants' larger sociocultural positions. In so doing, one can better understand the ways in which communities pass along ideas about themselves and how they mask or make ideological norms more transparent.

Thus, there are two underlying theoretical assumptions at work when we approach texts from a CDA position. First, because online discursive interactions are also sites of social interaction, they must be understood as *reflections* of a "knowledge base" that reveals larger offline social structures, situations, and norms about language and language use. Second, these knowledge bases are sites for the *reproduction* of other social structures, situations, and norms about language and language use. In this sense, when members of an online community participate in the production of discourse, they negotiate meanings and form newer ones to suit their needs, but these discourses are never free from the cultural norms and histories to which participants are bound. As Potter and Wetherell note, critical analysis of a discursive event isn't as much about the content as it is about the interpretations of it.[54] Thus, a critical approach allows us to appreciate the development of new forms of discourse while still interrogating the conditions under which longstanding ideologies are reproduced and maintained throughout.

Norman Fairclough's approach to CDA is most instructive here, and provides clear and useful analytical strengths for understanding the power of dedicated sites for youths and the larger racialized online communities.[55] His is a three-step method that involves describing the linguistic features within the text, interpreting the relationships between the discursive processes and that of the text, and, finally, explaining the relationships between discursive processes and larger social processes.[56] Rather than explain and address each of the steps individually, as is fairly standard in CDA, this section presents some of the illustrative findings from my seven-year case study, so as to underscore the dominant rhetorical strategies and techniques, themes, and ideologies with which young people can expect to engage when they are in dialogue about race and ethnicity on dedicated sites. My research findings suggest that (1) there is a relationship between topic titles, participation rate, and age of participants in the Heritage and Identity forum; (2) race-based essentialism operates more as an implicit element in these dialogues and is rejected outright when made explicit; (3) knowledge of the community's history is used to establish one's authority and authenticity, and in many cases history is treated uncritically like the physical sciences (as immutably factual, objective, and free from interpretation); and (4) a healthy sense of racial identity is one of the key parameters based on which participants are judged.

To better understand the role that discussions of race and ethnicity play on these sites, samples of exchanges in the Heritage and Identity message board forums were used exclusively.[57] A total of 3,027 threaded forum messages were considered for this particular analysis. This accounted for 415 messages on Asian Avenue, 1,735 messages of BlackPlanet, and 877 messages on MiGente. All the data were analyzed over time according to CDA, with multiple critical readings over time for the purpose of identifying salient discursive patterns, structural features, and repetition of themes. The messages under analysis were taken from a

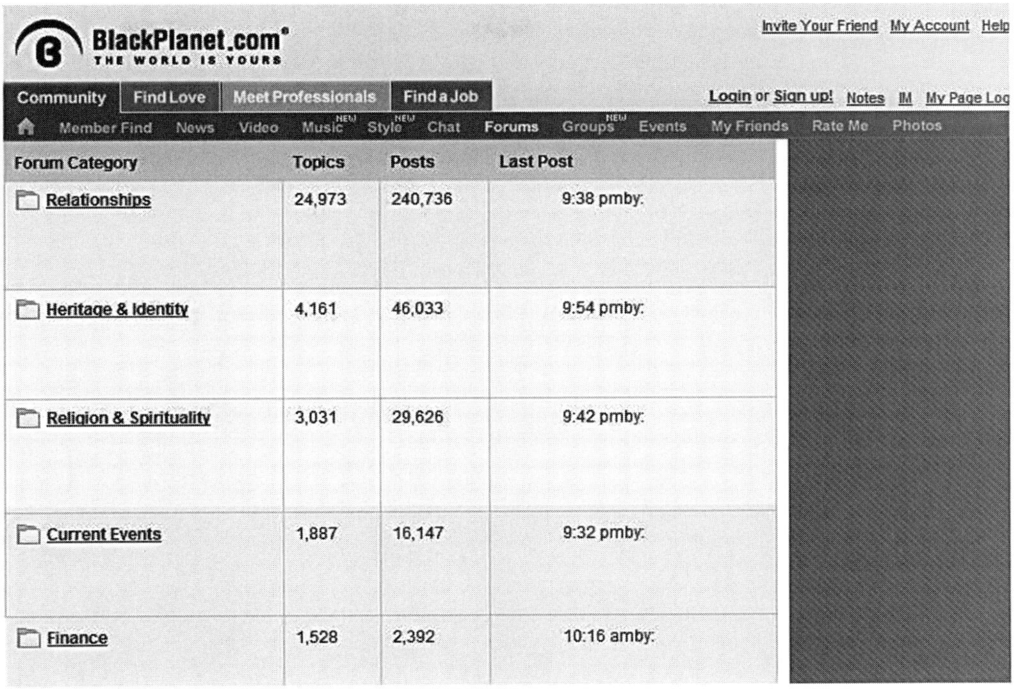

Figure 1

larger pool gathered from random visits over a seven-year period.[58] Only those discussions that generated responses from more than five participants were considered in an effort to pay closer attention to dialogic characteristics of a particular issue. Threads with fewer than five participants did not yield as many exchanges. Rather, participants responded to the original posts without engaging with or building on the contributions of members before them. Some of these discussion threads had few participants, were flooded with advertisements, were repeat postings, or were off-topic exchanges between online friends. Similarly, because the sizes of these communities range in the millions, the volume of daily message board postings is quite considerable. Many discussion threads do not receive more than a few responses because there are so many new topics each day. In the case of current events, several threads may present the same issue, thus lowering participation across all of them.

Nonetheless, even when accounting for the participation issues described above, the Heritage and Identity forum is still the centerpiece of interaction on two of the sites. As the January 2007 screen capture from BlackPlanet shows (Figure 1), the 4,161 discussion topics located in this forum generated 46,033 responses. In comparison, the second- and third-ranked forums were Religion & Spirituality and Current Events, where the combined participation is comparable with Heritage and Identity.

This pattern is fairly similar on MiGente (Figure 2). Whereas Religion & Spirituality currently has more topics and more responses than the others, Heritage and Identity has a comparable rate of participation per thread. For example, each of the 112 topics in Heritage

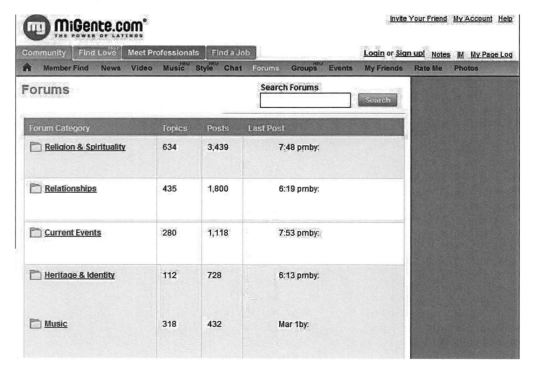

Figure 2

and Identity that were still receiving posts in January 2007 had more than five participants. On the other hand, Religion & Spirituality had 634 topics, but many of them asked users similar questions over the course of the day or the week, and in those cases there were few or no responses.

It must be noted that AsianAvenue discontinued its message boards for reasons currently unknown to the author.[59] However, until 2005 (about the time it was removed), participation in the Heritage and Identity section also outnumbered that of the other forums, and was the site of participation from various ethnic groups. It is interesting to note that the AsianAvenue chatrooms, which are the only remaining places CCI provides for group interaction, separate members by ethnicity (Figure 3). For example, there is a chatroom for DESIs (i.e., South Asian descent), East Asians (i.e., Chinese, Japanese, etc.), and Filipinos. At the time of this writing, separation by ethnicity does not occur on either of the other two sites.

The most popular discussions in Heritage and Identity are those that explicitly ask questions about race or ethnicity. Appearing at least once a day, a post may ask members to relate how racial identity impacts their way of life. Not only are these threads most prevalent, but they also tend to rank highest in participation, especially when the race of the community or the group under discussion is mentioned in the thread title. For example, on BlackPlanet, when looking at two threads with the same topic like, "I'm Black and I Voted For Bush . . . Are U Crazy"[60] and "War,"[61] the originators of the threads asked essentially the same question about whether black people should support President Bush and the war in Iraq. However,

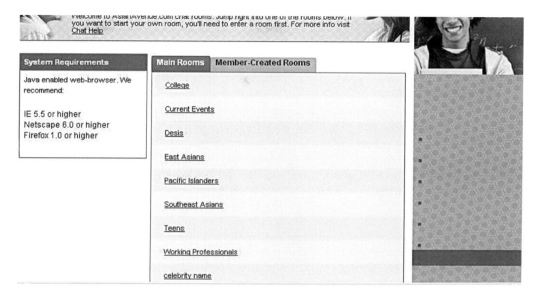

Figure 3

forty-one people responded to the post in which race was noted, and only eight responded to the post in which it was not. Similarly, of the topics generated from May to June 2006 on MiGente, each of the most popular threads included the words *Brown*, *Puerto Rican*, *Taino*, *Latino*, or *Mexican*.[62] On AsianAvenue, threads like "Do U Consider Hmongs to be like us?"[63] "Filipinos: Latino or Asian?"[64] and "What makes DESIs Asians?"[65] were among the most popular, each receiving responses well into a year after they were started.

As of 2006, CCI has given participants the option of revealing their age in their profiles. When looking at the age of participants in the BlackPlanet and MiGente forums over a two-month span, there also seems to be a relationship between explicit use of race and age range of participants within discussion threads. Of those whose ages were visible, all were over the age of 30 in the "War" thread, while those in the "I'm Black and I Voted For Bush" thread had seven participants under 25. Likewise, "Blacks and the military" attracted participants ranging in age from 19 to 40, while the "9/11 and Bush" thread had fewer respondents and none who were younger than 35. In the MiGente threads "Race Confusion Among So-Called Latins"[66] and "If You Are Latino and Dont Speak Spanish Does This Make You Hispanic?"[67] the average age of the respondents was 22, with the youngest participants aged 17 and 16, respectively. However, in "your take on the war?"[68] much like on BlackPlanet, participants were, on average, eight years older, with the eldest contributor being age 45.

Years ago, it was typical for participants to claim their communities rhetorically by declaring their cultures or heritages before engaging with a particular question. As was described in the previous section, when members responded to labellalatina1001's question, "What are you," they frequently qualified their "Latinoness" as their rite of participation in the forum. As a rhetorical strategy, qualifying one's Latinoness makes one an authority and implies that one is a credible source of information about community issues. In this way, respondents make clear that racial proximity to community is tied to one's right to influence decision making. Today, however, this relationship seems to have gone underground. While race or ethnicity is still the benchmark for participation, very few members or users actually state who they are. In response to a question about whether speaking Spanish defines one's Latinoness, one respondent states, "The problem with Hispanics is that we don't network like [Jews], [Europeans] do,"[69] while another retorts, "No one should consider themselves [*sic*] Hispanic we are LATINO."[70]

Rather than provide evidence that either one is Hispanic or Latino, the use of the inclusive term *we* establishes that both participants are part of the dominant group and thus are capable of legitimately contributing to conversations about the community "problem." While this shift away from qualifying one's identity can be the result of ongoing interaction, the prevalence of this pattern may also suggest that the default assumption is that participants are indeed in dialogue with members of the dominant group, unless otherwise stated. Moreover, the presumption is that the site is more or less free from outsiders, and that being from the dominant CCI racial community group still determines one's right to weigh in, particularly when weighing in means being critical of that particular group.

So assumed is membership in the racial/ethnic dominant group that participants are shocked when CaseyCanada, the originator of the seventy-three-page thread (and counting) "How Do You Feel about 'Whites' on BP," reveals that she is white and participates in the site because she prefers "the company of blacks" over her own.[71] (Notice that this very popular thread names a race in the title.) Responses, which vary from, "You white?" to "What u doin on [here]?" to "Wow had no idea," show that even with a picture beside her name, most thought CaseyCanada was black because she had not stated otherwise.[72] Her use of "you" in the thread title shows that she, too, assumes that everyone else responding will be black. Ironically, the quotation marks around *whites* suggests that she is skeptical about race-based categorizing even when she proceeds to normalize her experiences, being "unwelcome" in several threads, as representative of black views on the whole. Though most simply acknowledge their surprise and continue to offer very candid responses, some abandon the question altogether and interrogate her connection to the community. Respondents try to understand her relational position as much as she feels compelled to explain and justify it. As is frequently the case with outsiders on these dedicated sites, signifiers of interpersonal relationships (i.e., "my best friend is," "I grew up near," or "my girl/boyfriend is") are offered as evidence of participants' alliances and intentions. For example, CaseyCanada posts:

I joined BP to interact with people not to pretend to be something [I'm] not. My reasons for [preferring] the company of black people (over my own) is mostly because: I have spent my whole life living amongst black people its what I've come to be comfortable with. I feel "out of touch" when Im around my own as crazy as it sounds.[73]

Embedded in CaseyCanada's statement above is the understanding that not wanting to be among one's own is simply not normal, and that by "living amongst black people" and by becoming "comfortable with" them, she is "out of touch" with her natural state of being—an outsider among whites. Seemingly unaware of the implications of her statement, CaseyCanada fails to understand why respondents accuse her of being racist, no different from "others," and just another example of how white power manifests itself time and time again. Since she didn't "say" anything racist and rather "prefers" being around black people, CaseyCanada deduces that this is yet another instance of how race is a "[delinquent] subject and one word out of context can cause havoc!"[74]

Members tend to scrutinize outsiders who present themselves as allies with much more rigor than they do explicitly racist ones. For example, when AryanNationPrincess created racist posts (before her account was deleted), participants humorously quipped that her hatred must have been the result of a sexual relationship gone bad, or that "massa" was just "pissed" that she now has to purchase natural black features in order to get attention from white men. AryanNationPrincess's post received a mere twenty-one responses from seven participants in total, none of them really analyzing it with the care and attention paid to CaseyCanada. It must be noted that respondents quickly establish that a romantic interest in the opposite sex is the primary motivation for both CaseyCanada and AryanNationPrincess to join BlackPlanet. This pattern appears on all three sites, whether respondents are critically engaging the poster or humorously dismissing him or her. The particular community's sexualized history frequently undergirds its discursive interactions with outsiders.

But simply belonging to any one of CCI's dominant racial or ethnic groups does not guarantee that participants' contributions to these sites are welcome either. Knowledge of community history (or the willingness to learn) is just as critical as knowledge of a participant's own genetic makeup. In fact, familiarity with the community's origins, how the "race" really came to be, and how it has developed are typically offered as historical "facts" that vouch for both the "authenticity" and the authority of the poster. When LiLing2K (age unknown) details her schoolyard experiences with Japanese racism in Seattle, Washington, and connects this with centuries of Japanese–Chinese conflict, respondents congratulate her for being a "good girl" and for keeping her eyes on "who she is," in spite of her American influences. It is assumed here that LiLing2K's ability to interpret these experiences stems from cultural pride, and by extension a healthy sense of racial identity. In this way, LiLing2K becomes the model citizen in the discussion thread because she is born Chinese and is also conscious of the "undeniable facts of our history" that distinguish her from others grouped under "Asian." This consciousness is then associated with racially, and often gender-, appropriate behaviors. While youth demographics are not specifically at issue here, I believe we can extrapolate that, in this informal learning context, youth will indeed learn which attitudes they must subscribe to in order to become full-fledged members of their on- and offline communities.

As is evidenced above, there is an underlying assumption in the rhetoric that there are essential properties to one's racial or ethnic identity. Although participants never seem to agree on what that essence is—food, music, geography, blood, slavery, white domination, disenfranchisement, and skin color are some of the frequently occurring themes—their responses imply that this essence of race and ethnicity exists nonetheless. Examples of the ways in which participants on all three sites engage with the notion of "mixed blood" will demonstrate this ideological belief. Responses can run the gamut from "since I am *only* half I don't know if I can say"[75] (emphasis added), "am Haifa and proud. The best of both bloods in me,"[76] or "I [don't] care what anybody says [I'm] black cuz I got half [black] blood."[77] These few statements show how simple words like "only half," "both bloods," and "half black blood" contribute to a prevailing ideology that being born into a particular race largely determines who you are. But when faced with more overt essentialist notions, participants typically reject them, noting instead that there is so "much diversity of our race [defining] us is impossible."[78] As the following illustrates, when AsianAvenue's LeeK asks why Asians try to act like "the inferior race" by speaking "ebonics"—is it the popularity of hip-hop culture or is it reflective of deeper reasons such as identity or cultural displacement—his extremist position is admonished by the group, he is labeled a racist, and worse yet, he is viewed as being no different from whites. Responses increasingly address the inappropriateness of his comment, the way it does not account for diversity, how it threatens peace within and across communities, and how, ironically, it reveals his self-hate, insecurity, and overall ignorance.[79] LeeK's desire to reduce all blacks to inferior "ebonics" speakers or to propose that Asians who speak it are "less" Asian, is vehemently opposed. In spite of this, most participants on other threads tend to agree that speaking another language changes them, and that to be real Asians means that they must speak their real languages.

The view that language is tied to *being* and identity is echoed on MiGente. When one poster asks why Latinos prefer Ebonics over Spanglish, a conversation that takes place in English on the English-speaking Latino site, many agree that it is because "[Latinos] are losing their way, have no pride, don't remember where [they] come from."[80] The premise of LeeK's post, that a community ought to speak its natural language, is understood, perhaps applauded. Whereas overt essentialism in LeeK's post is the focus of critical attention, a similar, albeit less obvious form, goes relatively unnoticed in the MiGente thread. Furthermore, those overt claims left LeeK open to charges of being ignorant and lacking in real self-worth, "Why else wouldn't [*sic*] you feel so threatened by blacks being on this site."[81] On MiGente, participants conclude that not to speak Spanish means that *those* Latinos are trying to be something they are not. The connection between speaking and *being* is a fairly recurring theme in the Heritage and Identity forum. Although several respondents on MiGente assert that Spanish is not the "natural language" of any Latino, such views are rarely the subject of intense dialogues. The more popular view supports the idea that Spanish is indeed a distinguishing feature of one's Latinoness.

Because consensus or group cohesion plays a large role in community life, it is fairly common for members to silence, modify, or limit the fullness of dissenting voices in favor of the dominant opinion within the thread. Even though some respondents in LeeK's thread remarked, "I hear what you're saying but you're going about it the wrong way," or "No comment," clearly indicating that they had alternative, perhaps even supportive, views, such sentiments were never elaborated upon.[82] Given that LeeK's question was not only met with unfavorable replies but was also used to determine that his was a self-esteem desperately in need of repair, it is no wonder that no one publicly sided with him. If we draw from these emotional issues and their consequences for young participants, we can see how easily dominant beliefs are passed on through the discourse, informing them that simply being born Asian, black, or Latino is not enough. Furthermore, there are opinions, views, and ways of acting online that are significant components of an authentic Asian, black, or Latino identity. Indeed, young participants on all three sites will learn which views will be applauded and which ones will be admonished. They will also learn that there are inherent discursive rules for *acting* or *being* online, and that these rules determine whether one has a healthy sense of racial pride, as well as whether one is a credible source of knowledge in the community.

As this discussion shows, discourse about race and ethnicity on social networking sites is rather complex. On the one hand, participants tend to object to the notion that they can be reduced to shared or essentialist racial or ethnic characteristics, frequently citing the diversity of personalities, appearances, and interests among their interpersonal networks as evidentiary. The most vehement opposition, though, comes about when they are faced with what is perceived as racist ideologies, particularly those that posters feel exemplify the continuation of white supremacist attitudes. On the other hand, participants also play active roles in reinforcing some of these prevailing notions, often inadvertently, by implying that there are definitive ways of being Asian, black, or Latino. Given that these forums are the centerpiece of public life for a cross-section of participants, particularly young people, there are profound implications when considering that what is said about race, and how it is said, determines how the community interprets the value of each participant's contribution.

Part III: The Future of Dedicated Sites

As I have argued throughout this chapter, dialogues about race and ethnicity are purposeful discursive events taking place on dedicated sites. It must be reiterated that these conversations are not inevitable consequences of holding membership in such sites; rather, participants willingly contribute to race-based discussion topics out of the myriad of others available to them. The Heritage and Identity forums have consistently been loci of public life, and with the addition of the age feature, it appears that these forums attract a fair share of the sites' young members. As loci of public life for several years, these online forums are where ideologies are likely to be developed, promoted, contested, and institutionalized. Furthermore, for any participant who has a stake in the community, weighing in about race becomes a fundamental component of large-scale community engagement. That these conversations are likely to bring with them taken-for-granted beliefs is certainly nothing new. Demonstrating what critical language theorists mean when they say that discourse reflects the sociocultural material affecting producers of that discourse, some ideologies are so deeply embedded in the common sense of their cultures that participants inevitably reify values that, when otherwise made conscious of them, they would oppose.

But unlike other forms of media, participants in these online networks—many of whom are youth—are active producers of their content and exert a real sense of ownership over these spaces. It is much easier under these conditions to naturalize various ideological strains, because it appears as though what is circulated as discursive truths originate from the communities that utter (type) them. Because consensus in such peer-communities is inherently bound to community status and degree of racial pride, participants are also less likely to critique these truths, further allowing them to be upheld as the standard. As a result, becoming critical of and interrogating such below-the-radar ideologies is made more difficult (though not impossible), especially when adherence to them is the benchmark of identity, participation, and public life. This situation is further complicated because young people are more susceptible to the influence of their peers, whether positive or negative, and are participating in these communities at a time when their needs for acceptance, approval, and belonging are highest.

Given that these beliefs are produced and consumed—learned and taught—by those that have been troped by them underscores the need for theorizing about what young people consume as participants in these informal learning spaces, and for developing effective tools for helping them to engage with them more critically. Aside from learning the rules about initiating, structuring, and participating in large-scale discussions with others from around the world, members are constantly learning and teaching each other about the overall effect that the individualized act of voicing opinion has on collective thinking and action. The latter element could well be one of the most important discursive acts taking place on these sites. For those who may not yet be granted full access to the public sphere offline (if ever), participants have the opportunity to speak and be heard on what they see as more equal ground. By virtue of their contributions to public life, members learn the importance of consensus, as both a measure of collective reasoning and as a mechanism for silencing or ignoring those opinions that are out of favor with the majority. Informal citizenship schools with no prescribed curriculum so to speak, participants effectively learn and teach each other about which aspects of race and ethnicity are fundamental for public engagement. In learning how to speak about, listen to, or repress certain ideas about race and ethnicity, participants also forge a much deeper understanding of the connection between online politicking and offline social structures. Interaction on these sites becomes a fundamental aspect of relationship-building under conditions like mass participation, which inevitably teaches them about the complex ways in which racial identifications continue to serve as common ground, especially in an increasingly globalized, multicultural world. With so many members, millions dialoguing in larger conversations, participants not only learn to form community but they learn the different styles of communication within their respective diasporas.

For participants in these learning environments, online literacy skills will be useful tools in providing them with the ability to read and interpret texts of which they are both consumers *and* producers. Though much has been said about critical literacy skills elsewhere[83] and the ways in which such tools have been used historically to empower communities of color, we must also listen to the cautionary words of scholars like Adam Banks who argue that for a society in which racist ideologies run so deep, literacy skills alone cannot guarantee the kind of material, functional, experiential, and critical access that is needed for young users of color to see themselves as "users, producers, and even transformers" of the varying technologies informing their day-to-day lives.[84]

As ripe with potential as these online forums are—imagine the possibility of Malcolm X ushering a call to 16 million African Americans in 1960—there has yet to be any real hypothesizing or organizing around key issues that each community deems important to its offline life. By real hypothesizing or organizing, I mean that group discussions about issues like police profiling, discrimination in restaurants, improper translation of ballots, flying while Muslim, or driving while black do not include ways of translating this level of community consciousness into the type of collective action or decision making that is part and parcel of any public sphere. What is rarely heard or seen in seven years' worth of observations is the sense that "something can be done" to counter the varying forms of hegemonic control participants encounter offline. Although examples can be called upon where communities of color have deliberately used online networking to impact offline conditions (part II of this chapter provided just a few of them), public life for the more than 16 million participants on CCI's sites has yet to produce the kind of action consistent with the level of discourse about racism and social justice taking place. My most recent work on BlackPlanet has shown that, while youth are clearly engaged in conversations about issues of common concern to the larger black community, these discussions never moved beyond a discursive level of civic engagement. In fact, when I analyzed postings about Hurricane Katrina and genocide in Darfur, participants who suggested that the group should "do something" were either summarily dismissed, called "irrational," or placated with polite acknowledgments.[85]

Developing new ways to combat the pernicious effects of the "why bother" rhetoric I witnessed in these discussions is of chief importance because young participants must see that there is a fundamental relationship between collective voice and social change. Likewise, helping young people to see that such sites are public forums that are useful vehicles for civic engagement is necessary, especially for black and Latino communities, who continue to internalize the otherwise immobilizing rhetoric of the digital divide. Teaching them about the potential of such connective capabilities will have real consequences on how young people of color think about the possibilities of new media, and themselves, in bringing about material change.

Despite the range of challenges discussed above, for young people, participating in dedicated social networking sites is especially important because they can be useful vehicles for strengthening their cultural identities, for teaching them how to navigate both public and private dimensions of their racial lives, and for providing them access to a more globalized yet unfixed conversation about their community histories. Scores of contemporary research studies show how important cultivating intragroup cultural networks is to minority youth.[86] Much like the world offline, participating in online cultural communities will help them to develop a healthy sense of racial identity, what psychologists argue is necessary to resist the pernicious effects of racism. In likening a healthy cultural identity to a healthy psyche, Marcia suggests that without it, an individual is unable to adapt easily in more diverse environments.[87] These findings also underscore why minority youth must have access to dedicated online spaces, not just mainstream or "race neutral" ones. Seeking out and logging in to online communicative spaces is a central component of the lives of all young people today; however, participating in those that are more likely to value the raced experiences of minority youth not only teaches them that who they are offline bears as much relevance to who they are online, but it also teaches them that talking about this aspect of social life can help them redress the impact of racism.

Notes

1. Delpi, Why Are So Many Whites Here? *Asian Avenue*, April 9, 2000. Retrieved May 28, 2000. http://www.asianavenue.com/Members/Forums/FORUM=13501.

2. The names of CCI participants quoted in this chapter have been changed to protect their identities. Although the rules for conducting online research are not firm, I have followed some of the guidelines prescribed by Norman K. Denzin, Cybertalk and the Method of Instances, in *Doing Internet Research: Critical Issues and Methods for Examining the Net*, ed. Steve Jones (Thousand Oaks, CA: Sage, 1999), 107–126. Throughout this study, I have never interacted with any of the participants cited nor have I asked for permission to quote directly. Such practices are fairly common, given that all of the information included in this chapter is "public" and available to anyone who registers on the particular CCI site. Nonetheless, I have changed the participants' names and have not provided the URLs to their specific posts. Instead of URLs to the posting, I have included the URL for the thread, the site name, and date the post was created.

3. Because members are not restricted from opening multiple accounts, it is likely that the number of subscribers per site is not representative of the actual number of individual members. For example, in 2004, BlackPlanet boasted a whopping 18 million subscribers; in 2006 the number hovered around 14 million. Although users are worldwide, the majority are based in the United States. In 2004, Forrester Research estimated that Asian Americans, African Americans, and Latinos accounted for over 18 million Web users combined, and that in 2000, 3.8 million African American households were online. Nonetheless, the combined membership of these sites is still likely to be well in the millions.

4. Gee defines *Discourses* (with a capital D) as our ways of being in the world. Every Discourse has a "tacit theory" as to what determines a normal person within discourse, and this defines what is the right way for each person to speak, listen, act, value, and think. See James Paul Gee, *Social Linguistics and Literacies: Ideology in Discourses* (London: Taylor & Francis, 1999). According to Josephine Peyton Young, Discourse is like a "club with [implicit rules] about how [members] are [to] behave." See Boy Talk: Critical Literacy and Masculinities, *Reading Research Quarterly* 35, no. 3 (2000): 312. For example, BlackPlanet member BigWhiteBlob (name used with permission) posted a rather interesting response to a forum question that asked whether it is possible to "know" with certainty that someone is Black in cyberspace. He stated that

"it isn't really the sprinkling of faces that are like your own, that is nice, but it is really about the content, I can tell by the expressions used on people's pages or the way they describe themselves that I am in my real community." Interestingly, BigWhiteBlob refers to the ways in which members speak (quite frankly type) as evidence of their insider/outsider positionalities. That seeing a picture of someone who looks like you is not enough suggests that some transference of real-world communicative modalities is necessary to gain full access. Discourses (and language choices) function as boundary markers, signs of proximity to territory, mapping who is inside or outside, what is authentic, and who belongs, as well as a host of historical, political, and epistemological understandings of realities, knowledge(s), texts, and selves.

5. According to Norman Fairclough, Critical Language Studies (CLS) analyzes "social interactions in a way which focuses upon their linguistic elements, and which sets out to show up their generally hidden determinants in the system of social relationships, as well as hidden effects they may have upon that system." See *Language and power* (London: Longman, 1989), 5. With these postulations on the relationship of language and power, along with the contributions of Foucault, CLS becomes an "alternative orientation to language studies which implies a different demarcation of language study into approaches or branches, different relationships between them, and different orientations within each of them" (Ibid., 13).

6. Ibid., 5.

7. See Community Connect, Inc., "About us." Retrieved May 4, 2002. http://www.communityconnect.com/about.html.

8. Ibid.

9. Ibid.

10. John Gangemi, A MySpace That Speaks Your Language, *BusinessWeek.com*, September 2006, http://www.businessweek.com/smallbiz/content/sep2006/sb20060920_307149.htm?chan=search. Retrieved October 11, 2006.

11. Ibid.

12. In spite of the decline in daily participation on the CCI sites, the company has managed to maintain its foothold as the leading special-interest Web publisher for American ethnic groups, and remains in the top fifty of Web content publishers for the last eight years. Web trafficking sites like Alexa and comScore are useful resources for comparing the daily participation of these sites.

13. Vorris Nunley, Hush Harbors: Barbershops, Rhetorical Theory, and African American Expressive Culture (Doctoral dissertation, Pennsylvania State University, 2005), 1–19.

14. Ibid., 16.

15. Norman Fairclough, *Language and Power* (London: Longman, 1989), 26.

16. labellalatina1001, What Are You, *MiGente*, February 10, 2003, http://www.migente.com/Members/Forums/28392. Retrieved March 8, 2003.

17. OrelleAngelle, What Are You, *MiGente*, March 20, 2004, http://www.migente.com/Members/Forums/28392. Retrieved March 21, 2004.

18. *In Modernity and Self-Identity*, Anthony Giddens notes that "[a] person's identity is not to be found in behaviour, nor—important though this is—in the reactions of others, but in the capacity to keep a particular narrative going. The individual's biography, if she is to maintain regular interaction with others in the day-to-day world, cannot be wholly fictive. It must continually integrate events which occur in the external world, and sort them into the ongoing 'story' about the self." See *Modernity and Self-Identity: Self and Society in the Late Modern Age* (Palo Alto, CA: Stanford University Press, 1991), 54.

19. Habermas argues, through a Kantian analysis, that civil society allows man "to engage in a debate over the general rules of governing relations in the basically privatized but publicly relevant sphere of commodity exchange in social labor." See Jurgen Habermas, *The Structural Transformation of the Public Sphere*, trans. Thomas Burger (Cambridge, MA: MIT Press, 1989), 27. For Kant, civil society in Europe relied on the private man's public use of his reason. See Immanuel Kant, *Foundations of the Metaphysics of Morals and What Is Enlightenment*, trans. Lewis White Beck (New York: Macmillan, 1990). For a discussion on alternative public spheres, read Nancy Fraser, "Rethinking the Public Sphere: A Contribution to the Critique of Actually Existing Democracy," in *Habermas and the Public Sphere*, ed. Craig Calhoun (Cambridge, MA: MIT Press, 1992), 109–142.

20. Sherry Turkle, *Life on the Screen: Identity in the Age of the Internet* (New York: Simon & Schuster, 1997), 14–16.

21. Lisa Nakamura, *Cybertypes: Race, Ethnicity, and Identity on the Internet* (New York: Routledge, 2002), 102–123.

22. Stuart Hall, Culture, the Media and the "Ideological Effect," in *Mass Communication and Society*, ed. James Curran, Michael Gurevitch, and Janet Woolacott (London: Edward Arnold, 1977), 318–323.

23. The list of scholarship on identity and cyberculture is very extensive. Some recent publications on race or online communities include Darin Barney. *The Network Society* (Cambridge, UK: Polity Press, 2004); John Rodzvilla, ed., *We've Got Blog: How Weblogs Are Changing Our Culture* (Cambridge, MA: Perseus, 2002); Leah A. Lievrouw and Sonia Livingstone, eds, *Handbook of New Media: Social Shaping and Consequences of ICTs* (London: Sage, 2002); Manuel Castells, ed., *The Network Society: A Cross-cultural Perspective* (Northampton, MA: Elgar, 2004); K. Ann Renninger and Wesley Shumar, eds., *Building Virtual Communities: Learning and Change in Cyberspace* (New York: Cambridge University Press, 2002); Beth Kolko, Lisa Nakamura, and Gibert Rodman, *Race in Cyberspace* (London: Routledge, 2002); and Alondra Nelson, Thuy Linh N. Tu, and Alicia Headlam Hines, *Technicolor: Race, Technology, and Everyday Life* (New York: New York University Press, 2001).

24. Sherry Turkle, Constructions and Reconstructions of Self in Virtual Reality: Playing in the MUDS, *Mind, Culture and Activity* 1, no. 3 (1994): 158–167.

25. Emily Noelle Ignacio, E-scaping Boundaries: Bridging Cyberspace and Diaspora Studies through Nethnography, in *Critical Cyberculture Studies*, ed. David Silver and Adrienne Massanari (New York: New York University Press, 2006), 186–187.

26. Ibid., 187.

27. Steven Rosenbush, News Corp.'s Place in MySpace, *Businessweek*, July 19, 2005, http://www.businessweek.com/technology/content/jul2005/tc20050719_5427_tc119.htm. Retrieved August 12, 2006.

28. Robert Young, Why Rupert Murdoch Really Bought MySpace? *GigaOM*, August 6, 2005, http://gigaom.com/2005/08/06/why-murdoch-bought-myspace/. Retrieved August 12, 2006.

29. News.com, MySpace.com Creates Own Record Label, *News.com*, November 2005, http://news.com.com/MySpace.com+creates+own+record+label/2100-1027_3-5930390.html?tag=nefd.top. Retrieved August 12, 2006.

30. Ibid.

31. GlobeandMail.com, Google, MySpace Ink Deal, *ReportOnBusiness*, August 8, 2006, http://www.theglobeandmail.com/servlet/story/RTGAM.20060807.wgoog0807/BNStory/Business. Retrieved August 12, 2006.

32. Benedict Anderson, When the Virtual Becomes the Real: A Talk with Benedict Anderson, http://www.nira.go.jp/pube/review/96spring/intervi.html. Retrieved August 18, 2006.

33. News.com, MySpace.com Creates Own Record Label.

34. Peter Kollock, The Economies of Online Cooperation: Gifts and Public Goods in Cyberspace, in *Communities in Cyberspace*, ed. Marc A. Smith and Peter Kollock (London: Routledge, 1999), 220–239.

35. Howard Rheingold, *The Virtual Community: Homesteading on the Electronic Frontier* (Reading, MA: Addison-Wesley, 1993), 57–58.

36. Kollock, 225–239.

37. For further discussion on imagined communities, see Benedict Anderson, *Imagined Communities* (London: Verso, 1991).

38. ROFL is netspeak for "rolling on the floor laughing"; LOL is netspeak for "laughing out loud."

39. John G. Ruggie, Territoriality and Beyond: Problematising Modernity in International Relations, *International Organization* 47 (1993): 139–174.

40. Kenichi Ohmae, *The End of the Nation State* (New York: Free Press, 1995).

41. Arjun Appadurai. *Modernity at Large: Cultural Dimensions of Globalization* (Minneapolis, MN: University of Minnesota Press, 1996).

42. Jan Aart Scholte, The Geography of Collective Identities in a Globalizing World, *Review of International Political Economy* 3 (1996): 565–608.

43. SK and NYCTony posting to African American Chat 261, *Yahoo!* August 1, 2006, http://www.yahoo.com/chatrooms. To access Yahoo! chat rooms, one must have a Yahoo! e-mail address and install Yahoo! Instant Messenger.

44. Anna Everett, The Revolution Will Be Digitized: Afrocentricity and the Digital Public Sphere, *Social Text* 20, no. 2 (2002): 131, 139.

45. John Rawls, *Political Liberalism* (New York: Columbia University Press, 1993), 4–44.

46. Ibid., 13–23.

47. I visited some of these MiGente members pages on MySpace and, in most cases, they reproduced their MiGente content.

48. Keith Boykin, Black Gay Bloggers Unite Against Homophobic Artists, *KeithBoykin* blog, July 11, 2006, http://www.keithboykin.com/arch/2006/07/11/black_gay_blogg; EURWeb, Black Gay Bloggers Launch Protest: Target Is Music Industry's Anti-Gay AIDS Concert, July 11, 2006, http://www.eurweb.com/story/eur27394.cfm. Retrieved August 15, 2006.

49. Fox News Online, NYC Reggae Concert Canceled after Protests, *FoxNews.com*, July 12, 2006, http://www.foxnews.com/wires/2006Jul12/0,4670,ReggaeProtest,00.html. Retrieved August 15, 2006.

50. BlackPlanet, 911 Response to Unsaddened Blacks, *BlackPlanet*, http://www.blackplanet.com/forums/thread.html?thread_id=18603. Retrieved August 21, 2006.

51. Ibid.

52. Ibid.

53. Ibid.

54. John Potter and Margaret Wetherell, *Discourse and Social Psychology: Beyond Attitudes and Behaviour* (London: Sage, 1987).

55. Norman Fairclough, *Critical Discourse Analysis* (London: Longman, 1995).

56. Ibid., 97.

57. In order to gain access to all of the features that each of these sites offer, participants must register and disclose their sex, age, level of education, and racial or ethnic characteristics. Interestingly, the identity categories and requirements differ on each site. Identity on AsianAvenue is denoted by one's ethnicity, with members choosing from among twenty-one ethnic groups. From 2000 to 2005, BlackPlanet members only had five choices available to account for their identities: Black, Asian, Latino, Native American, and White. By 2006, with its site redesign, members can choose "other" or type in a specific ethnicity. MiGente registrants can choose from among ethnic origin and race. There are twenty-five ethnic categories like Dominican, Cuban, and so forth and the same five racial categories available on BlackPlanet. Commenting on the click-box identity, Lisa Nakamura argues that the process of choosing identity in this way forces users into dominant notions of race. Arguably, the various changes to these categories in the site redesign may be indicative of an increased social awareness of the inadequateness of these categories. Nakamura, *Cybertypes*.

58. CCI has twice revamped its sites and, as a result of this, older threads and discussions that may have been brimming with meaning were deleted. The discussion forums were disabled during the time of the redesign, and in the case of AsianAvenue, discontinued altogether.

59. It appears as though AsianAvenue has undergone the most drastic modifications in comparison to the other two CCI sites. I suspect that these changes are in an effort to keep up with current social networking trends used on sites like MySpace. As such, there is no general public forum for the entire AsianAvenue community.

60. Blackplanet, I'm Black and I Voted For Bush. . . Are U Crazy, *BlackPlanet*, http://www.blackplanet.com/forums/thread.html?thread_id=1851. Retrieved June 9, 2006.

61. BlackPlanet, War, *BlackPlanet*, http://www.blackplanet.com/forums/thread.html?thread_id=185. Retrieved June 9, 2006.

62. For example, on MiGente, see threads http://www.migente.com/forums/thread.html?thread_id=2720; http://www.migente.com/forums/thread.html?thread_id=658; http://www.migente.com/forums/thread.html?thread_id=2511; http://www.migente.com/forums/thread.html?thread_id=2200; http://www.migente.com/forums/thread.html?thread_id=373; and http://www.migente.com/forums/thread.html?thread_id=1567.

63. AsianAvenue, Do You Consider Hmongs To Be Like Us? *AsianAvenue*, http://www.asianavenue.com/Members/Forums/viewforum.html?   VIEW=THREAD&PID=17036&RID=17036&FORUM=1011. Retrieved May 4, 2000.

64. AsianAvenue, Filipinos: Latino or Asian? *AsianAvenue*, http://www.asianavenue.com/Members/Forums/viewforum.html?VIEW=THREAD&PID=18726&RID=18726&FORUM=1011. Retrieved May 4, 2000.

65. AsianAvenue, What Makes DESIs Asians? *AsianAvenue*, http://www.asianavenue.com/Members/Forums/viewforum.html?VIEW=THREAD&PID=182340&RID=182340&FORUM=27375. Retrieved May 8, 2000.

66. MiGente, Race Confusion Among So-called Latins, *MiGente*, http://www.migente.com/forums/thread.html?thread_id=619. Retrieved June 16, 2006.

67. MiGente, If You Are Latino and Dont Speak Spanish Does This Make You Hispanic? *MiGente*, http://www.migente.com/forums/thread.html? thread_id=1802. Retrieved June 16, 2006.

68. MiGente, Your Take on the War? *MiGente*, http://www.migente.com/forums/thread.html?thread_id=192. Retrieved June 16, 2006.

69. MiGente, If You Are Latino.

70. Ibid.

71. BlackPlanet, How Do You Feel About 'Whites' on BP? *BlackPlanet*, http://www.blackplanet.com/forums/forum.html?forum_id=156. Retrieved February 1, 2007.

72. Ibid.

73. Ibid.

74. Ibid.

75. BlackPlanet, Interracial Chaos, *BlackPlanet*, http://www.blackplanet.com/forums/thread.html?thread_id=2162. Retrieved August 18, 2006.

76. AsianAvenue, Haifas Identify [Yourselves], *AsianAvenue*, http://www.asianavenue.com/forums/thread.html?thread_id=1910. Retrieved May 20, 2000.

77. MiGente, Blacarican??? *MiGente*, http://www.blackplanet.com/forums/thread.html?thread_id=1078. Retrieved July 9, 2006.

78. Ibid.

79. AsianAvenue, Chronic Ebonics, *AsianAvenue*, http://www.asianavenue.com/Members/Forums/viewforum.html?VIEW=THREAD&PID=187034&RID=187034&FORUM=27375. Retrieved May 20, 2000.

80. MiGente, Spanish Spanglish English, *MiGente*, http://www.migente.com/Members/Forums/viewforum.html?VIEW=THREAD&PID=18575&RID=18575&FORUM=4377. Retrieved July 9, 2006.

81. AsianAvenue, Chronic Ebonics.

82. Ibid.

83. See, e.g., Cynthia Selfe, *Technology and Literacy in the Twenty-first Century: The Importance of Paying Attention* (Carbondale, IL: Southern Illinois University Press, 1999); and Barbara Warnick, *Critical Literacy in a Digital Era* (Mahwah, NJ: Erlbaum, 2002).

84. Adam Banks, *Race, Rhetoric & Technology: Searching for Higher Ground* (Mahwah, NJ: Erlbaum, 2005), 138.

85. Dara N. Byrne, Public Discourse, Community Concerns, and Its Relationship to Civic Engagement: Explaining Black Social Networking Traditions on BlackPlanet.com, *Journal of Computer Mediated Communication* 13 (2007), http://jcmc.indiana.edu.

86. Janet E. Helms, ed., *Black and White Racial Identity: Theory, Research and Practice* (New York: Greenwood, 1990); Harvey P. Oshman and Martin Manosevitz, The Impact of the Identity Crisis on the Adjustment of Late Adolescent Males, *Journal of Youth and Adolescence* 3 (1974): 207–216; Mary-Jane Rotheram-Borus, Ethnic Differences in Adolescents' Identity Status and Associated Behavioral Problems, *Journal of Adolescence* 12 (1989): 361–374; and James E. Marcia, Identity and Intervention, *Journal of Adolescence* 12 (1989): 401–410.

87. Marcia, Identity and Intervention, 401–410.

Separating Race from Technology: Finding Tomorrow's IT Progress in the Past

Tyrone D. Taborn

Career Communications Group, Inc.

Saying that the Digital Divide is closing because minorities have greater access to computers is like saying minorities have a stake in the automobile industry because they drive cars.[1]

Myths, if recited often enough, become self-fulfilling prophecies. Two such myths, turned prophetic, run counter to the low participation rates of minorities in the science, technology, engineering, math (STEM), and technological arts fields. First, popular opinion holds that mathematics is a loathed subject and an area of particular weakness for students of color. However, there are studies that find more minority students rate math as their favorite subject than do their white counterparts.[2] Second, there is a familiar myth that blacks, especially, and other minority youth by extension, are slower to adopt technologies that connect them to the nation's information infrastructure. However, the National Telecommunications and Information Administration report, which several subsequent studies support, shows that despite the divide, blacks are coming online in increasing numbers, and that they are actively keeping pace with the purchases of products that link them to the communications infrastructure.[3]

The fact that minorities have a propensity toward math raises the question about why there are so few of them in advanced math courses leading to a track in STEM careers. Other studies have revealed that a similar misperception about math incompetence among women is common as well. Young girls actually score higher in these subjects than do boys. Yet, as they advance in school, they lose interest. The point here is that we need to be more concerned with why there are, and how to prevent, such outcomes and misperceptions that have very real consequences for already underserved minority youths and girls.

It is not only the failure of organized programs to bridge the digital divide that concerns us here. There is another problem where race and technology intersect. Walk into any classroom (majority white or minority, rich or poor) and quiz students on whether they know Kobe Bryant. Then, query them on Dr. Mark Dean, the African American engineer who played a critical part in developing the modern-day IBM personal computer. Sadly, most students will not know much about the latter. This demonstrates the lack of awareness and self-knowledge minority youths show when it comes to identifying black role models in technology. Still, experiences are not identical for all minorities. The African American story—the fact that few black youths know African American computer scientist Dr. Mark Dean—has much in common with the rest.

"I Want to Be Like Mike"

The lack of visible role models in science and digital media technologies represents an enormous problem for closing the technology gap. A number of surveys indicate that many technology professionals entered the field because of a role model (ITAA).[4] For white youths, the odds are on their side for opportunities to interact with role models who reflect their values and culture in today's new information society. The situation is not the same for minorities. As our Kobe Bryant–Mark Dean example above attests, the small pool of minority technology professionals makes it very unlikely that minority youth will have meaningful and life-changing interactions or encounters with information technology (IT) role models that look like them.

A *US Black Engineer & Information Technology* magazine survey showed that 23 percent of respondents cited an advisor's role in influencing their career choices.[5] Twenty-one percent cited a family member, and 30 percent said a role model working in the IT field had influenced their choices. For minority youth, many of whom lack access to professional role models, contemporary media images and history take on critical roles in shaping their relationship to science and technology, and even their positions in the ubiquitous computing culture that defines much of their everyday lives. Underlying this problem is the fact that the significant achievements of minorities in scientific and technical fields have been obscured by history and popular culture representations. Even more sinister is that what gets erased is minority communities' historical practices of embracing technology, and their record of producing some of humanity's greatest IT innovations. So precious little of this important history is taught or documented. Therefore, having neither identifiable role models nor historical records to consult, minorities see technology and the world of science as places where very few of their kind are reflected, and spaces where none of them can enter and flourish.

Bruce Sinclair, author of *Technology and the African-American Experience*, argues that it will take more than writing blacks and other minorities back into history to remedy the problem. Understanding how whites have presented themselves is crucial as well. He says, "From the eighteenth century on, white Americans described themselves as an inventive people. They claimed to have a natural disposition for quick and novel solutions to the practical problem of life."[6] Of course, this characterization is an exaggeration. If minority youths were familiarized with their impressive IT history, they might not be so easily intimidated, or their early passions for mathematics so readily extinguished. Part of the reason for low minority participation (beyond consumerism) in science and technology, and in digital media culture, is that the technological discourse has been separated from the larger issue of race in the United States. In spite of progress in providing minority communities and schools with technology artifacts like computers, longstanding racial issues continue to be formidable obstacles to minority pipeline development for future science and technology workers and educators.

So, we ask now, why is it that black and brown students are still failing to change this technological imbalance and increase their ranks in the science and technology fields? To find answers, we now turn to other factors. One, minority youth don't feel welcome in many STEM and other IT classes. Two, negative attitudes and perceptions of instructors persist. And, three, there are very few people who look like them teaching the courses.[7] For many minority students, the consequence is a lack of self-confidence, feelings of isolation, and, finally, a loss of interest in these subjects. However, perception plays a far larger role than the academic community seems willing to acknowledge. What the research demonstrates is that among the factors that influence the low participation rates of women and minorities in science and technology are the following:

- Lack of self-confidence
- Feeling of isolation
- Lack of interest
- Financial problems
- Not being accepted into a department
- Feelings of intimidation
- Poor advising

A study at Iowa State University entitled "An Engineering Student Retention Study," by Cheryl Moller-Wong and Arvid Eide, printed in the *Journal of Engineering Education* in January 1997,[8] organized attrition factors into the following five categories:

- Background (existed for the student prior to enrollment)
- Organizational (admissions, scheduling, financial aid, academic, and social services)
- Academic and social integration (social life, friends, contact with faculty members, appropriate study skills)
- Attitude and motivation (self-confidence, sense of development, individual stress, desire)
- Institutional fit (family traditions, peer pressure, or perception of need to obtain a degree from a specific institution to be successful).

The reality is that technological growth for students of color follows a model of positive feedback; that is, it reinforces itself. Relevant feedback and reinforcement leads to technological development, which leads to newer technology skills, which, in turn, leads to technological development for the nation. Hence, the nation's need for technological development will only grow—increasingly faster and more voraciously—as larger numbers of women and minorities embrace technology opportunities. For the country to prosper internationally, and for America to ensure its leadership in the global IT marketplace and information society, the nation can't afford a culture that is content to have a population of technology have-nots. At the same time, it is important to acquaint underrepresented youths with fully articulated histories of IT pioneers, innovators, leaders, creators, entrepreneurs, artists, and activists from their racial and ethnic backgrounds. We will address some of this little-known history in what follows.

Connecting to the Past

America's minority groups share an equally insidious experience of obscuration of their contributions to earlier science and technology histories, as well as to the more contemporary histories of IT development. As Sinclair aptly puts it, "The history of race in America has been written as if [minority communities'] role in technology scarcely existed, and the history of technology as if it were utterly innocent of racial significance."[9] He supports this thesis by calling attention to the scarcity of established literature that "explores this relationship" and the nonexistent "body of teaching that unites the two subjects." For the most part, the image of minorities was unflattering, limiting their relationship to technology either to the role of consumers or of operators of the technological wizardry created by whites.[10]

Early Participation in Technology (1945–1980)

History will mark World War II (1939–1945) as the beginning of the computer information age, and the turn of the twentieth century as the moment in history when digital technology became firmly entrenched in all segments of society. Technology played an important role in helping the Allies defeat Japan and Germany. And mass production, ushered in by Henry Ford in the automobile industry, allowed high-volume manufacturing of finished goods and increased productivity. Worker gains came with huge investments in automation and mass production techniques. However, while mass production was becoming prevalent in the United States, Japan and Germany were still using slower, ineffective manual labor in their factories.

Also during World War II, military research resulted in scientific breakthroughs that would soon be of commercial value. War department investment in both research and applied sciences enabled "many major technologies [to be] used for the first time, including nuclear weapons, radar, proximity fuses, jet engines, ballistic missiles, and data-processing analog devices (primitive computers). Every year, piston engines were improved. Enormous advancement was made in aircraft, submarine, and tank designs, such that models coming into use at the beginning of the war were long obsolete by its end. One entirely new kind of ship was the amphibious landing craft."[11]

From a cursory glance, it would appear that the contributions of women, minorities, and blacks (in particular) were nonexistent during this social transformation, but nothing could be further from the truth. Take the case of Admiral Grace Hopper. The computer futurist is best known for her contribution to the invention of the compiler, the computing program that translates English instructions to a language understood by computers. Hopper paved the way for the discipline of computer science with her contributions to the Mark I and Mark II radar programs towards the end of War World II.

Another example is Grace Brewster Murray. She graduated from Vassar with a B.A. in mathematics in 1928, and worked under Oystein Ore at Yale for her M.A. (1930) and Ph.D. (1934). She began teaching mathematics at Vassar in 1931. A decade later, Murray achieved the rank of associate professor, when she won a faculty fellowship for study at New York University's Courant Institute for Mathematics.[12]

There was also the African American inventor Otis Boykin, born in Dallas, Texas, in 1920. He is responsible for inventing the electrical device used in all guided missiles and IBM computers, plus twenty-six other electronic devices, including a control unit for an artificial heart stimulator (pacemaker).[13] One of Boykin's first achievements was a type of resistor used in radios, television sets, and a variety of electronic devices. Boykin's improvement to the electrical resistors contributed to today's digital age and the growing pervasiveness of digital technology. Boykin certainly wasn't alone in contributing to the four revolutionary advancements in computer-based technology since World War II. Women and blacks played a major role in the war's industrial complex. However, in 1944, a *Saturday Evening Post* headline asked, "Are Women Doing Their Share?"[14] The tone of the article implied that women were little more than mere housewives, and it seemed to scold them about the need to do more to support the war effort. In reality, some 5 million American women, and blacks, filled the jobs vacated by men entering the armed forces. By the end of 1942, the defense workforce was composed almost entirely of women, African

Americans, and other minorities—the largest previously untapped labor pools. Their contributions to the development of technology have not been fully acknowledged or rewarded, because more than 4 million lost their jobs to GIs returning home at the end the of the war.[15]

Nonetheless, women and minorities participated in all technological advancements from automation to IT to the personal computer, and now to digital technologies. And though many of their contributions have been minimized at best and, at worst, erased from history altogether, the fact remains that without them the modern world would not enjoy the advanced technology, research, science, and telecommunications that define our current era.

The Information Age, 1960–1985: From the Factory Floor and Government to Corporate America

By the late 1950s, the information technology age had arrived. One sure sign was Bank of America's adoption of a mainframe computer system for data and check processing. This period saw computers move from being very large, energy-hogging tube technology to more effective and smaller-scale transistors. Computers were also being transformed from performing simple, repetitive operations to more complex information storage and retrieval. The information technology age would transform business and everyday life in industrial nations. ATMs were developed, information would flow at the speed of light as mainframes were networked, and financial data became accessible in real time and on demand, driving global economic growth. While the numbers of women and minorities would remain low, they continued to play an integral part just the same.

A decade later, Hispanic Engineer Edson de Castro emerged as one of the contemporary IT pioneers of his generation. His early career in the 1960s was as a design engineer at Digital Equipment Corporation (DEC), where he led the team designing the famous PDP-8 mini computer. In 1968, he left DEC to co-found Data General. He grew the company revenues to more than $3 billion and captured 11 percent of all minicomputer sales nationwide. His blunt speaking earned him a reputation for forthrightness and honesty so that the *Boston Globe* said gave him a "brash renegade" image.[16] De Castro was a prophet of technology's future. Predicting all businesses would embrace technology, de Castro said, "Most, even what we'd consider old line industries, are beginning to get themselves very involved in technology because technology is what they need to encourage the productivity to remain competitive in their industries. They're starting to work with all kinds of new things in automobile companies, such as General Motors and their Saturn Project. Those are pretty technologically intensive undertakings. I think some of our older line industries may in fact have been napping for a while. But now they're wide awake."[17] Clearly, most of de Castro's prophecies seem outdated today. GPS and other technologies are standard in automobiles, utility companies and digital technologies are morphing into one, and the list of extinctions is mounting for the old-line industries failing to bridge the technological divide.

And de Castro is largely overlooked by mainstream histories of technology development. In 1997, *Business Week* magazine made an effort to correct the story with an excerpt from *The Soul of a New Machine* by Tracy Kidder. "A chapter of DEC's official history, a technical work that the company published, describes the making of a computer called the PDP-8. DEC sent this machine to market in 1965. It was a hit. It made DEC's first fortune. The PDP-8, says the official history, "established the concept of minicomputers, leading the way to a multibillion-dollar industry." But the book doesn't say that Edson de Castro—then an engineer in his twenties—led the team that designed the PDP-8. The technical history mentions de Castro only once, briefly, and in another context. They expunged de Castro.[18]

De Castro also made two other notable contributions during his career at Data General. The company introduced one of the first portable IBM-PC portable computers. It would be a forerunner to the laptop. As innovative as that was, Data General would be one of the largest U.S. computer makers to produce its first personal computer at a Japanese plant. Ed de Castro would later explain that the business climate in Massachusetts was less than ideal for growth.

The PC Revolution (1970–2000)

Because of Mark Dean, Ph.D., the African American engineer who coinvented components of the IBM computer, the computer would move from labs to millions of desktops and homes in less than thirty years. The power of the personal computer fundamentally changed the world, as programmers, designers, and manufactures brought ideas and new business models to life. Just as important, the affordability of computing power allowed for new players in the technology field.

The personal computer revolution made technology artifacts available to countless millions, and as they came under the digital sky, technology workers were needed to implement technologies in the workplace and create services and applications. High-tech replaced blue-collar, manual occupations as being the surest path to the American dream. On average, where electrical engineers make slightly more than $62,000 per year, the information systems manager averaged $75,000. The engineering and IT fields will add more than 2 million jobs by 2014. According to the Bureau of Labor Statistics, jobs requiring technical skills will be in great demand for the foreseeable future, with rapid growth for computer engineers, analysts, and support specialists.[19]

Earl A. Pace Jr. and the late David Wimberly did not miss the significance of this burgeoning field nor its importance for minority technology workers. After a meeting in 1975 where they discussed their concerns about the low numbers of minorities in the data processing field, the two founded the Black Data Processing Association (BDPA) in Philadelphia. According to BDPA's official history, "There was a lack of minorities in middle and upper management, low recruitment and poor preparation of minorities for these positions, and an overall lack of career mobility."[20] In the intervening years, BDPA has grown from an organization of just thirty-five members to thousands of members throughout the United States. Consequently, the organization became and continues to be an important catalyst for professional growth and technical development in the IT industry.

The midseventies also saw the rise of Native Americans in the science, engineering, and technology fields. In 1977, American Indian scientists, engineers, and educators created the American Indian Science and Engineering Society (AISES) to address high dropout rates and low college enrollment and graduation rates of American Indians, along with the historical underrepresentation of American Indians in science and engineering.

AISES has a focus in helping American Indian and Native Alaskan students prepare for careers in science, technology, engineering, and business. The organization's mission reads,

The American Indian Science and Engineering Society was founded in 1977 by American Indian scientists, engineers and educators. In view of the high dropout rates and low college enrollment and graduation rates of American Indians compared with all other ethnic groups in the United States, and the severe under-representation of American Indians in the science and engineering fields, these Native professionals resolved to create an organization that would identify and remove the barriers to academic success for Native students.[21]

Another notable organization was the Chinese Institute of Engineers. The CIE/USA National Council, a federation organization of CIE/USA, was established in 1986, with the Greater New York and San Francisco Bay Area chapters as its founding chapters. In the following years, the National Council was expanded to include a Seattle Chapter, an Overseas Chinese Environmental Engineers and Scientists Association Chapter, a Dallas-Fort Worth Chapter, and a New Mexico Chapter.

Minority Youth as Early Adopters

Samsung's slogan, "Technology that takes your life to a higher power," captures how digital, communication, and information technologies have become pervasive in the daily life and economic activity of Americans and in other industrial nations. The personal computer unlocks a multiplicity of means for individual expression and productivity. Rather than have technology happen to the individual, individuals would now embrace technology and have a share in its developmental outcome. Thus, the pervasiveness and accessibility of digital technologies has deeply impacted young adults and teens, minority youths included. Take the Internet, for instance. According to the Pew Internet & American Life Project, some "57 percent of online teens create content for the Internet. That amounts to half of all teens ages 12–17."[22] The Pew Content Creators report mentions that teens are most involved in activities like creating blogs and personal Web pages, and doing work on Web pages for school, for friends, and/or for organizations. They also use the Web for social networking, such as sharing artwork, photos, music, and videos.

Young people use the Internet to a greater extent for leisure and research. Eighty-four percent of young, black Internet users, compared to 64 percent of older blacks, used the Internet for no particular reason except to have fun. Youth adoption rates are just as high with online chats, music downloads, multimedia browsing, and Web-based activities.[23] Internet usage hasn't been the only area in which youth of all races have been early adopters of technology. Cell phone usage and other interactive technologies have had great appeal to teens and young people. Interactive technologies, in particular, have appealed to African American youth to a larger degree than to their white counterparts.[24] Again, we find that minorities have played significant roles in advancing these consumer technologies. Take the cell and terrestrial technologies, something that is second nature to just about every American youth. Hispanics have been right in the middle of the research, development, and businesses operations sides of those technologies.

On the research side, Maria Martinez, a computer scientist, developed and patented an algorithm for managing the magnetic defects in the telephone switching hardware. When the switching hardware isn't functioning properly, calls can't reach their intended destinations, much as when the wrong Web address is entered in an Internet search. Hispanic technology workers were key players on the business side as well. In the early 1990s, Eduardo Dardet, a project manager, was partly responsible for bringing Motorola's paging services to the millions of users in the United States and abroad. Around the same period, George Foyo and Ernie Rodriquez, both vice presidents at AT&T, brought digital, stored-program control telephone systems to Latin America. These individuals were representatives both of the technology users and of the developers and implementers of that technology.

Young people are also large users of gaming, and there are growing numbers of them moving into the development end of the business. For Ntiedo Etuk, games are serious business. Etuk is CEO of Tabula Digital, Inc., a New York-based educational video game company. Etuk's company focuses on teaching algebra by using video games. In an interview with *USBE & Information Technology*, Etuk said, "Algebra is a 'gating' subject for high school and college. Statistics show that you are five times as likely to go to college if you have passed algebra. It's also something a tremendous number of students don't do very well."[25] "As a result," Etuk continued, "Tabula Digital's founders thought that playing video games, demonstrated to be one of the most compelling media for teenagers and tweens, and combining that with a critical need, you are adapting your educational tool to a format kids are used to." Etuk backs up his theory with eye-opening statistics:

A child born today will watch 20,000 hours of television, see 400,000 commercials, and spend 10,000 hours on video games before age 21. That's a total of 416 days. For the MTV generation, a group that grows up multitasking between e-mails, IMs, homework, and listening to the radio, everything is happening at the same time. And when you go into the classroom, you're still teaching from blackboards and teaching out of textbooks. Our theory was: you're losing them. There are 145 million video game players in the U.S., about half the population; 34 percent are your K-12 population, that's 53 million people.[26]

Although analysts are still assessing opportunities in serious games markets—education, government, health, military, corporations and industry, first responders, and science—some estimates have put total figures in excess of $100 billion. More conservative estimates have put market share for serious game development work at $1 billion.[27]

Historically black colleges are taking notice. Howard University's College of Engineering, Architecture and Computer Sciences recently held its first one-day computer and video games workshop. The workshop assisted the university in positioning itself as a supplier of creative talent for the games industry and as a conductor of leading games research. Panelists Nichol Bradford, senior global brand manager of Vivendi Universal, one of the leading black females in the games industry, John Nordlinger, a Microsoft Research games evangelist, and Adam Clayton Powell III, director of the Integrated Media Systems Center of the National Science Foundation's exclusive Engineering Research Center for multimedia and Internet research, described the present and future states of the game industry in discussions about research, curriculum, and business considerations.

Mario Armstrong, of NPR technology, sees increasing participation of minority youth on the consumer side, but not on the business side. "As for who is missing," he adds, "nonprofits, foundations, venture capitalists, video game publishers, and the entertainment side of the industry are all missing from the equation. I'm also concerned that the baby-boomer generation in communities of color is not paying close attention to this pivotal and profitable industry; I feel to some degree that another viable opportunity may be passing right by us."[28]

The Military as a Gateway

What few people may realize is that the U.S. military has led the nation in minority and women affairs that ultimately bear on our present discussion. Years before the civil rights activities of 1964 there was the passage of the Armed Services Integration Act of June 1948. One year later, in September 1949, Annie L. Graham became the first black female to enter the U.S. Marine Corps. Even before 1948, blacks made historical advancements unheard of outside of the military. On October 25, 1940, Benjamin O. Davis Sr. became the nation's first black general in military service. Fifteen years later, his son—Benjamin O. Davis Jr.—became the first black general in the U.S. Air Force. Others followed: Samuel L. Gravely Jr., the first black Admiral in the U.S. Navy; Frank E. Petersen, the first black general in the Marine Corps; and Hazel Winfred Johnson, the nation's first black female general. Minorities in the military also made great strides in science, engineering, and technology. Air Force General Bernard Randolph, the second black four-star general in the history of the Air Force, controlled a staff of nearly 53,000 scientists and engineers in the Air Force Research and Development program.

Benjamin F. Montoya, a Mexican American growing up in rural Indio, California, was a trailblazer for many Hispanics in the military in the late 1950s. Montoya's career took a trajectory to its full conclusion when he became one of three Hispanic Admirals in 1986 and took command of the Naval Facilities Engineering Command. Admiral Montoya would comment that it was his parents who most greatly influenced him: "There were also very strong discussions in my family about what it means to be an American. My four brothers and I were brought up with a philosophy which said, 'you are equal to anyone. Don't let anyone take advantage of you. Have self-pride. There's nothing wrong with being poor, but there's a whole lot wrong with being a thief or a liar. You might be poor, but you're clean.' As a result, all of us learned to value education."[29]

The Digital Age Pioneers (2001–)

There is another aspect of the digital divide. These are the stories of many women and minorities who have successfully "crossed" the tech divide to forge successful, valued, and influential careers. The tragedy is that these tech leaders go largely unnoticed by the nation's youth, regardless of race and ethnicity. For these minorities and women offer our best hope for pulling others across the divide. They personify the rewards and opportunities of pursuing technology-based careers and technology integration. They should serve as a testament of success in IT fields for many of the nation's youth. The point is that minority youths should become as intimately familiar with these leading scientists and technology innovators of color as they are with celebrity entertainers and athletes. The reality, of course, is that popular culture celebrates the evanescent victories and singular wealth of entertainers and athletes of color rather than the compound value acquired over decades by their engineer and IT specialist counterparts.

Let's now take the case of Katherine G. Johnson (1918–). In July 1969, the nation was spellbound when Neil Armstrong and Buzz Aldrin descended to the lunar surface. The famous moon landing comment "A giant leap for mankind" could have easily been substituted with Katherine Johnson's "It was a time when computers wore skirts." Without Johnson, who was a key contributor in the understanding of orbital dynamics, and who calculated the orbits for the Mercury series of suborbital flights for several historic space missions, there could have been a very different outcome in the U.S. space program. With the launching of Sputnik and the subsequent "Space Race," many engineers and computer scientists were occupied with defense and rocket development. That left the detailed attention and time-consuming mathematics to women. Literally and figuratively, women became the computers of the space age.

Linda Gooden: The New Global Leader

A more contemporary role model is Linda Gooden, an African American executive at Lockheed Martin. She represents the new face of minority technology trailblazers—someone whose activity is not behind the computer or technology, but who is an innovator and thinker. Gooden had the extremely rare opportunity to build a company from scratch within a large organization. She built her own team, decided which business opportunities to pursue, and watched an idea grow from a conversation to a success by any measurement. As president of Lockheed Martin Information Technology, she grew Lockheed's IT division from $22 million to $2.6 billion. With a performance like that, every company in the industry wants her.

Tianna Shaw

Tianna Shaw grew up on the Hupa Indian Reservation in northern California. She was one of the 1,732 Indians out of 2,140 of the Hupa Tribe who resided on the Reservation. The Hupa religion celebrated annual world renewal ceremonies for ten days in the fall. Today, Shaw continues that tradition of celebrating the earth, only now her celebrations include the sky. At NASA Ames Research Center, Tianna Shaw currently manages the Life Sciences Division's Facilities Utilization Office, providing oversight and leadership for a multidisciplinary team of civil servants and contractors supporting investigators' peer-reviewed science projects in the ground-based Center for Gravitational Biology Research. In English, she manages the ground test facility complex and provides expert technical direction and oversight of contractor support activities.

Shaw has always valued her tribe. She was an active promoter of Native American access to science careers, and was a founder of the first high school chapter of AISES, in which she remains active. Later, in graduate school, she cofounded another chapter and served as president. At NASA Ames Research Center, she is the founding chair of the Native American Advisory Committee and the current vice president and past president of the California Professional Chapter. Shaw majored in biomedical and electrical engineering at the University of Southern California, and went into the space program. Shaw also completed an MS program in biomedical engineering, specializing in medical instrumentation in 1994; but by that time, she had begun her career at the Jet Propulsion Laboratory and moved on to the NASA Ames Research Center. Shaw exemplifies the need for our success in marrying minority cultural values to technology skills acquisition.

Pablo Iglesias

Pablo Iglesias, Ph.D., knows the importance of growing critical technology leaders. From his classroom at the Johns Hopkins University campus in Baltimore, Maryland, Dr. Iglesias teaches students how to apply tools to problems. In a rapidly changing world, students won't always know what problems they will face, but they will be able to solve problems if they have the educational and critical literacy tools.

One innovative approach is his use of everyday model helicopters and cars to teach students how to design computerized control systems. Because of his creativity, a dry theoretical course has been turned into one in which students learn theory through practical applications. At 39 years of age, this Venezuelan engineer is at the helm of changes that will create a new generation of critical thinkers. And it is no small task. Ten years ago, the National Science Foundation responded to the high dropout rate of the nation's engineering students by funding alliances of engineering schools to explore the reasons behind students' leaving engineering. Two factors appeared on the lists of resources. One, universities needed professors who had just as much passion for teaching as for research; and two, real-world experiences should be part of the first two years of the engineering curriculum. Iglesias has turned his control systems course into a practical experience in which students explore real-world applications of control technology. Being a classroom instructor who teaches students the principles of why things work is the most important job to him.

But research is equally important to Dr. Iglesias. His current interest is the exploration of how the Internet can be used to control unmanned vehicles or robots over long distances and in telesurgery. Such research can close the distance between those in need of expert support and the experts themselves, such as having a surgeon in Baltimore perform surgery on a patient in a remote Central American village. It is critical thinkers like Dr. Iglesias who will shape America's future in the global digital marketplace and help bring along underrepresented youth into the IT education fold.

Dr. Aileen Van-Nguyen

Aileen Van-Nguyen was a ghost to countless Americans who merely gave a passing glance at the young Asian woman bagging their groceries at a supermarket back in 1975. What they did not see was that this supermarket bagger would someday be a microbiologist inventing bio-insecticides that would protect plants and the very foods they would take home to prepare for their families. Aileen Van-Nguyen came to the United States as a war refugee, making the perilous boat pilgrimage over the Pacific at the end of the Vietnam War in 1975. After mastering English, Van-Nguyen worked her way up the job ladder, continuously pursuing education.

By 1982, she had a B.S. in microbiology from the University of Illinois at Champaign-Urbana. She joined the DuPont Company, working in the Plant Disease Group, and then stepped up to DuPont's Discovery Program, where she managed an effort to develop *Bacillus thuringiensis* (Bt) bio-insecticides. She also managed risk-assessment studies, identified research collaborations with institutions around the world, and led commercialization of Bt products.

Then Van-Nguyen crossed the Atlantic to complete her Ph.D. in molecular biology and biochemistry at Cambridge University in England. Back home in Delaware, Dr. Van-Nguyen rose to senior research microbiologist, and then to alliance manager and contract administrator in the Regulatory Sciences Department. She has won awards for her research on sulfonylurea soils, development of a microbial insect control discovery program, genetic engineering of *Helicoverpa zea* nucleopolyhedro virus for insecticidal control of Heliothine pests in cotton and vegetable crops, and leading the registration effort for four Dupont Crop Protection products.

A Nation at Risk and Some Historical Milestones

For the first time since the Second World War, America's position as global market leader is not guaranteed. Increasingly, political leaders are acknowledging that, in a knowledge-based economy, it will be the nation with the best-trained people that will lead the global economy. With the worldwide competition for talent, will America at last come to appreciate the vast untapped pool of talent in minority communities, and finally muster the will and financial resources to encourage and train underrepresented youth to enter and excel in science and technology fields? Appearing on the April 23, 2006, edition of NBC TV's *Meet the Press*, Senator Ted Kennedy (D-MA) addressed aspects of these concerns and warned that America could be a second-rate country within 25 years. An excerpt of that show's transcript follows, and bears quoting at length:[30]

Mr. Russert: You also, in your book, say this about education: "I propose that every child in America, on reaching eighth grade, be offered a contract. Let students sign it, along with their parents and Uncle Sam. The contract will state that, if you work hard, finish high school, and are accepted for college, the federal government will guarantee you the cost of earning a degree."

Sen. Kennedy: Right. That's right.

Mr. Russert: Where are we going to get that money?

Sen. Kennedy: Well, we don't have an alternative, Tim, in the areas of education. The Chinese now are graduating 650,000 engineers a year; the Indians, 350,000 engineers a year. We're at 72,000, and half of those are foreign students. We're either going to equip every young person in this country to be able to deal with globalization, every worker to get continuing training, or we're going to be a second-level country in another 25 years. And that's going to take education; it's going to take investment on that. *If we are spending $10 billion dollars a month $10 billion dollars a month*—on Iraq, if we're going to spend a trillion dollars, which is Mr. Schultz's estimate, who's the Nobel Laureate, he says it's going to cost a trillion dollars, we ought to be able to educate every child, provide continuing training, and make sure that our American young people and older people are going to be ably equipped for globalization.

In his 2006 State of the Union Address, President Bush said,

> We need to encourage children to take more math and science, and to make sure those courses are rigorous enough to compete with other nations.... Tonight, I propose to train 70,000 high school teachers to lead advanced-placement courses in math and science, bring 30,000 math and science professionals to teach in classrooms, and give early help to students who struggle with math, so they have a better chance at good, high-wage jobs. If we ensure that America's children succeed in life, they will ensure that America succeeds in the world.[31]

On one level, President Bush and Senator Kennedy are correct: At a time when the use of technology is growing exponentially, and the nation's need for technology workers has never been greater, fewer students are pursuing science, engineering, and technology studies. African American engineer and scientist John Brooks Slaughter points to the chronic shortage of technology workers facing America.[32] Each year, nearly half of a million minority students graduate from high school. Only 32,000 will complete the necessary math and science courses to be considered for entry into engineering schools. Of that number, 15,000 will enroll. At the end of four or five years, only 4,000 will graduate and add to the ranks of the 72,000 U.S. college engineering graduates.

In recent years, several major reports have warned of the United States' diminishing technology leadership. Three factors have contributed to this. One, the dwindling supply of immigrant technology workers; two, the retiring of the baby-boomer scientists and engineers; and, three, the steady decline of American students in the science and technology pipeline.[33]

Lockheed Martin Chief Executive Officer Robert J. Stevens argues that America's preeminence in technology is declining because of the United States' shrinking technology workforce. Stevens predicts that, in three years, Lockheed will need to add 44,000 engineers per year to its talent base. American colleges and universities are currently producing only 62,000. Stevens warns, "The blooming tech talent shortfall will have an impact far beyond any single firm or sector. Science and engineering aren't just crucial for national security; they're critical for economic growth."[34] The loss of the immigrant technology worker has had profound consequences on U.S. industry. Prior to 1970, Asians represented 2 percent of all scientists and engineers in the United States. By 1990, that percentage had jumped 7 percent from 21,000 to 150,000. Of all the Asian scientists and engineers, 83 percent were foreign-born. In Silicon Valley, Asians made up 21 percent of the workforce at top technology companies.[35]

Like industry, the federal government is facing a wave of retirement, and there are few technology workers to replace those who are retiring. Within the next 10–15 years, more than 40 percent of the federal technology workforce will retire from the payroll.[36] In the current heightened security climate, augmenting the workforce with foreign workers is not likely. One solution for meeting the growing need seems obvious: Turn to the nation's minority population, just as the country has done throughout history. Only this time, the country will not exploit their skills and labor, but finally make space for minorities as full partners in society. Minorities are well positioned to seize these emerging opportunities, but it doesn't seem to resonate. This must change or, as Senator Kennedy said, America will be a "second-level country in another 25 years." America can ill afford to leave this talent pool underdeveloped as the global economy becomes more competitive. The question, though, is how to get minority youth to embrace a STEM career path in greater numbers. The answers are in our past and in our future. If we fail, the costs are grave for them and for industry.

At this point we might begin to recognize that many answers to problems of the future often can be found in such experiences of the past, as we have been discussing. This truism is especially pertinent as we strive to move beyond the digital divide, comprehend the limitations of the government's approach to closing the technology gap, and grasp the consequences of the continuing underrepresentation of racial and ethnic minorities in STEM education and career paths. This is equally true for underrepresented racial minorities in IT-based humanities and arts education. The problem becomes quite clear when we realize that, despite billions of dollars spent by American school systems for the acquisition of digital technology infrastructures, students of color are not pursuing or utilizing humanistic and science-related educational paths, career options, and cultural practices in sufficient numbers to keep pace with today's information society. So the pertinent questions that must be raised include (a) what intrinsic value has digital technology added to further or increase technology pedagogy for students of color; (b) why are these students failing to grasp the relevancy of STEM opportunities and information communication technologies (ICTs) in the arts and humanities; and (c) why, at this historical moment, should we, as a country, care? The short answer: Our future will surely depend on it.

In recent years, the campaign to close the digital divide galvanized the nation and spurred hope that technology would diminish or minimize the gap between the information haves and have-nots.[37] Some scholars argue persuasively that the availability of information from the Internet and peer-to-peer technology systems would empower the have-nots, leading to improvements in educational, health, and various other class and social spheres. Government reports, such as the U.S. Department of Commerce's "Falling Through the Net,"[38] corroborate this position. The Department of Commerce's report, a cross-cultural survey that documented the disparity in telephone and computer ownership and Internet access between whites and racial minorities, explained that, "While a standard telephone line can be an individual's pathway to the riches of the Information Age, a personal computer and modem are rapidly becoming the keys to the vault. The robust growth recently experienced in Internet usage illustrates this promise as new and individual subscribers gravitate to on-line services."[39] In 1999, another NTIA report went further, declaring that information tools, such as the popular personal computer and Internet, were becoming progressively critical to economic success and personal advancement.[40]

Responding to disturbing reports such as "Falling Through the Net," the federal government launched a number of initiatives to address the computer technology imbalance in the nation's poorest or underserved schools. One program charged with making a difference, the E-rate, has provided upwards of $2.25 billion per year to needy schools, specifically for the acquisition of digital technology infrastructures.[41] In appropriating these funds, special consideration was given to rural and urban schools that had limited computer and Internet access. Closing the digital divide by providing computer technology to underserved minorities was intended to enhance the methods of teaching technology and information-age skills to minority students. On paper, these technology programs appear to be closing the gap steadily. However, on closer inspection, the numbers tell a very different story. It is true that billions of dollars are poured into low-income urban and rural school systems and their inadequate to nonexistent computer programs, bringing into existence functional technology infrastructures of sorts where none had existed before. Yet, black, Hispanic, and Native American students' participation in STEM and digital media arts careers remains less than impressive.

The Engineering Workforce Commission survey, for example, revealed that African American freshman engineering majors dropped from a high of 8,924 in 1992 to 8,192 in 2001. Latinos/Latinas had a slight increase during that same period, from 5,624 to 6,157. Native Americans went slightly down from 633 to 629. Overall, minority participation in engineering programs during the Clinton–Gore administration (1993–2001) declined from 16.3 to 14.9 percent. Given these apparently little-known statistics, it is easy to see how rhetoric on the digital divide would lead to the mistaken belief that more potential minority technology professionals are emerging from the nation's schools in substantial numbers to justify such expenditures. But as troubling as it is, the facts indicate otherwise, the major consequences of which now confront us as a society. There is much to answer for in our nation's lackluster commitment to bridge the digital divide for youths of color.

Symptomatic of this denial are people I call "tricknologists"—those who narrow the definition of the divide by saying that mere computer ownership and Internet usage are somehow effective measures of minority participation in the new, high-tech economy. They claim, further, that the divide is closing, pointing to statistics which show that minorities are closing the gap in becoming consumers of technology, even though they are not producers of or equal partners in the nation's technological revolution. In fact, some "tricknologists" miss the mark when they attempt to shift the focus away from this important collective problem by merely highlighting contemporary examples of individual minority successes, which is important. They fail, however, to provide larger historical, and especially culturally specific, frameworks for these minority successes—an important omission that I address above in my own survey of minority technology pioneers and visionaries. For example, they will name Roy Hoth, a Native American inventor at IBM; Nancy Stewart, Wal-Mart's African American vice president of information technology; Jim Padilla, the Hispanic engineer and the chief operating officer and chairman of Ford Motor Corporation Worldwide Auto Operations; and Duy-Loan T. Le, the first Asian woman to be named a TI-Fellow at Texas Instruments Inc. This is an impressive list, to be sure. But, out of context, it masks the true reality of America's growing paucity of up-and-coming minority talent. The unimpressive numbers speak plainly to the fact that simply providing minority students with classroom access to computers and the Internet does not result in getting more minorities to choose careers in science, technology, engineering, or academia. The reality counters and undermines the views of "many technologists and educators [who] argue passionately that computers and Internet connection in schools would be the great equalizer in American education."[42]

Understanding why these programmatic provisions of technology assistance to underrepresented minorities fail to develop a sector of minority technology providers requires a thorough investigation into what digital divide efforts did not accomplish, more so than what minor or exceptional results occurred, as outlined above. For example, although the Clinton administration intended to wire every poor and underserved school, it failed to forge connections between modern technology systems and the culturally rich pasts of minority students, thus rendering worthless skills accrued for a digital age without ties to a culturally relevant curriculum. As Bonnie Bracey, author of *Harnessing the Potential of ICT for Education: A Multistakeholder Approach*, cogently puts it, "Many of today's schools may have a wire that does not connect to anything."[43]

This is not to say that the gains in the Clinton administration's goals for universal access to information technologies were not commendable; far from it. Appearing with Bill Gates at the Microsoft Government Leaders' Forum Africa in Cape Town, South Africa, on July 11, 2006, former President Bill Clinton was clear about his objectives for his administration's efforts at the end of the millennium:

This is a question that consumed a lot of my time when I was president. I worked very hard on increasing Internet access, for example, and bridging the divide between rich and poor and middle class within the United States. We had about 35 percent of our schools on some sort of Internet connection when I became president. We were at almost 100 when I left. We went from 30 percent to 63 percent of our classrooms being connected.[44]

However, Adam J. Banks, author of *Race, Rhetoric, and Technology: Searching for Higher Ground*, argues that these limited "material access" gains in hardware may have come at the cost of teacher development. Banks observes that educators invested in grant writing and program creation to connect their schools in anticipation that these networked computers would help to improve classroom teaching and create added motivation for students. They quickly discovered, however, that few resources actually existed for teacher and student training and technology implementation plans. As it turns out, this was a costly oversight. Bracey echoes this conclusion and remarks, "Many teachers have little meaningful professional development. . . . In many cases there is a tech person, but the teacher has had minimal training in technology use, at whatever level there is technology for their use."[45]

Clearly, then, accessing information is not the same as acquiring useful knowledge and advancing technological literacy. Access to the Internet opened the door to an explosion of information services and Web sites, but it did not inevitably mean that students of color or their teachers were able to turn that information into useful and practical knowledge, apply new analytical skills, or make successful inroads in the digital economy. Furthermore, we recognize that providing digital artifacts (i.e., computers and Internet connectivity) has not necessarily changed the way students of color are being taught. In fact, it could be argued that networked computers in schools and Internet access perpetuated the same ineffectual classroom practices, only now with the aid of faster media. In fact, renowned African American scientist Carter G. Woodson advanced the argument of the futility of educational methods that disconnect students from their heritage early in the twentieth century. Woodson was a vocal critic of an educational system that considered the dissemination of information to students more important than the development of their critical thinking skills. In his influential book *The Mis-Education of the Negro*, Woodson is scathing in his criticism of mainstream educational practices exerted on African Americans more than a century ago. Unfortunately, his words still ring with just as much truth today. He viewed mainstream or Eurocentric educational models and approaches as tools that disconnected the Negro or African American from his history, cultural moorings, and surroundings. According to Woodson:

The same educational process that inspires and stimulates the oppressor with the thought that he is everything and has accomplished everything worthwhile, depresses and crushes simultaneously the spark of genius in the Negro by making him feel that his race does not amount to much and never will measure up to the standards of other peoples. The Negro thus educated is a hopeless liability of the race.[46]

Woodson's arguments apply with equal veracity to other minority groups, when we consider the failures of digital divide programs targeted at underrepresented minority youths. In fact, he points out that the system also fails Europeans. Woodson writes:

Education, like religion, is conservative. It makes haste slowly only, and sometimes not at all. Do not change the present order of thinking and doing, many say, for you disturb too many things long since regarded as ideal. The dead past, according to this view, must be the main factor in determining the future. We should learn from the living past, but let the dead past remain dead.[47]

Years later, Postman and Weingarner observed that the advantaged student has a financial interest in willingly engaging, because there are more tangible payoffs that are unavailable to disadvantaged students. Postman and Weingarner postulate that schools offer little encouragement in the development of youth who can "question, doubt, or challenge any part of society in which they live." In other words, the prevailing views rely on the notion that closing the digital divide is primarily about providing technological artifacts, not creating technological literates. The attention paid to the digital divide was not effective in addressing the significant matters that created the divide in the first place—race and class disparities.

An educational system undergirded by the benefits of wealth and, conversely, the liabilities of race has stacked the deck against upward mobility for the poorest citizens—racial and ethnic minorities. In *The Shame of the Nation: The Restoration of Apartheid Schooling in America*,[48] Jonathan Kozol explains how little has changed in minority education, even with improved technological access. In light of the billions of dollars invested in digital technologies, the findings of Kozol's study are disturbing. At a South Bronx school with a predominantly minority population, only twenty-eight of the fifty faculty members had ever taught a class before assuming teaching duties that year. One fourth-grader had four different teachers in one year. Reports like Maisie McAdoo's "Just Passing Through . . . A Look at Teacher Retention" (United Federation of Teachers)[49] highlight the challenge in retaining public school teachers. These cases point out that there is the direct link between poverty and racial, as well as economic, segregation. Some 86 percent of schools in predominantly black and Latino neighborhoods qualified for free or reduced lunches, while only 15 percent of majority white schools qualified.[50] In addition, researcher Barbara Monroe reminds us that no matter how much equipment is placed in underserved schools, the poorest students will still be at a material disadvantage compared to those with historical and entrenched material wealth.[51]

In this context, it is worthwhile to consider the value of technology in the classroom. As a result of inadequate computer infrastructures, poorly trained instructors, and insufficient technical supports, urban students generally use computers for the most basic tasks: typing and word processing, skills that are now redundant for any high-level technology career. By comparison, in majority white schools, computers are used for sophisticated, collaborative projects and social networking that require high-level technological skill sets which prepare white youths for the most challenging positions in industry and society. Therefore, higher levels of technology use are grooming whites for better-paying jobs in the workforce, while minorities are destined for menial jobs in the digital world. Both Kozol and Moore suggest that it is "oxymoronic" to believe that poor children can receive a good education in high-poverty schools where more of the nation's blacks, Hispanics, and Native Americans attend. To reiterate, in often-misguided efforts to bridge the digital divide, we often overlook the reality that providing schools with digital technology does not address or change, in meaningful ways, the systems that limit minority youth and, ultimately, the well-being of our society.

Answers and Solutions

George Santayana, the Spanish-born philosopher, said, "Fanaticism consists in redoubling your effort when you have forgotten your aim."[52] In many ways, that describes most of the political contributions to the discourse on meeting our future workforce needs. Senator Kennedy's proposal meets the financial obstacles that many disadvantaged students face. But the nation must go farther than promoting the European cultural values of individualism and pulling oneself up by the bootstraps. To increase minority participation, programs that reach the entire community and helps minorities and women connect to their heritages is critical.

The same is true for President Bush's plan to hire 70,000 high school and science teachers. This is another important step, and will undoubtedly add value to the nation's teaching workforce, which consists of many poorly trained and overworked teachers. Quite ironically, according to a recent survey, it is at elementary and middle school levels that many minority technology professionals decide on technology careers.[53] Of the survey respondents, some 74 percent made their decisions to enter engineering between the ages of 12 and 21, and 46 percent made the decision between the ages of 12 and 18. Also significant is the role informal science education programs had on their career choices. Forty-six percent of minority engineers participated in precollege engineering or science programs as students (*US Black Engineer*, 2005[54]).

New media offers promising new techniques that have the potential to change the paradigm of how educators can connect to minority youth and women in moving beyond the digital divide. As the above examples of successful minority technology workers reveal, racial and ethnic minority students may be empowered to move between two cultures without sacrificing their cultural core values.

Digital Media Cultural Mentoring (A Useful Exemplar)

Mentoring takes on an expanded and more relevant purpose with the integration of virtual technology and traditional mentoring methods. Traditionally, mentoring has been a one-on-one experience, and the dissemination of information from mentor to the protégé. But again, there is a huge lack of minority professionals available to make meaningful, personal connections with the nation's 50 million K–12 students. To connect with today's students, we must change our concept of mentoring, look to the past, and use today's real, living technology innovators to help students move beyond the digital divide.

Digital media cultural mentoring uses the environment of the student to convey positive images of their cultural connection to science and technology. The technology provides on-demand cultural content aligned with curricula introduced in the classroom; it focuses on organizing the community, village, or tribe members into active participants in the mentoring process by providing easy-to-implement life-skills methodologies; it helps students make the connection between knowledge and real life; and, lastly, it builds a sense of worth for self, family, and community.

Ying-Shao Hsu, assistant professor in the Department of Earth Sciences at National Taiwan Normal University, has shown that computer hypermedia and networking technology can be powerful tools in stimulating students' "motivation, scientific attitude and learning efficiency."[55] Hsu's research centers on the thesis that learning occurs when students are successful in connecting the real-world situation with the academic theories. Students' interest in science increases when they make the real-world connections. Two parts of Hsu's research have direct relevancy to digital media cultural mentoring. The first is animation design that displays the students' realistic life situations. In this digitally mediated environment, students see representations of themselves that help in the connection of theory. The second is online collaboration that promotes communications and exchange of information. Here again, the concept of a virtual community that is representative of the youth stimulates their interest in science and technology. This program is called cyber mentoring.

When used effectively, cyber mentoring has produced promising results in students' academic achievement. The cyberspace mentoring project, Journeying into the Rain Forests, gives a glimpse of the possibilities that digital media cultural mentoring might offer students. This team of cyber mentors consists generally of student teachers that interact with participating first- and second-graders located more than 45 miles away from the university campus. The student teachers are linked to the elementary school students through the university's project database. FileMaker Pro software was used to capture writing assignments from the grade school students and comments from the cyber mentors. The goal of the classroom teacher was to raise the performance level of the students with an interactive collaborative project with university students. The project "demonstrated the ability to address several reading and writing strategies within a single online activity."

The first contact was social in nature. Cyber mentors exchanged greetings with the students with friendly personal introductions. Students were then encouraged to post their essays to the database. The cyber mentors avoided making editing and grammar corrections to the essays. They engaged the students with probing questions about the direction and content. As the exercise progressed, students embraced the collaboration and looked forward to the interaction with their cyber mentors. Cyber mentoring seemed to excite and motivate students about their writing assignments. The academic improvement was also noteworthy, with 95% of the class achieving GPAs of 3.8 out of 4.0. The cyberspace mentoring project Journeying into the Rain Forests revealed that cyberspace could bridge the geographic distance between students and mentors, and enhance the educational experience of the students.

George Santayana's words cry out to us, "Those who cannot remember the past are condemned to repeat it."[56] And regarding the future, Terry Tempest Williams, naturalist, pleads, "The eyes of the future are looking back at us and they are praying for us to see beyond our own time."[57]

Notes

1. This is my own view of how limited perspectives often appear when the digital divide is the subject of discussion.

2. B. Dundee Holt, *NACME Journal: The State of Minorities in Engineering and Technology* (New York: The National Action Council, 2001-2002): 40.

3. John T. Barber and Alice A. Tait, eds., *The Information Society and the Black Community* (Westport, CT: Praeger, 2001), 47.

4. The Information Technology Association of America, *Untapped Talent: Diversity, Competition, and America's High Tech Future* (Arlington, VA: ITAA).

5. US Black Engineer, Minority Professional Choice Survey, Career Communications Group, Inc., http://www.blackengineer.com/artman/publish/article_433.shtml. Retrieved June 13, 2007.

6. Bruce Sinclair, ed., *Technology and the African-American Experience: Needs and Opportunities for Study* (Cambridge, MA: MIT Press, 2004).

7. National Collaborative on Diversity in the Teaching Force, *Assessment of Diversity in America's Teaching Force* (Washington, DC: National Education Association, 2004), 5.

8. Cheryl Moller-Wong and Arvid Eide, An Engineering Student Retention Study 1997, *Journal of Engineering Education* (1997): 7–15.

9. Sinclair, *Technology and the African-American Experience*, 1.

10. Martin Kevorkian, *Color Monitors: The Black Face of Technology in America* (Ithaca, NY: Cornell University Press, 2006).

11. Wikimedia, 2007, February, s.v., World War II, http://en.wikipedia.org/ wiki/World_War_II.

12. San Diego Supercomputer Center, Women in Science, http://www. sdsc.edu/ScienceWomen/hopper.html.

13. See the African American Registry, Otis Boykin: Inventor! in The African American Registry [database online], 2005, http://www.aaregistry.com/african_american_history/1474/%20Otis_Boykin_Black_inventor (accessed June 13, 2007).

14. Aja Sorensen, Rosie the Riveter: Women Working During World War II 2004, National Park Service, http://www.nps.gov/pwro/collection/website/rosie.htm. Retrieved June 14, 2007.

15. Sorensen, Rosie the Riveter.

16. Jane Poss, Data General Founder Ousted by His Creation, *Boston Globe*, December 13, 1990, Economy section, City Edition.

17. Tyrone Taborn and Grady Wells, Corporate Profile: Edson D. de Castro, *Hispanic Engineer* 1, no. 1 (1984, Fall): 20–23.

18. Tracy Kidder, Book Excerpt: *Soul of a New Machine, Business Week Online*, 1997, http://www.businessweek.com/chapter/kidder.htm. Retrieved June 14, 2007.

19. Bureau of Labor Statistics, U.S. Department of Labor, *Occupational Outlook Handbook, 2006–2007 Edition*, Engineers, on the Internet at http://www.bls.gov/oco/ocos027.htm. Retrieved June 25, 2007.

20. Black Data Processing Associates, About BDPA, Black Data Processing Associates, http://www.bdpa.org/portal/index.php?option=com_content&task=view&id=16&Itemid=43. Retrieved June 14, 2007.

21. American Indian Science and Engineering Society, About AISES, http://www.aises.org/about (accessed June 14, 2007).

22. Amanda Lenhart and Mary Madden, *Teen Content Creators and Consumers* (Washington, DC: Pew Internet and American Life Project, 2005). http://www.pewinternet.org.

23. Susannah Fox, John Horrigan, and Amanda Lenhart, *African-Americans and the Internet* (Washington, DC: Pew Internet & American Life Project, 2000).

24. Barber and Tait, *The Information Society*, 47.

25. US Black Engineer, Perspectives on Serious Games Summit 2005, Career Communications Group, Inc, http://www.blackengineer.com/artman/publish/article_457.shtml. Retrieved June 14, 2007.

26. US Black Engineer, Perspectives on Serious Games Summit 2005.

27. Ryan Kim, Games Get Serious: Among Options Are Military Training, Fighting Cancer, Designing a Peace Plan, *San Francisco Chronicle*, May 22, 2006, C section, city edition.

28. US Black Engineer, Perspectives on Serious Games Summit 2005.

29. Carmela Mellado, Hispanic Engineer of the Year: Rear Admiral Benjamin F. Montoya, *Hispanic Engineer*, 1989, Fall, 35.

30. *Meet the Press*. Television. Anonymous New York: National Broadcasting Network, 2006, http://www.msnbc.msn.com/id/12407213/page/4/. Retrieved June 24, 2007.

31. C-Span, State of the Union Address by the President, http://www.cspan.org/executive/transcript.asp?cat=current_event&code=bush_admin&year=2006. Retrieved June 14, 2007.

32. John B. Slaughter, *Black History: A Time for a New Chapter in Science and Technology* (Laurel, MD: Johns Hopkins University, 2005); John B. Slaughter, *The Search for Excellence and Equity in Higher Education: A Perspective From An Engineer* (Atlanta: Georgia Institute of Technology, 2003).

33. Committee on Science, Engineering, and Public Policy. *Rising Above the Gathering Storm: Energizing and Employing America for a Brighter Economic Future*. Committee on Science, Engineering, and Public Policy; Policy and Global Affairs, 1st ed. (Washington, DC: National Academies Press, 2007).

34. Robert J. Stevens, Social Engineering, *Wall Street Journal*, April 19, 2006, Commentary section, national edition.

35. Public Policy Institute of California, Silicon Valley's Skilled Immigrants, *Generating Jobs and Wealth for California* 21 (1999): 1–2.

36. Office of Personnel Management (OPM), *Retirement Readiness Study* (Washington, DC: OPM, 2006), Foreword.

37. Barbara Monroe, *Crossing the Digital Divide: Race, Writing, and Technology in the Classroom* (New York: Teacher's College Press, 2004), 7–10.

38. US Department of Commerce, National Telecommunications and Information Administration, *Falling Through the Net: A Survey of the "Have Nots" in Rural and Urban America* (Washington, DC: NTIA, 1995).

39. Ibid.

40. US Department of Commerce, National Telecommunications and Information Administration, *Falling Through the Net: Defining the Digital Divide* (Washington, DC: NTIA, 1999).

41. The International Society for Technology in Education, E-Rate "Window" Closes with Over 30,000 Completed Applications, http://www.iste.org/Content/NavigationMenu/Advocacy/Policy/Washington_ Notes/19982/May8/May.htm. Retrieved June 14, 2007.

42. Adam Banks, *Race, Rhetoric, and Technology: Searching for Higher Ground* (Mahwah, NJ: Erlbaum, 2006), 40.

43. Bonnie Bracey and Terry Culver, eds., *Harnessing the Potential of ICT for Education: A Multistakeholder Approach* (New York: United Nations Publications, 2005), 28.

44. William J. Clinton, speech at Microsoft Government Leaders' Forum, Cape Town, South Africa, July 11, 2006. http://www.microsoft.com/presspass/exec/billg/speeches/2006/07-11GLFAfrica.mspx.

45. Bracey and Culver, *Harnessing the Potential*, 8.

46. Carter Woodson, *The Mis-Education of the Negro* (New York: AMS Press, 1977), xiii.

47. Ibid., 158.

48. Jonathan Kozol, *The Shame of the Nation: The Restoration of Apartheid Schooling in America* (New York: Crown, 2005).

49. The Council of the City of New York, *Teacher Attrition and Retention* (New York: NYC, 2004).

50. Jonathan Kozol, *The Shame of the Nation*, 20

51. Monroe, *Crossing the Digital Divide*, 11.

52. Robert Andrews, Mary Biggs, and Michael Seidel, et al., *The Columbia World of Quotations* (New York: Columbia University Press, 1996). http://www.bartleby.com/66. Retrieved June 25, 2007.

53. US Black Engineer, Minority Professional.

54. US Black Engineer, Minority Professional.

55. Ying-Shao Hsu, Lesson Rainbow: The Use of Multiple Representations in an Internet-based, Discipline-integrated Science Lesson, *British Journal of Educational Technology*, 37 (2006): 6.

56. George Santayana, *The Life of Reason; or, The Phases of Human Progress* (New York: Scribner's, 1905).

57. Tavis Smiley, ed., *The Covenant With Black America* (Chicago: Third World Press, 2006), preface.

PART II: OPPOSITIONAL ART PRACTICES IN THE DIGITAL DOMAIN

Hip-Hop 2.0

Raiford Guins

Old Dominion University, Department of Communication and Theater Arts

Down for the Cause: Digital Learning through Hip-Hop Culture

Type "www.guerrillafunk.com" into your search engine. A header displays the title "Guerrilla Funk Recordings" in powerful graphics. Despite listings for new music as you would expect to find on a music label's Web site, another menu is equally apparent. You are provided with a "Thought Box" column displaying headlines like "America's Endless Race Wars and Massacres" and "Hip-Hop and Net Neutrality: Battle for the Internet." Are you on a news Web site or visiting a Web site for purchasing music by Guerrilla Funk artists? You may ask yourself such a question as this mixed media space willfully conflates hip-hop culture with global politics, learning with Internet democracy.

This conflation is blatantly absent from newsstand hip-hop magazines aimed at young consumers, like *The Source*, *XXL*, and *Vibe*, as well as Web sites for hip-hop labels like Def Jam Recordings, Shady Records, Bad Boy Records, and Interscope Records. In these more well-known institutions from the mainstream hip-hop marketplace, a music label's Web site is dedicated to promoting and distributing the artist-commodity and selling lifestyle (the cache of contemporary cool branded in the appellations of "black" and "urban") as opposed to active involvement in political discourses directly affecting young people in the so-called post–civil rights era of American empire.

Double-clicking "multimedia" from its side menu loads a selection of digital videos. Users are given the option of viewing titles like "Crack The CIA," an archived talk by Cynthia McKinney, the first African American woman to represent Georgia in the House of Representatives, on ending the war in Iraq, and an exposé on the Carlyle Group, a private investment bank taking the lead in rebuilding Iraq's infrastructure in Western interests. Hardly the type of subjects we commonly associate with young people and hip-hop culture; jiggling hotties, pimped rides, million-dollar cribs, and chiseled six-packs are absent. When visiting guerrillafunk.com, a hip-hop fan can select to stream the "The Diamond Life." It's a documentary distributed and produced by "GNN" (Guerrilla News Network) on the mass murders of the Revolutionary United Front (RUF) of Sierra Leone and the De Beers Company's inhumane ties to the industry of conflict diamonds. Gruesome scenes of RUF random executions, complete with decapitated victims and mutilated children are streamed. Guerrillafunk.com pairs this video stream with user-generated essays on "bling" (a term for mass ostentation that found its way into the *OED* in 2003) that connects the "ghetto fabulous" with an exploitative and murderous industry. Executions such as these, as well as media content critical of the United States' violent imperialistic actions will, most likely, not reach the eyes and ears of young people tuned into broadcast media, unless they are aware of alternative public spheres like guerrillafunk.com. In the twenty-first century, a hip-hop music label becomes an indispensable source for learning: a young person's resource for information otherwise suppressed by industry regulation, federally censored, or not considered "newsworthy" across corporate broadcast modes of distribution. Malcolm X's compelling dictum "any means necessary" now includes Internet distribution as an electronic means for survival. This is hip-hop 2.0: from the streets to your networked computer screen.

Founded by Paris, "the black panther of hip hop," who is the militant voice behind politically conscious albums such as *Sleeping with the Enemy* and *Sonic Jihad*, Guerrilla Funk is a "musical organization" for the distribution of music to counter media censorship and an educational voice of opposition to racism, state violence, war, civil and human rights violations. Paris—and we could add Public Enemy, The Fine Art Militia, Dead Prez, Mos Def, Immortal Technique, Common, Talib Kweli, and Kanye West—come under the heading of "conscious rappers" or creators of "politically conscious hip-hop," whereas Nelly, 50 Cent, Lil' Kim, Foxy Brown, DMX, Snoop Dogg, Nas, Jay-Z, Lil Flip, and scores of others are lumped into categories like "gangsta," "thug," or simply "mainstream."[1] The previous grouping warrants the title "underground" on account of not receiving airplay on Viacom's music television monopoly (it owns MTV, MTV2, VH1, and BET) and U.S. corporate oligarchy/oligopoly that dooms radio broadcast to Clear Channel's heavily regulated, sponsorship-driven, programming. Given that hip-hop's political practices are manifest in diverse forms across social positions and occur in varied relations to power and capital, we should be careful not to accept this polarization as a static state. Sean "Diddy" Combs, Jay-Z, and Master P's ascents to mega-stardom are hardly without political ramifications despite the MTV gloss. In his book *The Hip Hop Generation*, Bakari Kitwana clarifies that hip-hop's political agenda is as diverse as its culture, and has identifiable concerns focused on issues of education, employment, reparations, the state of urban subsistence, poverty and disease, the criminalization of young people, violence, and imperialism.[2] Moreover, this spectrum attests to the rich diversity of black cultural production at work that constantly traverses the parameters of hip-hop culture that now is well into its third decade. It has become synonymous with U.S. popular culture, and further afield, global mass culture. From Ralph Ellison's claim that "Negro Americans" give U.S. culture "color"[3] (a raced metaphor for style, language, identity) to Greg Tate's assertion that African Americans have become the "masters of the nation's creative profile,"[4] black cultural production—in the forms of hip-hop aesthetics— may very well define youth culture in the United States. Its styles, argot, practices, and creative expression are increasingly hegemonic in the marketplace while repeatedly counterhegemonic in cultural politics.

This balancing act is not lost on Guerrillafunk.com's unapologetic collapse between hip-hop as cultural form, commercial culture, educational site, political, and politicizing force. While the measures of political practice in hip-hop are far reaching throughout its historical lineage and global present, I'd like to consider hip-hop's innovation and early adoption of technology for the mediation of its culture, its cultural practices for negotiating urban spaces, and—in the context of networked computing—the Internet music label as a learning space. Hip-hop's historical arsenal of sonic and communicative technologies has received a great deal of scholarly study and I will discuss these in the section entitled, "Techniques and Technologies: Bring the Noise." This discussion will establish the importance of the black public sphere's emergence into a digital space through Mark Anthony Neal's notion of a "digitized aural urban landscape." The Internet, Internet radio, and digital distribution have, only recently, received attention in the continued engagement of the broader subject of race and technology.[5] For it is within networked computing, I posit in the next section, "Record Label for the 21st Century: More Than Music," that we can locate practices for evading the music industry's management of all facets of music while coming to regard the politically conscious hip-hop label as constitutive of a counter public sphere. Here, young people can learn about strategies for surviving in the music industry alongside larger social and political issues confronting them.

The contention here is that the Internet and Internet distribution of music expressed by guerrillafunk.com and, as we will see, Chuck D's rapstation.com and slamjamz.com, demonstrate how cultural politics aimed at young people in the form of hip-hop, activism, and cultural entrepreneurial practices are conducted and practiced through networked digital media. Turning to S. Craig Watkin's assertion that the Internet serves as a "town square" for hip-hop culture, I will examine how such Web sites provide an educational space where young people can interact, learn, and discuss real-world problems via their commitments to popular culture. Through these practices we witness the full realization of the Internet's democratizing possibility at a time when these freedoms are not ensured, both off and on-line. These Internet music labels "sell" more than music and broaden how entrepreneurial production and citizen initiatives can be reinterpreted by non–broadcast-based media while constituting a public sphere for political activism and learning. Of course, hip-hop is not exempt from generational differences. Public Enemy, for instance, cannot convincingly be considered "youth," although its music still informs "youth culture." Nonetheless, its cultural and economic currency is exchanged to different ends as both Paris and Public Enemy engineer online initiatives to educate younger generations—through the distribution of alternative models of hip-hop, enterprising technological practices, and the cultivation of an alternative public space for young people—for whom hip-hop culture largely informs their identities, social relations with others, and perspectives on their world. Guerrillafunk.com's content, for instance, negates the stereotypes of violence and sexism that often dog hip-hop in the public eye, to offer young people provocative images of the world that extend well beyond their neighborhoods, while illustrating the need for social/civic responsibility in one's own neighborhood. A growing need to recognize and understand hip-hop's "lesson plan," as well as how online music labels provide an alternative public space for teaching young people, is our task.

The triangular assemblage of artist–activist–entrepreneur is, in my conclusion, "Flip the Script: Hip-Hop's Other Novel Teaching Strategies," contrasted to the hip-hop moguls' emphasis on financial prestige and status within the culture industry. These Internet sites and the communities built around them have become essential technologically enabled spaces for disseminating politically conscious rap that does not conform to stereotyped images of hip-hop, determining what forms of youth culture receive mass airplay and how hip-hop can be positioned within the global market place as a type of blackness. Although the phrase "positive role-model" is often discredited when addressed in relation to hip-hop, the triangular model demonstrates a cultural producer whose currency is education, knowledge, and social change rather than diamonds, gold, and dope rides.

Hip-Hop 2.0 suggests that knowledge production, access, action, information dissemination, discussion, politics, as well as how young people interact with and through culture, looks and sounds radically different in the twenty-first century. For many young people today, popular culture is, perhaps, the inroad to civic life and political awareness, since so many are disillusioned by established political parties in the doldrums of the United States' two-party system. Increasingly, popular culture is a textbook for materializing the mediation of politics via everyday practices with technology . . . and as a cultural practice, hip-hop mustn't be dismissed or trivialized on account of its cultural politics and productions. This sentiment is expressed well by Ellis Cashmore in *The Black Culture Industry*, where he alerts readers that "to have cultural power is to have power, period."[6] Mediation of this power and young people's place within it are my subject, and we ought to engage with hip-hop's cultural models to ascertain how race and ethnicity are experienced and articulated across digital media, and how these emergent social functions of communication technology disperse and decentralize democratic ideals in a networked public sphere in the form and styles of hip-hop culture.

Such an engagement is especially critical as major forms of electronic mediation—like television, music, and the Internet (those most pertinent to the identities of young people)—are increasingly regulated and privatized. Once Chuck D famously declared, "Rap music is the CNN of black America." Today he would most definitely retract his analogy, as major news sources fail citizenry and democracy while the likes of blogs, wikis, podcasts, social-networking sites, and—of particular interest here—Internet radio, and Internet music labels, provide much-needed alternative means of coverage, debate, critical spaces, communication, and the distribution of information beyond the heavily controlled and orchestrated worldview of corporate broadcast and governance.

Techniques and Technologies: Bring the Noise

Robin D. G. Kelley's *Yo' Mama's Disfunktional: Fighting the Culture Wars in Urban America* has given the study of hip-hop an enduring image to assess its utilization of technology: "Their music and expressive styles have literally become weapons in a battle over the right to occupy public space. Frequently employing high-decibel car stereos and boom boxes, black youth not only 'pump up the volume' for their own listening pleasure, but also as part of an indirect, ad hoc war of position. The noise constitutes a form of cultural resistance not to be ignored."[7] Kelley's account of late twentieth-century cultural production, in the sundry forms of U.S. hip-hop culture, also includes technologies of spray paint, "bombed" New York City subway trains, the turntable as musical instrument, salvaged drum machines, the emergence of digital samplers, an MC's voluble microphone, the ghetto blaster sounding out the city, and bass frequencies drowning out Los Angeles, Oakland, and Miami as the automobile became a mobilized sound-system. From this well-played overview—one preserved fresh in the PBS television documentary *Style Wars* (Henry Chalfant and Tony Silver, 1982), the independent docu-drama film *Wild Style* (Charlie Ahearn, 1982), and the inevitable Hollywood exploitation vehicle *Beat Street* (Stan Lathan, 1984)—we see that hip-hop abides by its own distinguished forms of technocultural practice consciously assembled from communication and sound reproduction technologies.

In considering this annotation we ought not to restrict it to a historically produced series of specific technologies cultivated by hip-hop culture, but rather view it as illustrative of a relationship to technology that regards the surrounding environment of postindustrialization as a potential resource for cultural production and carefully engineered urban socialization. We also see a broad understanding of technology at work: one that is simultaneously a way of acting on the world, knowing the world, and a strategy for creating alternative worlds within the existing one. In complementary and creative ways, all the above mediated hip-hop culture's early formation in the contestation of public space:

through the ether, the stage, on vinyl and magnetic tape, and across the surfaces of urban infrastructures.

Kelley's passage also speaks to a general consensus among scholars of hip-hop that disenfranchisement, along class and racial lines, neither equals technophobia nor passivity, as is often attributed to marginalized people's relationship to emergent technology. The polarity of consumption and production is skewed, as is the belief that racial minorities or people of color are alienated from and victims of technology. Social forces shaping hip-hop assist in the production and understandings of cultural technology, for it is, in the case of hip-hop culture, transformative and enabling. For example, and to expound upon one of Kelley's examples of expressive styles, hip-hop aesthetics tweaked the everyday. A "personal" portable stereo audio device like a radio/cassette player (emerging in the mid-1970s) and later, in the 1990s, portable CD players, became *not just* a device for listening to music but also a mobile sound system outfitted with wheels, pulled in a wagon (as common in my old neighborhood), or carried on the shoulder because of enormous sizes and weight, as was common in the early 1980s. The presence of this device transforms public space (the stoop, streets, corner, or courts) into spontaneous social happenings. A lesson learned well for this first generation of hip-hop is that its practices and modes of production signal an active and inventive approach to the amorphousness of technology through various acts of creative expression and technical expansion in the political context of "the right to occupy space." This bespeaks the period within which hip-hop formed its social and cultural responses to economic and environmental conditions affecting the South Bronx in the late twentieth century. Technology, in its nonhierarchical manifestations plundered by hip-hop's right to "refuse," in both senses of the word, enabled a response: a means to reshape and redefine in order to survive an oppressive environment. "Refuse" has been encapsulated beautifully by Tricia Rose's well-known observation that "hip hop *is* black urban renewal."[8]

To invest in hip-hop as a complex of social, political, economic, cultural, and aesthetic discourses and practices for articulating youth's engagement with digital technology, we cannot remain crazy-glued within the historical context of postindustrialization and the technocultural practices emblematic of hip-hop "back in the day," despite how enticing narratives of authenticity—fat laces, white gloves, and a thumping Panasonic RX-5050—can be. The avant-garde of hip-hop studies is historically bound, historically responsible, and therefore requires rethinking and reevaluation when hip-hop of the late twentieth century is met by networked computing, Internet radio, and online music distribution. Furthermore, in the twenty-first century, hip-hop exists in its post-subcultural present—consumed en masse across class and racial divides by blacks, whites, Latina/os, and Asians youths—as a global mass culture and billion-dollar culture industry, complete with its own moguls. Hip-hop, it ought to be stressed, *is*—at once—old school *and* next generation.

Mark Anthony Neal engages with digital technology's place and influence within hip-hop culture in his *What the Music Said: Black Popular Music and Black Public Culture*. Neal opens his final chapter, "Postindustrial Postscript: Digital Aural Urban Landscape," by assigning Kelley's passage (cited above) the rank of epigraph. For Neal, Kelley's account is cast upon the social and economic backdrop of the standardization of digital sound reproduction in the music industry beginning to occur in the 1980s, and the challenges facing the historical black public sphere—the black church, black liberal bourgeois, black music and the oral tradition, black arts movements, civil rights, black nationalism—in the postindustrial era. Yet, we should note that Kelley's passage bears no semblance to digital technology, as his description is firmly latched onto broadcast radio, cassette tapes, and possibly CDs. Digital technology can no longer remain a postscript in the study of race and technology. It's more likely that Neal aims to emphasize Kelley's discussion of "cultural resistance," and his argument is not a dedicated account of technology, despite its interconnectedness with hip-hop. Hip- hop, in the digital era, is a direct benefactor of this technological transformation for the production of recorded—as well as performed—music, and introduces a notable contrast to previous forms of black music like blues, rhythm and blues, and soul. I have elected to quote Neal at length to address this difference and its impact on the black public sphere and hip-hop:

In the case of the urban blues, which received stimulus from the development of the phonograph, and rhythm and blues, which benefited from the electrification of instruments and the development of the transistor, advancements in technology have often served to distribute the popular narratives of African-Americans beyond limits of their insular communities, often to the detriment to those in communities. Given the structural transformations that hip-hop was in part a response to, digitized recordings of hip-hop theoretically served to distribute the critical narratives of an isolated working class and underclass youth culture across the disjointed African-American diaspora via the marketplace.[9]

We have to be careful not to celebrate digital media as achieving a sweeping newness otherwise impossible through existing forms of electronic mediation. "Digitized recordings," as described by Neal, seem no more capable than magnetic tape, radio broadcast, vinyl, or even music video (when black artists were finally featured on MTV during its teething years). The digital here, unfortunately, appears as nothing more than an "improved" commodity (the CD) following the market distribution network of other sound recordings. I'd like to position digital technology as *more than* another mode of distribution or shiny new storage medium for the consideration of digital learning and youth.

Neal assigns the significance of hip-hop's relation to new digital technology as a response to the postindustrialization of black urban spaces whereby the music form and style constitute a "vehicle for forms of critique uniquely suited for the dispersed and disjointed nature of contemporary black communal formations."[10] The erosion of social institutions and spaces indicative of the black public sphere finds hip-hop satisfying this void: "hip-hop recordings began to resemble digitized town meetings in which the black community and the very traditions of hip-hop were open to debate and critique."[11] Debate and critique, according to Neal, are exemplified by hip-hop lyrics that are critical of hip-hop itself, as well as social conditions confronting African Americans. Accordingly, "hip-hop artists," Neal insists, "have reclaimed the critical possibilities of popular culture, by using popular culture and the marketplace as the forum to stimulate a broad discussion and critique about critical issues that most affect their constituencies."[12] Popular culture is the source and substance through which young people interact with their worlds. To reclaim the popular as a critical forum for rebuilding/redesigning the black public sphere is to broaden what popular culture can consist of, how it can be called upon to function in provocative and educational ways for engaging with youth.

I am not going to dispute Neal's claims about the political possibilities of popular culture. I agree with him wholeheartedly. Rather, I will suggest that his approach to digital technology is limited to *digitized* forms of media and does not consider other emerging digital media technology and information technology's impact on hip-hop culture, young people's acquisition, and technology's formative role for the maintenance of a black public sphere. Published in 1999, *What the Music Said* makes no reference to computers, the Internet, digital distribution, or online music. In the period within which Neal sets his postscript on the digital, online music already existed. It took the forms of purchasing CDs online, Internet radio, RealAudio for streaming audio via the Internet, MP3 players, music downloads via Liquid Audio (launched in 1996), and MP3.com (launched in 1997). All of which would add fuel to the fire of ownership and copyright that greatly transcend hip-hop's legal battles over royalties disputes surrounding its propensity for sampling.

The Internet experience at present is different from the period within which Neal wrote, and the hip-hop experience online is different as text-based pages are built on platforms (like the Web development technique AJAX, Asynchronous JavaScript and XML) that allow for more interactive Web applications. Web sites are more useable as Web content is not static but dynamic, as are our experiences. In other words, when studying hip-hop's relation to network computing and software applications, we immediately learn that it isn't just downloading the latest hits, but a full social experience that parallels the vibrant energy of black cultural production within a larger context of digital democracy. Without a broader consideration of emerging media, Neal's "digitized town meetings" and the social agency they hope to perform appear limited to recorded music where imaginary citizenry cannot be vocal, interact, debate issues, form opinions, but must simply listen to prerecorded lyrics, which, it can be said, maintains the one-to-many principle of broadcast media that is hardly interactive. In this case, young people can only be active within this imagined town meeting as consumers and listeners. They are not afforded an active role in participating in knowledge exchange, and not part of a learning environment conducive to any form of democracy.

Neal's town meeting is little more than a battle rap and an undemocratic public sphere where only contracted recording artists are capable of speech and can "represent." Here, "public" becomes "publicity."[13] This "digitized aural urban landscape" remains terrestrial as networked computing, discourses on digital democracy, and the potential of an electronic public sphere eludes his consideration to delimit hip-hop's communicative abilities severely, along with the radicality Neal himself affords its cultural politics. As the subject of my chapter attests, Internet radio, Internet record labels, and digital distribution introduce expanded nodes into the black public sphere, to maintain an engagement with Neal's important work, as the participatory principle of networked computing and file-sharing reciprocity allows for more to participate in a global community of many-to-many social agents. For it is through the continued innovation of black technocultural production and practices that digital learning finds a place within hip-hop culture. After all, this was a major reason that scholarly attention was first afforded to hip-hop: its transformative vibrancy.

Record Label for the 21st Century: More Than Music

Where Neal posited the digitization of rap as constitutive of a town meeting for a dislocated and morphing black public sphere, S. Craig Watkins assigns this function and responsibility to the Internet as "new town square." "More than radio, corporate rap, or music video," he proclaims, "the Internet has become the new town square in hip hop, a vital public sphere for building an imagined community, organizing political initiatives, and conducting provocative debate about the state of hip hop."[14] The decentralized, or distributed, network of the Internet and the interconnected network of the World Wide Web, as well as software that continually drives and shapes digital computing, mediates our heterogeneous complex of understanding and communicating in the world, whether on- or offline. Watkin's claim further endorses the rich lineage of hip-hop's embrace (if not embodiment) of technology, while offering more of a networked space for conceiving of black community, social awareness, participatory communicative exchanges, and digital learning than recorded music allows per Neal's conceptualization.

The Internet, under this pretext, is imagined, mediated, and occupied along the lines of Pierre Lévy's "knowledge space,"[15] whereby the Web's dissemination of knowledge and information may enlarge participatory actions, lead to the development of alternative forms of citizenship, and expound on community without geographical restrictions. Members of this knowledge space cogenerate knowledge exchange and development as a collective endeavor, a collective intelligence. A common thread that unites this collective participation is hip-hop, which becomes the object cogenerated across artist, label, fan, activist, entrepreneur, innovator, and prosumer. Witnessed in my account of guerrillafunk.com, music—while no doubt a vital cultural form of expression, sonic experimentation, and political mediation within hip-hop culture—isn't enough to tackle critically and communicate local and global issues facing young people in the United States. We find the foundational stylistic accoutrements of hip-hop rocking the computer screen with broader criticism of power relations, as we will see below, in the forms of activist journalism, video-streamed news coverage, documentaries on world events, and critical commentary on the music industry.

In Watkins' chapter "The Digital Underground" from *Hip Hop Matters: Politics, Pop Culture, and the Struggle for the Soul of a Movement*, he informatively plots Chuck D's Internet ventures throughout the 1990s to the formation and prolongation of rapstation.com and slamjamz.com. While the music industry was transfixed on the "illegality" of P2P file sharing and the copyright infringement surrounding Napster, the Internet was adopted as an "alternative industry and ideology"[16] by Chuck D and Public Enemy, who regarded digital distribution as a means to shift power outside and away from corporate holders, thus expounding upon the possibilities of cultural power enabled by emergent media. Public Enemy attempted to release free downloads of its *Bring the Noise 2000* until Polygram Records (which purchased Def Jam in 1994) threatened legal action over its ownership of the master tapes. The release of *There's a Poison Goin' On* (1999) was the first major record released in MP3 format, released through the Internet in partnership with distributor Atomic Pop Records. In November 2004, *Wired* released a free CD, (-*Rip. Sample. Mash. Share.*), compiled under a Creative Commons License that contained the track "No Meaning No," by Chuck D and the Fine Arts Militia. Networked computing offers enterprising hip-hop artists and their fans the opportunity to rethink their relation to ownership, artistic control, egalitarian business practices, cultural capital, and the function of a record label, while redesigning how production, distribution, consumption, and content can benefit substantially online, where FCC regulation does not apply.

Founded in 1996, slamjamz.com is a "label site" where visitors can download free singles of various artists. According to Chuck D, this practice isn't a risk, as artists can turn a profit "on the back end—through T-shirt sales or the fans will shell out for a boxed CD,"[17] a lesson learned from radio's promotion of singles. Existing as an Internet-based label or "label site" (as Chuck D refers to it), slamjamz grew *on account of digital technology*, versus reluctantly moving to the technology to remain competitive in a changing market (as have major music labels). Also, the label can take risks on artists that the corporate strategies of major music labels cannot, owing to the uncertainty of the market held hostage by generic restrictions, formulas of the star system, and distribution constraints. A do-it-yourself ethic is yet another lesson of hip-hop 2.0. Small-budget artists, and artists who aren't considered "radio friendly" because of their political positions, are afforded a means of distribution beyond mass appeal. This becomes increasingly important as broadcast radio, MTV, and even CD sales are heavily regulated affairs scared of "controversial" artists on account of FCC fines for "indecency" (raised by Congress in June 2006 to the highest levels in U.S. history), media watchdog protest and congressional hearings, and the largest retailer of music—Wal-Mart—refusing to stock CDs that carry parental advisory warnings. Serving as a label site and distributor of music, slamjamz.com is a public space generative of free speech and democratizing principles. In its spaces, youth can listen without the oppressive regulatory apparatuses that restrict musical content on the radio, in music stores, and on MTV.

The label site also enables music ventures, otherwise impossible without networked computing and digital distribution. I'm referring to slamjamz artists, Crew Grrl Order. Hailed as "the world's first virtual woman rap squad," the group's members are based in Georgia, Colorado, and Ohio. Hip-hop's ties to the local that defines a sound and attitude are confounded when the group's members do not hail from the same city and, instead, assemble their sound through the networked space of the Web. Where the cultural discourse of transnational communication and sonic dialogues took the form of sampling in the history of hip-hop, the Internet label is a platform where national—as well as intranational—artists can amass, thus connecting cultural producers who reside outside of cities most associated with hip-hop culture, while further diversifying hip-hop's style and flava.

Equally, the risk taking of slamjamz is a political manifesto to counteract banal and nihilistic forms of hip-hop maintained by big labels and mainstream constructed tastes. Kembrew McLeod's work on microlabel practices affirms this position. He writes, "We can hear a greater diversity of expression than is allowed through the gates of big record companies—with their narrow ideas about what kind of music is profitable. For instance, if you knew hip hop only from what you heard on the radio or MTV, you'd rightly come to the conclusion that it's about nothing but bitches and money."[18] Many do reach this conclusion in their condemnation and vilification of hip-hop for its "violence," "misogyny," "homophobia," and "sexism," while others imitate and validate as alternative models remain invisible. In her post to the MacArthur Foundation's online discussions about digital media learning, youth, and race, videographer Helen H. Park voices a similar concern over her students' lack of awareness of alternatives to the scenario that McLeod describes. She writes:

Many of these young people look at an image of 50 Cent, perhaps download a ring tone or watch his videos on YouTube, and they see a representation of a man of color that they respect, perhaps even believe they relate to. But what are the other options? What other representations are they getting? The Game? Both of these "artists" gross a lot of money, even in their public brawls (perhaps also because of their public brawls). So why show anything else when billions can be made, even at the expense of young people who try to emulate what they see, which is a lifestyle of violence, misogyny, bling.[19]

The label sites studied in this chapter attest that alternatives do—in fact— exist, and many young people are active in supporting and participating in these counterpublics and digital practices. Granted, the steps being taken by guerrillafunk.com and rapstation.com are difficult to see compared to the massive capital behind 50 Cent and others, who are cash cows for the music industry while further affirming marketable images of blackness. It requires an ongoing process to make young people aware of this discrepancy—through initiatives such as this series, community projects, activism, pedagogic practice, and, of course, politically aware hip-hop—and actively participate in building critical dialogues to work toward social responsibility and change. Slamjamz's roster of artists already looks a lot different than what reaches the eyes and ears of young people via broadcast: the afrofuturist sounds of Basheba Earth, the genre-bending of rock and hip-hop by The 7th Octave, the soul of Kyle Jason, and the fusion of country and western with rap by Bonnie Cream. Slamjamz refuses to allow the mic and turntable model to dominate its creative output, and challenges the confines of hip-hop's intelligibility within the marketplace.

The communicative element of slamjamz's public presence is not only expressed by its micro-label politics, counterbalancing tactics of re-representation, but also found in its information dissemination known as the "backboard." A term borrowed from basketball, the backboard *supports the net* and provides a surface on which to make shots, and for slamjamz it is a portal to active forums about hip-hop where members can converse, network, and post views on articles that range from music, hip-hop culture, black history, politics, sports, and celebrity. The backboard also connects to forums shared with Chuck D's other Internet venture, rapstation.com. Internet radio maintains a distribution outlet for underground or marginalized hip-hop artists. Rapstation.com boasts 5,907 registered users who have generated over 9,000 articles. User-generated subjects discussed on the boards include reparations, exploitation and slavery, violence at hip-hop gigs, the war in Iraq, calls to impeach Bush, racism (and racism within the online postings), police violence during "black" spring break, Eazy E's AIDS quilt, sex, and world hip-hop. Also, many who post provide links for related materials that they've researched on the Web. On November 25, 2002, the member "Vision" posted on Cuban "raperos": "A rebellion has taken root in Cuba, nourished by a stifling trade embargo, the collapse of the Soviet Union, and racial inequality. But these rebels use lyrics, not guns, and they dance instead of march."[20] The article is linked to cnn.com.

In addition, rapstation's "Digital Affairs" menu option provides rap lyrics in its "Lyrics of the Week" link, hosts a "rapstation swapmeet," where users can file-share music and videos, and provides an information source called "Hip Hop University." Referred to as the "empowerment zone" and "advice from the trenches," the article "Material Love," by Cedric Muhammed, focuses on images of conspicuous consumption dominant in mainstream hip-hop music videos. He shares his experience of working in the music industry with users by questioning why hip-hop is "so flooded, at this stage, with visual images that emphasize material possessions, violent acts, language and sexual imagery?"[21] Users can post comments in response. Other lessons provide advice for young artists to manage their relationship with music labels, the attributes of digital recording for the independent artists, and information on purchasing a home for first-time buyers in a market that continues to discriminate.

Again, music is only one facet of this informational resource and social space. The "Today in Hip Hop" menu option offers a wealth of information on music as well as a forum for engaging with issues confronting the black community. For instance, coverage of the second National Hip-Hop Political Convention held in Chicago tackled the problem of "urban radio's" lack of relevant news coverage, especially local election issues, as these are sidelined for "gossip-filled entertainment." Long-time black community activist Afrika Bambaataa, along with his Universal Zulu Nation, have initiated a nationwide campaign to mix up the type of hip-hop in constant rotation on radio playlists that highlight violent activities. The campaign captures many of the concerns that Park raises for young people's need for alternative voices. Neal and Watkins' claim that hip-hop mediates a town meeting/square is best embodied by rapstation's support and transmission of the interactive forum, "Urban Campfire," a virtual town hall meeting produced by New World Culture of San Francisco. Furthermore, a public sphere for critical debate and opinion formation is fostered by Adisa Banjoko's (a.k.a. "The Bishop of Hip Hop") journalist coverage of social issues facing African Americans, Islamic culture, and world hip-hop. While in the late 1980s and early 1990s, hip-hop concentrated on the black community as an American condition concerned with racism and economic inequalities, in the twenty-first century this concern remains, but is joined with an emphasis on human rights and war that stretches well beyond U.S. borders. Like a hip-hop recording, on these sites the "local" and the "global" are mixed.

The responsibility of leading, or at least helping to cultivate, an accessible digital public sphere for the creation of dialogues and learning for youth currently not being served by big media conglomerates, rests on the optimism afforded to technology as an enabling power, a transformative measure, and critical levy for active participation in democratic practices. We cannot regard democracy and freedom as inevitable results of networked computing, but rather as ongoing struggles while new legislation threatens to inhibit further our constitutional right to assemble peacefully even in the public space of the Internet and engage in its myriad social functions (e.g., federal requirements of Internet filters in schools, ICRA Web-content ratings, and the Communications Opportunity Promotion and Enhancement, which threatens net neutrality in the interest of telecom companies). The public sphere, as Mark Poster rightly asserts, "is at the heart of any reconceptualization of democracy"[22]— even one that consists of electronically mediated discourse and distributed communications systems.

So if we are to pursue Neal's and Watkins' investment in digital technology as contributing to the reconstruction of a black public sphere through the popular forms of hip-hop, as I believe we should, then we have already witnessed what George Lipsitz argues is a "new public sphere that uses the circuits of commodity production and circulation to envision and activate new social relations."[23] Lipsitz is not referring to digital technology in making this claim yet, as I've already briefly mentioned, the likes of guerrillafunk.com readily mashes up commodity production, activist practices, and the management of a record label and Web page in forging social relations to the world through hip-hop. In regards to Lipsitz's claim I'd also like to suggest that hip-hop, in the manner articulated within this chapter, fully realizes the available circuits of the commercial market that the music industry has traditionally feared and attempted to extinguish through copyright infringement lawsuits against alternative means of music distribution, namely file-sharing and Internet distribution. Hip-hop isn't simply piggy-backing, (i.e., using an available means), but experimenting with new business models based on digital technology and leading the redesign of the distribution, consumption, and culture of music.

The threat posed to oligopoly music market hegemony (Sony-BMG, Universal, AOL-Time Warner, and EMI) is not only manifest in shifts in formats evidenced by the flexibility of digital audio encoding (CDs, MP3 files, and related formats) as compared to obsolete dedicated storage media like reel-to-reel, 8-track tape, cassette-tape, and the 33-1/3 LP, but also through challenges to gatekeepers of officialdom who define economic and social relations between artists and consumers. Digital distribution reverberates with an ideology of direct access to music by consumers and an artist's ability to control her or his content while not being "owned" and exploited by a label for little or no compensation so that the label can recoup its production, promotions, and distribution expenses. What artist requires a record label when one can self-produce via music software for mixing, bypass radio altogether to distribute songs in MP3 format to vast audiences directly via social-networking spaces like myspace.com, file-sharing music sites like Gnutella, and commercial sites like Artistdirect.com? The artist can also avoid MTV's major-label-only promotional music videos by releasing his or her own video made with FinalCut Pro and posting it on user-generated Youtube.com. And one doesn't have to bow to Wal-Mart's dogma of family and clean-version CDs on account of not having a tangible commodity in need of pricey shelf space. Of course, this is a simplistic view that fails to consider the various interconnected divisions of the music industry, such as agents, publishers, and promoters/marketers, as well as related services like Ticketmaster's monopolized control of concert venues, Clear Channel Communication's music promotions, and the suspect practice of payola by which record companies pay to have their singles in heavy rotation (those radio hits aren't accidental but well-financed). Regardless of this simplicity, it does signal a do-it-yourself conviction that Chuck D and Paris have put to work in their construction of an online public sphere for Internet distribution of marginalized artists and content.

Rapstation.com, as well as Chuck D's affiliation with progressive talk radio, Air America, demonstrates the importance, viability, and need for Internet radio when the quality and heterogeneity of broadcast has been severely curtailed with the passage of the Telecommunications Act of 1996, which further deregulated media services and policies by increasing competition between corporate providers and restructuring the telecommunications industry. An overhaul of the Communications Act of 1934, this juggernaut included provisions for cable, television, the Internet, telephone, and radio... the new proindustry act lifted the ownership restrictions on how many radio stations a single company could own. The previous limit was set at forty nationwide (no more than four stations in a single market), and the sky's-the-limit model of ownership consolidation marks the looming death of local radio... the most noticeable effect being shorter playlists in cahoots with the majors' payola scheme that results in a lack of choice and difference. Radio is devalued as a public resource, if not sold off entirely for sponsors' revenue and major label distribution. *Wired*'s story on radio demonstrates that "big radio" increases "revenue by adding more and more commercials,"[24] broken up briefly by a hits list and prerecorded DJ voices on automatic pilot programmed via satellite. Before we could say "radio changed overnight" radio had already changed. Stations were acquired by aggressive companies like Clear Channel, which previously (in 1997) owned 173 radio stations and currently owns 1,207 stations. Rivals include Cumulus Media Inc., Disney, Emmis Communication Group, Cox Communications, Entercom Communications, Infinity Broadcasting (owned by Viacom), and Citadel Broadcasting. The "local" in "local radio" has dissipated as community programming is given over to high-paying sponsors, bland demographics, and the tyranny of the Wal-Mart business model for our ears.

Aside from big radio's homogenous programming and dominance of the radio market, the ontology of the medium is restricted to what German media theorist Bertolt Brecht condemned as a "distribution apparatus" in his 1932 manifesto, "The Radio as an Apparatus of Communication." For Brecht, the emancipatory possibility of radio resides in reclaiming the medium as "the finest possible communication apparatus in public life."[25] Brecht's Weimar vision for radio with its "vast network of pipes" consisted of listeners becoming "suppliers." This vision is more fully realized in digital communications and Internet user-generated content as seen with rapstation.com. The "supplier" model for Internet radio allows digital distribution to be unlike the "supply business" of Brecht's era, and counteracts big radio dominance and programming by providing programming that is not indentured to the majors, while providing a space and "truly public character to public occasions" in digital format.

Another damaging aspect of corporate radio consolidation is its control over content. With consolidation comes efficient control and regulation as difference is easily quashed to reach the largest market while appeasing sponsors. This is mostly achieved by tight control of content. It is well known that Clear Channel Communications, without any federal mandate, compiled a list of 164 songs—"songs with questionable lyrics"—the day after the September

11, 2001, attacks. Regarded as a "suggestion" rather than ultimatum to its stations, the list amounted to a direct ban as Clear Channel affiliates regurgitate a programming playlist. Clear Channel's 1,207 stations composed a nationwide ban on music ranging from any song that references an airplane (e.g., Peter, Paul, and Mary's "Leaving on a Jet Plane") to songs about peace (e.g., John Lennon's "Imagine").[26] Such a ban, and Clear Channel's general content control, powerfully demonstrates its influence on what the public can hear via the airwaves, while all but defining what the radio-as-public-sphere will consist of: patriotic car advertisements with Alan Jackson country twang that became the fitting anthem of "United We Stand" mythology. Since 9/11, Clear Channel has consistently not played music critical of U.S. actions in Afghanistan and Iraq, and broadcasts a variety of right-wing talk radio hosts such as Glenn Beck, who referred to hurricane Katrina survivors as "scumbags."[27] Whose voice is accessible and whose voice can articulate social issues and world events is at stake in such an example of corporate control. If, like voting, radio too has been relegated to democracy's Room 101, then hip-hop's utilization of Internet radio is an attempt to maintain community, access, informative services, and communication.

None of Paris' music appeared on Clear Channel's list of "suggested" bans, as his music receives no radio play: "nowadays radio makes it harder to bring real shit to the people" he raps on "Tear Shit Up" on *Sonic Jihad*. An album striking out against the Bush–Cheney regime and its response to 9/11, the corporatization of hip-hop, and media regulation, Paris uses the space of Guerrilla Funk's Web page to discuss the visual poignancy of the album cover: a commercial aircraft is depicted crashing into the White House. Instead of clinging to arguments on artistic license and freedom-of-speech banter common to musicians who publicly defend their work (the old taped mouth schtick), Paris seizes the opportunity to transform the "controversial" into a stimulus for a critical forum on the United States' "war on terror." In the "Thought Box" column (discussed previously), Paris' article, "The War on Terror," pits an image of the rapper literally going head-to-head with Cheney, Ashcroft, Powell, and Bush. His essay articulates the constitutional and civil rights violations of the Patriot Act (while providing links to the actual document for visitors) coupled with an engagement of the ACLU's objections to the act. Again, hip-hop is a hyperlink to a much bigger universe and social responsibility beyond the role of listener as young people are provided with access to federal documents unavailable and off curriculum in U.S. high schools (as well as absent from many university survey courses on Western civilization). Paris goes on to discuss the free market expansion as the modus operandi of capitalism, and the United States' economic benefits from wars in the Middle East, while connecting the need and ability to speak out against such actions in the midst of corporate control of hip-hop. In other words, Paris situates domestic cultural affairs—young people listening to and identifying with hip-hop culture—on a larger playing field, where hip-hop becomes a necessary resource for information increasingly difficult to obtain as broadcast radio content is subject to Clear Channel Communication's policy. If Blue Öyster Cult's "Burning For You" was banned after 9/11, we have little hope in relying upon radio as a crucial communication source.

The label, Guerrilla Funk, was originally founded in order to release *Sonic Jihad* globally, Paris explains in an interview with *LA City Beat*. This was necessary as labels would not touch the album: "We were indicting the Bush administration's involvement with September 11th. The climate was not conducive for anybody that expressed dissent at that time. It was so bad that there were even major independent distributors shunning material that was critical of the government, social conditions, and of the war."[28] The release of *Sonic Jihad* (which, in 2005, has sold 150,000 copies worldwide) allowed Paris to invest profits back into the label in order to produce the Public Enemy album, *Rebirth of a Nation*, as well as the work of The Coup (which raps on class issues), and TKASH (whose album *Turf War Syndrome* concentrates on America's urban life and social conditions after 9/11). A public space for information exchange and education, guerrillafunk.com provides in-depth interviews with artists. The space allows for a wide range of topics dedicated to social and global issues. It also illustrates Paris' polemic on hip-hop that "you don't have any business being a rapper if you can't talk to me about anything other than hip-hop and if your experience doesn't extend beyond your block. If that's all that's important to you, you aren't telling me shit. You gotta be value-added to the game."[29] Again, the label site expands beyond music in the form of its "suggested readings" menu. Here, an extensive book list (linked to Barnes & Nobel for immediate ordering) is provided. Subject matter is incredibly broad in scope, covering books on hip-hop, black activists and intellectuals (Cornel West, bell hooks, and Eldridge Cleaver, for example); Donald Bogel's classic study *Toms, Coons, Mulattoes, Mammies, and Bucks* on representation on blackness in Hollywood film; financial management; corporate farming; obesity; SAT test-taking skills; U.S. history and politics; criticism of the Bush regime; and the music industry. At guerrillafunk.com this broad scope constitutes hip-hop culture: young people are "redirected" into an electronic public knowledge space where popular culture is a political initiative and the label site is a communicative network running contrary to the music industry's promotion of hip-hop.

Flip the Script: Hip-Hop's Other Novel Teaching Strategies

As a communications infrastructure and public space, the likes of label sites slamjamz.com, guerrillafunk.com, and Internet radio, rapstation.com attest to the necessity of digital distribution when democracy is increasingly becoming a luxury bought and sold on global markets, and property for corporate conglomerates licensed by the federal government. Music—such a formative element in young people's sense of self, identity, community, and social discourse—is contested cultural terrain as hip-hop's Internet compliancy seeks alternative modes of distribution not just for music but also for a political and politicizing public space. I have stressed a triangular model (artist–activist–entrepreneur) for grasping the approach of Internet initiatives from within and expressive of politically conscious hip-hop. By way of a conclusion, I'd like to examine this model in a little more detail in regard to digital democracy and e-commerce, as well as the figure of the hip-hop mogul. As stated previously, I consider Paris and Chuck D moguls not in the variety of tycoons, but moguls dedicated to education and activism. Other models beyond the "get rich or die trying" bravado exist and are being made available to young people via the label sites discussed within this chapter.

Douglas Schuler has contributed to the MIT "Media in Transition" collection *Democracy and New Media*. He is cynical of loose language that opines the Internet as "immensely" or "inherently" democratic, while fully acknowledging democratic participation through user practices of the medium. To address claims of Internet democracy, Schuler reviews key elements constitutive of democratic processes. I would like to highlight a tension that he identities as detrimental to the potential of Internet democracy: e-commerce. Democracy requires active participation at various levels of its processes. Namely, egalitarian participation, access to public agendas, fair voting, and representation, are the attributes that Schuler identifies as necessary for democracy to function in the service of the people. Consolidation of radio, as we've seen, and the concentration of media ownership in corporate hands, denies democracy's basic tenets as electronic mediation is the main way that information, agenda building, and representation are possible today. The fear is that media ownership by the few (at the expense of the many) and the commercial forces that dominate the Internet with the end of net neutrality hanging in the balance, demonstrates that "infrastructure will likely focus on entertainment and that which brings in the most revenue—sex, violence, special effects—and devote little attention to services that educate, inspire, or help bring communities together."[30] In other words, democratic principles are threatened by the transformation of the Internet into a commercial space.

Certainly, the Communications Opportunity Promotion and Enhancement Act promises to do equal, if not more, damage than the Telecommunication Act of 1996 in further deregulating media for private interests while all but shutting down Internet democracy as private financial gain replaces ubiquitous communication. Yet, the triangular assemblage demonstrates that commerce and democracy ought not to be regarded as oppositional, as Schuler tends to place, for example, education at odds with entertainment. Hip-hop 2.0 incorporates both. "Merchandise," a menu option on all of the Web pages that I've discussed, provides access to commodities (CDs, posters, books, t-shirts) that are not devoid of cultural and political meanings. The fact that albums like *Sonic Jihad* and *Rebirth of a Nation* require digital distribution (as many corporate chains will not stock them) attests to democratic tenets of access, equality, representation, as well as inclusivity, while simultaneously demonstrating both the dangers of corporate consolidation and the Internet as a technology and space to thwart such efforts. Considering hip-hop as pedagogic practice, its digital practices illustrate the possibility of the Internet in that youth culture becomes an issue "inherently" tied to democratic debate and lessons in legality. Through commerce, hip-hop culture enters into a public space for active participation within democratic processes when broadcast media restricts knowledge acquisition and practices. Business practices of an Internet label and Internet radio testify to the pervasive demise of broadcast as a public resource and democratic institution.

My triangular assemblage also introduces a new figure—a radical role model, if you will—into the culture industry of hip-hop, a "mogul" not motivated by personal wealth and financial status, but political activism through cultural production and innovative investments in communications technology. Ellis Cashmore extends a reservation for claims of black entrepreneurship in the music industry. He writes that celebrities like Sean "Diddy" Combs "must be approached with the same kind of skepticism that once greeted the minstrel, themselves empowered by the money they earned yet constrained by the very environment in which they prospered."[31] Cultural entrepreneur does not account for the monetary reward and financial "empowerment" that accompanies the media celebrities that Cashmore studies (Berry Gordy, Michael Jackson, Prince, Russell Simmons), but engages with innovative practices that incorporate culture as a currency for political critique and protest. The rhetoric of empowerment is solely aligned with black ownership and modest financial gains compared to white ownership. In the late 1990s and into this century, the figure of the hip-hop mogul has emerged magnanimously, according to Christopher Holmes Smith, as an "icon . . . of mainstream power and consequently occupies a position of inclusion within many of the nation's elite social networks and cosmopolitan cultural formations."[32] The mogul, with his or her wealthy lifestyle and upward social mobility, is a surrogate figure for those who will never achieve such status and success, argues Smith. I want to cite Smith at length in order to erect a different mogul figure:

The mogul inspires his more downtrodden constituents to "buy in" to the emerging paradigm of accessible luxury and social status and in the process assumes an influential role as social mediator. Thus, the hip-hip mogul exemplifies the changing dimensions of African American political platforms for those generations born after the civil rights movement, particularly the changing regard for the residual modern social ideal of an "aspiring" mass social formation as a meaningful referent and basis for an activist-oriented black public sphere.[33]

This is not the only mogul figure to currently occupy hip-hop culture. In fact, it is one often chastised by a hip-hop intelligentsia critical of social divisions and music industry affluence.

The artist–activist–entrepreneur demonstrates that "status" and cultural influence are not only couched in terms of wealth but also social responsibility, education, and innovative practices aligned with hip-hop's history of technology. Achievements of social agency are expressed through commitment to social justice. Paris' first album, *The Devil Made Me Do It* (1990), was produced while he was pursuing his bachelor's degree in managerial economics at the University of California, Davis. Chuck D honed his Public Enemy persona as a radio DJ while attending Adelphi University. Rather than regard hip-hop as contrary to education, both found ways to fuse the two while expounding upon the limits of what hip-hop can be while rearticulating where and how knowledge acquisition can occur through black cultural production. This practice is furthered by investing in hip-hop culture as a stimulus for social change, business venture, and platform for humanitarian ideologies against injustice. To restrict hip-hop celebrity to the mogul is to reinforce mainstream conceptualizations of hip-hop culture while further endorsing media corporate consolidation as the only artery for its mediation. Greg Tate makes this point clear, "Within hip hop, however, as in American entrepreneurship generally, competing ideologies exist to be exploited rather than expunged and expelled—if only because hip hop culture and the hip hop marketplace, like a quantum paradox, provide space to all Black ideologies, from the most anti-white to the most pro-capitalist, without ever having to account for the contradiction."[34] Internet radio and digital distribution, in the forms we've studied, show "black ideologies" that are critical of those that receive mass dissemination, while positing a counter means to refrain from subsisting on a poor diet of McMusic.

Consider Chuck D's latest venture, Chuck D Mobile. Launched at the wireless trade shows Cellular Telecommunications & Internet Association (CTIA) and the Mobile Entertainment Content, Commerce of Applications Conference (MECCA) in Las Vegas in April 2006, the service intends to distribute a wide array of hip-hop songs and videos directly from artists to mobile phones. Here, wireless devices provide a new opportunity for open access and distribution as well as the freedom to build on creativity. In making politically progressive hip-hop content available to mobile phone users (literally placed in the hands of young people), Chuck D and M-Qube (mobile content provider based in Watertown, MA) hope to widen the "pitch" by having wireless carriers like Sprint, Verizon, and Cingular, distribute the service over their networks. Like the label site, the cell phone has joined the cacophony of hip-hop's techniques, not as a consumer device but as a prosumer instrument for connecting listeners to a wireless public sphere that knows no bounds. All of the practices discussed demonstrate that knowledge production and politics look and sound radically different in the twenty-first century. Black cultural production, in the form of hip-hop 2.0, remains at the forefront in developing innovative and creative practices that broaden access, distribute knowledge, and provide an interactive public space and critical learning forum for young people with its reconceptualization of democracy in the networked digital age.

Notes

1. According to Todd Boyd, *The New H. N. I. C.: The Death of Civil Rights and the Reign of Hip Hop* (New York: New York University Press, 2003), it's debatable whether or not hip-hop went to the mainstream or if the mainstream came to the margins.

2. Bakari Kitwana, *The Hip Hop Generation* (New York: Basic Books, 2002).

3. Ralph Ellison, *Going to the Territory* (New York: Vintage Books, 1986), 108.

4. Greg Tate, ed., *Everything but the Burden: What White People Are Taking from Black Culture* (New York: Harlem Moon, 2003), 3.

5. The invaluable pioneering studies of hip-hop culture by Tricia Rose, George Lipsitz, Nelson George, Mark Anthony Neal, and David Toop ought not be faulted; they have worked with the technologies through which hip-hop mediated itself during their respective periods of study, primarily the mid- to late 1990s. What proves detrimental to learning strategies in the twenty-first century concerned with questions of the "digital divide" and "race in cyberspace" is that these models do not provide sufficient analysis of digital media as hip-hop increasingly embraces and mediates itself through emergent forms of media well beyond the often-celebrated turntable. Where this reconfiguration to how hip-hop has been studied already resonates is within the study of the recorded voice and the sound reproduction technologies employed to articulate black presence sonically and the politics of cultural expression. I am referring to the work of Alexander G. Weheliye, Kodwo Eshun, and Paul D. Miller (a.k.a. DJ Spooky) grouped under the moniker of "Afrofuturism," that explores futurist ideals in the technological innovations of the African diaspora.

6. Ellis Cashmore, *The Black Culture Industry* (London: Routledge, 1997), 6–7.

7. Robin D. G. Kelley, *Yo' Mama's Disfunktional: Fighting the Culture Wars in Urban America* (Boston: Beacon, 1997), quoted in Mark Anthony Neal, *What the Music Said: Black Popular Music and Black Public Culture* (New York: Routledge, 1999), 159.

8. Tricia Rose, *Black Noise: Rap Music and Black Culture in Contemporary America* (Hanover: Wesleyan UP, 1994), 61.

9. Mark Anthony Neal, *What the Music Said*, 160.

10. Ibid., 160.

11. Ibid., 161.

12. Ibid., 161.

13. Mark Poster makes this argument when discussing the media as our new public sphere. See Mark Poster, *What's the Matter with the Internet* (Minneapolis: University of Minnesota Press, 2001), 178.

14. S. Craig Watkins, *Hip Hop Matters: Politics, Pop Culture, and the Struggle for the Soul of a Movement* (Boston: Beacon, 2005), 132.

15. See Pierre Lévy, *Collective Intelligence: Mankind's Emerging World in Cyberspace*, trans. Robert Bonomno (Cambridge: Helix Books, 1997).

16. Watkins, 129.

17. Chuck D, interview with Alberto Enriquez, Chuck Explains—Hip Hop Legend Gives His Rap on America, Media and Education, *Anchorage Daily News*, March 4, 2002.

18. Kembrew McLeod, MP3s Are Killing Home Taping: The Rise of Internet Distribution and Its Challenge to the Major Label Music Monopoly, *Popular Music and Society* 28, no. 4 (2005): 527.

19. Helen H. Park, Question 1: Do We Need to be Concerned about How Young People Encounter and Interact with Race and Ethnicity Issues Online and in Other Digital Media Technologies? And What Do Our Histories Teach Us? October 18, 2006, http://community.macfound.org/content/discussions. Retrieved October 12, 2006.

20. Vision, Cuban Hip-Hop: The Rebellion within the Revolution, October 21, 2002, http://boards.rapstation.com/viewtopic.php?=776. Retrieved September 14, 2006.

21. Cedric Muhammed, Material Love, http://rapstation.com/hiphop_university. Retrieved September 4, 2006.

22. Poster, 178.

23. George Lipsitz, *Dangerous Crossroads: Popular Music, Postmodernism and the Poetics of Place* (London: Verso, 1994), 12.

24. Charles C. Mann, The Resurrection of Indie Radio, *Wired*, March 2005, 106.

25. Bertolt Brecht, The Radio as an Apparatus of Communication, in *New Media: Theories and Practices of Digitextuality*, ed. Anna Everett and John T. Caldwell (New York: Routledge, 2003), 30.

26. See Steven Wishnia, Bad Transmission: Clear Channel's Hit List, *Lipmagazine.org*, October 24, 2001, http://www.lipmagazine.org/articles/featwishnia_142.shtml. For additional articles on Clear Channel's corporate censorship and September 11, 2001, see http://www.freemuse.org. Retrieved October 2, 2006.

27. Clear Channel's ultraconservatism should not come as a surprise. Vice President Thomas O. Hicks is a long-time investor in George W. Bush. In return for gubernatorial campaign donations, Bush cleared the way for the University of Texas Investment Management Company (UTIMCO), a private company that controls public funds, and appointed Hicks as its chair. Clear Channel's chair, Lowry Mays, also served on UTIMCO's board of directors. Hicks' company, Hicks, Muse, Tate, & Furst, Inc. is a regular contributor to the Republican Party.

28. Paris, interview by Donnell Alexander, *LA City Beat*, June 2, 2005, http://www.lacitybeat.com/article.php?id=2164&IssueNum=104. Retrieved October 13, 2006.

29. Ibid.

30. Douglas Schuler, Reports of the Close Relationship between Democracy and the Internet May Have Been Exaggerated, in *Democracy and New Media*, ed. Henry Jenkins and David Thorburn (Cambridge, MA: MIT Press, 2004), 70.

31. Cashmore, 175.

32. Christopher Holmes Smith, "'I Don't Like to Dream about Getting Paid': Representations of Social Mobility and the Emergence of the Hip-Hop Mogul, *Social Text* 21, no. 4 (2003): 69.

33. Ibid., 71.

34. Tate, 7.

Chicana/o Artivism: Judy Baca's Digital Work with Youth of Color

Chela Sandoval

University of California, Santa Barbara, Department of Chicano/a Studies

Guisela Latorre

Ohio State University, Department of Women's Studies

Introduction

Arnoldo's Brother (see Figure 1) watches us watching him from out of one of the most powerful digital media labs in the country, the César Chávez Digital Mural Lab, located in the Social and Public Art Resource Center (SPARC), a production facility devoted to creating large-scale digitally generated murals, educational DVDs, animations, community archives, and digital art. *Arnoldo's Brother*, a digital mural created by Chicana artist Judy Baca and UCLA students, is an avatar rising out of these technologies, a modern-day Chicano cyborg. Arnoldo is a fourteen-year-old boy, a figure created through the minds and souls of the young people who have come to the SPARC teaching facility, led by Baca, to testify and witness on behalf of their communities. Their offering to SPARC is a photo of one of these artists' younger brother, which they then Photoshopped into an artwork that tells one story of Chicana/o consciousness at the turn of the millennium. *Arnoldo's Brother* is here to speak actively back to history. His lips are closed. But warrior women noisily appear to the side of his forehead, their mouths open in revolutionary appeal. The boy's eyes are reflective. His overly large sunglasses mirror the city surroundings as well as our own bodies, the spectators as witnesses. In this image, street graffiti and matrix-like iconographies converge; youth and old age are syncretized; past, present, and future unite to suggest new social orders. The *shaded* vision of Arnoldo's brother vision is transformative.

Digital productions like this have emerged from the minds, souls, and digital art of the great public artist Judy Baca and the youth of color who have collaborated with her over the past ten years. Their workspace is SPARC, founded by Baca in 1996 and dedicated to the creation and support of community and public art in Southern California. But the digital art they produce is not only located in SPARC—it can be found in virtual installations globally, as well as on the walls of Los Angeles *barrio* housing projects and in the hybrid spaces of the Internet. We call their activity "digital artivism," a word that is, itself, a convergence between "activism" and digital "artistic" production. The digital artivism we find expressed through SPARC, we argue, is symptomatic of a Chicana/o twenty-first-century digital arts movement. Judy Baca as teacher, mentor, organizer, and as internationally renowned public artist, is at its heart. Her artivist sensibility, however, recognizes, as technoculture scholars Constance Penley and Andrew Ross do, that "cultural technologies are far from neutral, and that they are the result of social processes and power relations," while at the same time acknowledging, as Penley and Ross also insist, that "the kinds of liberatory fantasies that

Figure 1
Judy Baca and UCLA students, *Arnoldo's Brother* (1996), digital mural. © SPARC www.sparcmurals.org.

surround new technologies are a powerful and persuasive means of social agency, and that their source to some extent lies in real popular needs and desires."[1]

Thus the digital artivist movement advances the expression of a mode of liberatory consciousness that Chicana feminist philosopher Gloria Anzaldúa calls *la conciencia de la mestiza*, that is, the consciousness of the mixed-race woman. Like Alondra Nelson, who finds parallels between W.E.B. DuBois's concept of double consciousness and contemporary black digital activist sensibilities,[2] we also understand digital artivism as a manifestation of Anzaldúa's *mestiza* consciousness, which seeks to break down "the subject-object duality that keeps [the *mestiza*] prisoner and to show in the flesh and through the images in her work how duality is transcended."[3] Moreover, this consciousness is also not unlike what digital media scholar Anna Everett calls cyberwomanism, a sensibility in some women of color activists who articulate "new subjectivities and new knowledges for feminism in terms of race at that interface."[4] This chapter calls attention to this digital artivism that is enacted by Baca and the young people who are vested in the convergences between creative expression, social activism, and self-empowerment. In this text, we also present the contributions of SPARC to the development of youth populations, the contributions of youth to the development of SPARC, and their combined contributions to the global community art movements.

Chicana/o Artivism and *La Conciencia de la Mestiza*

Xican@ murals and digital murals are forms of tactical media entrenched in an historical and visionary politics of *barrio* consciousness that work in conjunction with other forms of oppositional politics.[5]
—John Jota Leaños, Chicano digital artivist and scholar, Arizona State University

The term *artivism* is a hybrid neologism that signifies work created by individuals who see an organic relationship between art and activism. As artivists, Baca and the young people we examine here are committed to transforming themselves and the world. The terms *artivism* and *la conciencia de la mestiza* reflect the same human–technology convergences that allow for creative work through digital media. Because digital media are capable of permitting multidimensional meanings, they have become favored artistic media for Baca and her crew at SPARC. Multidimensional meaning systems, as Anzaldúa argues, create the foundation of Chicana/o social activism. Like our definition of artivism, *la conciencia de la mestiza*, she contends, must provide access to a myriad of cultures, languages, and understandings, thus requiring the ability to negotiate multiple worldviews. Chicana/o artivism, like *la conciencia de la mestiza*, expresses a consciousness aware of conflicting and meshing identities and uses these to create new angles of vision to challenge oppressive modes of thinking. Ultimately, digital artivism is a form of political activism that seeks egalitarian alliances and connections across difference. It requires a mode of consciousness that replicates the digital potentialities and egalitarianism of cyberspace.

Digital artivism, however, does not blithely ignore the inequalities and oppressions that are also replicated within virtually all forms of technoculture, as Michelle Lee White reminds us: "Electronic technology, especially digital, seems to have pierced the protective bubble of fixed racial and ethnic identity by making it easy for us to create physically detached screen personas that transcend social realities. Yet in spite of the current cultural climate, which we like to believe has released us from the constraints of identity, the mechanisms of exclusion still persist."[6] Conscious of digital media's liberatory potential as well as its persisting exclusions, Judy Baca's artivism provides real-world and on-the-ground strategies for youth of color to enact empowerment through digital technology. "In practice...the democratic promises of the digital revolution remain as unfulfilled as the rest of our civil rights dreams," explains *New York Magazine* staff writer Logan Hill, "but there is hope."[7] It is this space of hope that Baca mines to its fullest potential.

Judy Baca's Youth Works and Digital Media

I've learned as much as I've taught from the youth I've had the good fortune to know by working alongside of them. They've taught me among other things how to laugh at myself, how to put play into hard work and how not be afraid not to believe in something. I am extremely grateful. —Judy Baca[8]

This chapter explores Chicana/o artivism through the analysis of SPARC and Baca's digital mural projects in Los Angeles. Baca has made a name for herself as an urban muralist who works closely with youth—many of whom are considered to be at risk. Their project over the past thirty years has been to create monumental public works of art, which have transformed the LA cityscape. These murals depict the histories of disenfranchised and aggrieved communities in the LA area and elsewhere. In part, Baca's intent has been to empower youth of color by having them assist her in the reconstruction of these histories. In this process, however, Baca also recognized that Chicana/o and Latina/o youth were insisting upon the production of artivist aesthetics, a recognition that contributed to Baca's own empowerment as a Chicana artist doing public art. The presence of young women and Baca herself in these public spaces also challenges the male domination of nearly every form of public art in Los Angeles, whether in practices of muralism or graffiti. By putting both boys and girls to work together in these public spaces, Baca challenges prescribed gender roles that too often relegate women to the private, domestic sphere.

Baca's work with youth took on renewed meaning in 1996 when she founded the digital mural lab within SPARC's premises. Officially called the UCLA/SPARC César Chávez Digital

Mural Lab, this facility introduced digital technology to the community mural movement as a new tool for the creation of public art. One mandate of this lab was to support and work "with youth, children and their families to produce public art expressing issues they identify through collaborative processes, which are then exhibited as public monuments, banners, murals, Web sites, prints, performances, video and DVDs."[9] These artistically rendered issues include immigration concerns, control over urban spaces, alliances between different ethnic groups, gender and sexuality matters, etc. This use of digital imaging technology has transformed both the aesthetics and praxis of mural-making. The Digital Mural Lab is equipped with high-speed computers, printers, and scanners and possesses its own server for the storage of images, which can be accessed remotely with a password. The murals are generally created with the latest version of Photoshop, which allows Baca and the young people who work with her to visually "scratch," synergistically combining preexisting imagery and original artwork seamlessly together in one composition.

The participation of youth is a critical component of this lab. Baca is well aware of the need for youth of color to overcome the discursive exclusions of the digital divide paradigm, a discourse that casts people of color "as casualties in the information revolution—a new permanent underclass in the information economy," as Anna Everett explains.[10] At the same time, Baca also recognizes how "digital culture" has increasingly been defined as the province of the "young." Participation in this lab provides Baca and her coterie of young people profound computer skills: Baca learns from and extends her own media-making abilities through the shared knowledge and expertise young people bring of other technologies, digital or otherwise, including ghetto blasters, turntables, lowriders, and—more recently—cell phones, MP3 players, iPods, and streaming digital video productions on YouTube.com and MySpace.com. Other Chicana/o artists have also recognized the recent proficiency of youth of color with technology, as was the case of performance artist Guillermo Gómez-Peña, who observed that his "hip generation-Mex nephews and my seven-year-old bicultural son, [were] completely immersed in and defined by personal computers, video games and virtual reality."[11] The combined use of digital media pushes SPARC, Baca, and all her apprentices to new levels of imaginative production. As such, Baca's working relationship with these young people can be regarded as a collaboration between intellectual and artistic equals, at the same time as it can be defined as a mentor–mentee type of association.

This chapter also focuses on Baca's role as a social enabler whose organization facilitates the development of a Chicana/o artivist consciousness. Baca's community work provides a powerful example of the ways in which youth creativity can be channeled, augmented, and empowered through the use of digital technology. The artist's innovative, resourceful, and proactive strategies to organize and forge community ties and coalitions reflect larger traditions of Chicana feminist activist praxis. Baca's work is treated here as a case study reflecting larger tendencies among those Chicana/o artivists who engage in similar forms of oppositional aesthetics. As such, digital technology is understood here as the means by which artivists like Baca deploy feminist understandings in the practice of public art. With her feminist interventions into the digital realm, Baca has disrupted what digital media scholar Jennifer Brayton calls "the patriarchal structuring of technology as a masculine space alienating to women."[12] Moreover, we also understand digital technology to function as a metaphorical and theoretical language that speaks to the nature of artivist praxis. The dynamic and fluid element in Chicana feminist consciousness, we argue, is not unlike the flickering and rhyzomatic forces that energize digital systems. This energy depends on the simultaneous establishment of networks, and links that work dependently, feeding on each other's input.

Who Are Digital Youth?

We regard youth—as a category of analysis and intellectual query—to be an unstable signifier that points to decisively fluid social and cultural identities. Who falls under the category of youth? Much of the scholarship on youth cultures focuses on social groups whose members range in age from eleven to twelve years (prepubescent youth) to the early twenties, as represented by cultural critics Joe Austin and Michael Nevin Willard in the book *Generations of Youth* (1998), and Andy Bennett and Keith Kahn-Harris's *After Subculture: Critical Studies in Contemporary Youth Culture* (2004), among others. But youth has also emerged as a category defined by a particular consciousness characterized, in part, by its rejection of established mores imposed by older generations and by a persistent need or desire for innovation and renewal. For example, we generally regard Chicana/o gang and graffiti cultures as youth-identified, yet many of its most influential members and practitioners are older individuals or *veteranos* who often take on the role of mentors or even parent figures to the younger folks. Similarly, computer gaming culture, while generally defined as youth-oriented, is also largely composed of adult players.

Even the Web site MySpace.com, a cyber portal associated with youth socialization and creative expression, has been found to be increasingly utilized by an older-age demographic; nearly 50 percent of its users are now thirty-five years or older.[13] We have found, therefore, that youth-identified cultural production is not necessarily a terrain restricted to adolescents and young adults. Moreover, although we recognize the importance of empowering young people through research and admit that—with the exception of Baca herself—most of the cultural producers discussed in this study fall within the chronological parameters of youth, we question approaches to youth studies that limit their scopes to strictly age-specified parameters, thus not recognizing the more qualitative factors that also define life experience and its construction across and between generations.

While we focus in this project on Baca's work with youth, we also argue that she, herself, engages in youth cultural production even though she is not a teenager or young adult. When speaking of her work with youth, Baca comments that she has "this affinity with teenagers, looking in a certain way, and I was always kind of a teenager myself."[14] Our point here, however, is different; it is that digital technology can foster *transgenerational* thinking, thus undermining clear distinctions between "youth" and "parent" cultures. As such, digital technology can effectively "age" youth while simultaneously "youthifying" older generations, thus allowing for more meaningful dialogues across different age groups.

Nevertheless, we situate our study within the larger field of youth studies, which successfully demonstrates that youth cultures are indeed critical sites of scholarly and intellectual inquiry. For example, youth studies have actively sought to overturn—or at least complicate—the dichotomous discourse that has emerged around the lives and activities of young people. These studies analyze the pessimistic vision of youth often espoused by the public media and other outlets that describe young people as inherently dangerous and irresponsible, and thus in constant need of social and parental control. Quite to the point, Joe Austin and Michael Nevin Willard have convincingly argued that "the practices of young people [have] become occasions for moral panic."[15] This alarmist discourse has most vehemently turned against youth of color who are usually branded as "animalistic, alien Others," as Austin and Nevin Willard tell us. These same pundits, however, swing to the other extreme to speak of youth as the hope for the future, a beacon of light in the dark corridors of the postmodern condition. These scholars thus believe that adults can control and shape the future of their own worlds by controlling and manipulating young people's lives. In both of these contradictory yet mutually dependent discourses, young people are stripped of their individual agencies, their identities solely defined by the fears, anxieties, and desires of adults. This is why, we would argue, dominant culture through its policing and criminalization of youth of color, can more effectively relegate minority communities—both children and adults—to the social margins.

The advent of digital technology and its overwhelming public adoption since the late 1980s has intensified this rhetoric of fear and hope directed at youth. Cyberspace now represents yet another public arena where children can be damaged or corrupted, and "thrown off" their course toward responsible and productive adulthood. Media studies scholar Julian Sefton-Green observed and critiqued similar anxieties in the wake of the digital revolution:

[Young people's access to digital technology] has led to as much anxiety as it has optimism. Are children going to have unrestricted access to pornography or be abused online? Can they participate in adult conversations and have equal access to information compared with their "adult peers"?[16]

Digital technology provides unprecedented means for young people to represent themselves outside of adult control; the fear here is that they are thus capable of further disrupting the "natural" evolution of social development. Ultimately, what seems most distressful to these analysts of youth culture is the idea that digital technology brings about a general destabilization of the categories of "youth" and "adult" themselves, categories that, in the past, maintained critical social hierarchies. In our analysis, we explore how Baca and her young apprentices critically and strategically undermine such categories to enact various forms of artivist aesthetics.

U.S. Latinas/os and Digital Technology

The digital work that Baca produces in collaboration with youth of color is directly and indirectly addressing a great social need among the Chicana/o and Latina/o community. Media study scholars and social scientists investigating issues of technology access and adoption among U.S. Latinas/os have observed that the levels of technology use among the Latina/o population fall well below the national average, marking one of the lowest rates among ethnic minorities in the United States. Josh Kun also reminds us that "the 'freedom' and paradigm shift discourse often tagged to digital media needs to be tempered by the reality of inequity. As globalization gathers steam as an economic and social force, so does the gap between those who participate in globalization and those who remain on the sidelines watching."[17] In 2002, the Tomás Rivera Institute, under the auspices of IBM, produced a report entitled *Latinos and Information Technology: The Promise and the Challenge*. Prepared by social scientists Louis G. Tornatzky, Elsa E. Macias, and Sara Jones, the report provided critical data on the status of the Latina/o population with regards to information technology.

According to their findings, only 40 percent of Latina/o households owned personal computers in 2001, 16 percent below the national average. Moreover, the report stressed the roles that institutions played in maintaining inequities with regards to information technology. Tornatzky, Macias, and Jones put particular emphasis on the educational system, observing that public schools with higher minority student enrollments were either ill-equipped or simply unequipped with computers and Internet access. Teachers in these schools also often lacked the proper training to teach students computer skills, even at the most basic level. The report, however, also provided recommendations for institutions—both private and public—to improve the situation, arguing that the concern over access "is a quality-of-use issue, rather than counting numbers of computers per capita."[18] Among these recommendations, Tornatzky et al. underscored the importance of placing role models in positions of mentorship to young people. These writers emphasized the positive impact for Latina/o children when they are surrounded by technology-savvy Latina/o adults, whether these individuals are operating in schools or in other settings. Together with mentorship, the authors of this report also argued that community-based organizations are in the position to make a significant contribution to technology adoption among Latina/os:

Community-based organizations [CBOs] tend to be very responsive to the needs of the community they serve, and they often support the more marginalized communities. Moreover, Latinos have demonstrated a willingness to turn to CBOs for technology skills and usage. As such, partnerships that include CBOs are likely to have a greater impact on Latinos and their families.[19]

By the mid-1990s when she founded SPARC's Digital Mural Lab, Baca had already fulfilled the recommendations that the Tomás Rivera Institute would propose some six years later. Her visibility and effectiveness as a mentor rested on the close relationship she cultivated with communities of color since the early 1970s, coupled with her national and international recognition as an artist. In other words, she had been respected and legitimized within two social spheres that were rarely in productive dialogue within one another: the mainstream art scene and the activist of color community. Moreover, SPARC—as a community-based organization—had become a focal point wherein minority youth from the Los Angeles area gained useful expertise in digital media, precisely the kind that would later be endorsed by the Tomás Rivera Institute. But Baca's work with SPARC, Chicana/o and Latina/o youth and digital media, went well beyond the Institute's assessments, data, and recommendations.

While the report called for initiatives that would make digital technology more "culturally relevant" to Latinas/os, it failed to engage in more qualitative types of cultural analyses. Instead, the report offered more quantitative assessments about technology use and adoption among Latinas/os. Perhaps Latina/os were not using digital technology in large numbers compared to other groups in the United States, but many activists were using it in innovative and subversive ways. From the onset of her work with digital media and youth, Baca always capitalized on this emergent use of digital technology among Chicana/o and Latina/o actvists, including youth, whose cultural productions were facilitated by the rise of these new technologies starting in the 1990s. Thus, Baca enhanced the quality of her work with youth and digital media by using and engaging this preexisting cultural capital already at work within Chicana/o and Latina/o communities. For example, by 1999, the influential media scholar Ray Santisteban observed that for many Chicana/o and Latina/o media makers, "no new medium offer[ed] as much potential...as the rapidly developing world of the Internet,"[20] further arguing that "media activists and cultural critics are increasingly using cyberspace as a way to present information, screen video and audio clips, and advertise alternative videos through Internet-based interactive Web sites."[21]

The Beginnings of Baca's Chicana/o Artivist Consciousness: Early Work with Youth

Pre-dating her adoption of digital technology by several decades, Judy Baca's work with youth goes back to 1970 when she began working in Boyle Heights, East Los Angeles, for the city's Department of Recreation and Parks. It was at this time that Baca came into direct contact with local youth in the area, many of whom were members of rival gangs. While she regarded these young men as troubled youth in need of guidance, she also took notice of the innovative forms of cultural production they practiced, namely, graffiti writing. Gang graffiti commanded urban space unlike any other form of expression by youth of color. Muralism thus offered these young people an opportunity to use their skills as taggers by rechanneling their creativity toward peaceful and nonviolent ends. Baca explains: "Redirecting gang members' inclinations toward public expression via my own artistic training as a painter, we began painting murals as a way to create constructive cultural markers."[22]

Baca's origins as a muralist, public artist, and community activist were all deeply connected to youth cultures in the Los Angeles *barrios*. The friendships and partnerships she forged with rival gang members across neighborhood lines were defined by earned mutual respect and creative exchanges; she taught them various painting techniques and they, in turn, shared with her tattoo and graffiti designs.[23] In addition, the mostly male youths who worked with her at this time in the 1970s also served as lookouts for Baca's mural crew. While the crew was up on the scaffolding working on a mural, the lookouts protected the muralists. The lookout's job was to whistle in warning when either rival gang or police officers (both of whom routinely harassed the artist and her young assistants) were approaching.

During this early phase in her artistic development, Baca had not yet adopted digital media, but her community work with youth was already exhibiting elements of digital artivism, which permits functioning both within and beyond the demands of dominant ideology. The artist's work at this time required her to negotiate with the city authorities in Los Angeles while addressing the needs of youth of color in Los Angeles' east side. Baca's capacity to move across the different spheres of a highly segregated and divided city reflected a consciousness becoming increasingly mobile, a quality shared with other artivists. In this sense, Chicana/o digital artivism functions as a differential mode of consciousness; a differential consciousness functions like the clutch of a car, the mechanism of which permits the driver to select, engage, and disengage gears in a system for the transmission of power. Artivists like Baca understand that systems of power, no matter how pervasive, possess interstitial spaces where agency for youth of color can be claimed and deployed. Thus Chicana/o artivism insists upon shifting locations, which means that the site of the artivist's differential politics will change depending on the circumstances that are being confronted. In this sense, Chicana/o artivism is part and parcel of what critics such as Donna Haraway and Gloria Anzaldúa have called a "cyborg life" and *la conciencia de la mestiza*, respectively.[24] While Haraway insists that individuals possessing a cyborg consciousness are "not afraid of permanently partial identities and contradictory standpoints,"[25] Chela Sandoval maintains that "peoples of the Americas have already developed the cyborg skills required for survival under techno-human conditions as a requisite for survival under domination over the last three hundred years."[26] Likewise, Anzaldúa's *conciencia de la mestiza* "constantly has to shift out of habitual formations. . . . The new *mestiza* copes by developing a tolerance for contradictions, a tolerance for ambiguity."[27]

Baca found her work with youth transformative. Yet she soon realized that the public locales of their work were deeply gendered spaces. "I had a hard time getting girls on the projects," Baca lamented, "at that time, boys were the only ones parents would allow"[28] in the program. Baca's community artivism developed in conjunction with the mural renaissance that took place in many *barrios* throughout the U.S. Southwest, an initiative largely fueled by the budding Chicano Movement of the early 1970s. What Baca found was that most of the mural projects in Los Angeles' east side were organized by men, many of whom were hostile to feminist ideas and to the presence of women in these public spaces.[29] As a result, Baca began to develop alliances and artistic connections with feminist artists and cultural producers, many of whom were working on the opposite side of Los Angeles, namely, the west side:

I had this problem at this point in which I was sort of divided because I had this life in the east side, which began after three o'clock, and then I had a life in Venice [in the west side], which was associated with other feminists. . . . But I always felt like I was a visitor [among the feminists] because there were not that many Latin or Third World women at all. [But] in my other world—in the eastside and in the area of Latin culture and Chicano culture—I was really an oddity. I wasn't the girlfriend of one of the men; I was an artist in my own right. I was neither treated seriously by the men nor considered a peer.[30]

The uneasy relationship that the artist established with the predominantly white feminist movement in the west side and the male-centered Chicano nationalism of the east side echoed broader concerns raised by Chicana feminist scholars. While Anna Nieto Gómez denounced the sexism of the Chicano Movement, Patricia Zavella underscored Chicanas' problematic relationship to white feminism.[31] Thus Baca's artivist and *mestiza* consciousness became a composite of two overarching schools of thought that rarely, if ever, conversed with one another at the time—namely, the Chicano and feminist movements. One of the results of Baca's new *mestiza* and artivist subjectivity was her resolve to recruit young women actively into her future public art projects, for she understood that gender, as much as race and class, systematically marginalized youth of color.

The Great Wall of Los Angeles (1976–1983)

Baca's next project implemented her new thinking about how to bring together different ethnicities, gang clans, and—most important—genders. She developed a unique pedagogy, which focused on helping youth work together in egalitarian modes. She raised the funds to employ more than four hundred economically disadvantaged and at-risk youth not only from different neighborhoods but also from various ethnic and cultural backgrounds, including women and girls. *The Great Wall of Los Angeles* was perhaps the most ambitious mural project undertaken by a Chicana/o artist to date. *The Great Wall* narrated an oppositional history of Los Angeles from the perspective of ethnic, social, and gender minorities, accomplished through a rigorous process of research and discussion with historians, community members, and youth. This visual history put people of color at the center of the city's development and growth. The mural, half a mile long, was painted on one of the cement troughs that comprise the San Fernando Valley flood-control system. "The work became a monument to interracial harmony," Baca later explained, "as methods were developed to work across the differences of race and class."[32] Many of the young women who worked on the project recounted how the experience profoundly transformed their lives, and radically changed their political and social consciousness.

The Executive Director of SPARC, Debra Padilla, explained to us that one of the most touching and moving examples of the young women working on *The Great Wall* was that of Ernestine Jiménez, who worked in the project from 1978 to 1984: "Ernestine came to *The Wall* when she was fourteen years old, pregnant and on PCP [phencyclidine]. Nobody believed in her, but Judy did. She came from a family of ten brothers and six sisters. At the end of it all, she stayed on *The Wall* for six years. She became a crew leader and supervisor."[33] Ernestine's own testimonial, which Baca and her staff recently posted in the form of streaming video on the SPARC Web site, reflects the various levels of social and political consciousness that awakened in the young girl's mind. Because of its complexity, it is worth quoting Ernestine's testimonial at length here:

The way I grew up, you fight through life.... It was a fight in my house all the time, and that's the way I believed you were supposed to have grown up, to fight through life. You don't like nobody but your own race and even sometimes don't like your own race.... There was a lot of tension [among the young people working on *The Wall*]; I think everyone wanted to fight everybody.... But after time, you just got to know that person as an individual instead of knowing them as you're taught to. Everybody became very good friends.... I wouldn't have gone back to high school because I wouldn't have had a role model to push me to go there. Education was Judy's number one thing. "As long as you stay in school, you can come back and paint the mural." Even though I got in trouble in school and fought and everything, that was my number one goal; I wanted to come back, I had to come back. What really freaked me out though was when we painted the mural of the Holocaust and I met the people that had the tattoos on them; that kind of blew my mind, it actually made me cry because I knew there was another world that was harder than mine.... Even when I am down and out, I still walk by here and I thank God that I did accomplish something in life and it makes me feel good. I think if it wasn't for this mural, for me to have my name on it and to have accomplished something, I don't know where I'd be.[34]

For Ernestine, *The Wall* became a site of healing where she could establish counterhegemonic alliances with other young people of color with whom she might have a hostile or even violent relationship otherwise. *The Wall* provided for her an alternative learning experience, one that was not given to her in the public school system but that yet compelled her to stay in school nonetheless. Many of the counterhistories narrated in *The Wall* resonated with Ernestine's own history of struggle and hardship, such as that of the Holocaust victims she met as she researched and painted the section on Jewish Americans in the mural. But what seemed most empowering about the experience, as evidenced in her testimonial, was that she directly participated in the process of history making and became one of the critical architects of a public and monumental work of art. Like Baca herself, Ernestine, as a young Chicana, also began to develop an artivist consciousness through her work on *The Great Wall of Los Angeles*. As her consciousness became increasingly flexible, she saw how her own life was intertwined with that of other disenfranchised communities in the city of Los Angeles.

The model for community interaction and intervention that Baca developed in the 1970s would become the foundation for a learning curriculum that the artist would employ in subsequent projects. This curriculum included an active learning process whereby youth are charged with responsibilities often given to teachers, adults, or other authority figures—such as planning and executing a mural. Through this process, the artist and the young people themselves would arrive at the understanding that their own life stories were not unlike those of those individuals featured in the murals. This understanding would eventually lead Baca to transform these personal narratives into the actual subject matter of the future murals she would create in collaboration with youth, many of which were executed through the use of digital media.

The Founding of SPARC and the UCLA/SPARC César Chávez Digital Mural Lab

One of the ways Baca enabled the empowerment of youth in sustainable ways was through the founding of SPARC in 1976. Through this nonprofit organization, Baca and cofounders

Christina Schlessinger and Donna Deitch were able to provide an institutional framework that would support the artist's mural work as well as that of other muralists working in the Los Angeles area. After many mural projects throughout the city and other parts of the world, Judy Baca made a critical decision. Her decision would deeply affect the course of mural history in California, as well as the way she collaborated with young people. She moved forward to create a digital mural lab in SPARC.

In 1994 Baca became a founding faculty member at the California State University, Monterey Bay, an institution created under the Bill Clinton presidential administration, which would become a model for the twenty-first-century university, with an emphasis on interdisciplinary teaching and information technology. While there, Baca was recruited by UCLA to become part of the César E. Chávez Center for Interdisciplinary Instruction. This campus unit was born out of a hunger strike enacted by students on campus to pressure the university administration to create a Chicana/o studies department. Baca accepted the invitation, and two years later founded the UCLA/SPARC César Chávez Digital Mural Lab, where she has been teaching her class "Beyond the Mexican Mural" and carrying out various mural projects ever since. In addition to the instructional purposes of the lab, it also functions as "a research and a production facility," Debra Padilla explained to us.[35] SPARC's digital mural lab supports the emergence of what anthropologist of antiglobalization movements Jeffrey Juris called "informational utopics," which involve "experimentation with new technologies and the projection of utopian ideals regarding open participation and horizontal collaboration into emerging forms of networked space."[36]

Baca's choice to make this SPARC facility into a *digital* lab came out of a long process of reflection regarding the emergence of this new technology in the arts and elsewhere. On the one hand, Baca was concerned with the ways in which people could use this technology to distort, fragment, manipulate, and disseminate her imagery and that of other artists without consent. She was also worried that the sphere of the digital was being claimed largely by a predominantly white male population who seemed to revel in these newfound powers. But rather than reject and disavow the digital, Baca embraced it, taking cues from hip-hop musicians who were using digital technology to create compositions through the process of "sampling" the work of others, effectively "eliminating the musician," she explains.[37] With the advent of digital media technologies, Baca witnessed a radical shift in the ways in which visual imagery could be created, disseminated, and consumed. She thus realized, as most Chicana/o artivists did, that she wanted and needed to adapt to this new reality. The artivist praxis that fostered her work with youth and that fueled her capability to bridge social, cultural, and political divides since the early 1970s, served her well in making this shift. In this process, however, Baca made an important discovery: digital technology could enhance methods, ideas, and strategies she had been using throughout her career:

I'm a technician kind of character. I draw hundreds and hundreds of sketches, look at things from thousands of different perspectives to make sure that I'm preparing a site well [for a mural or public monument]. With the computer I am able to see the work *in situ* and see it from a variety of perspectives and directions thus eliminating the need for hundreds of sketches. I could put things *in situ* without really being *in situ*. . . . I could also eliminate hours and hours of work doing compositional grids [for murals].[38]

This technology also provided a way for her to create longer-lasting murals by doing digital image-transfers onto tile, thus allowing her to produce murals more resistant to the elements. Rather than being marginalized by this new digital technology—as usual "digital divide" discourses purport about people of color—Baca became a determined practitioner and producer of digital cultural work. In this fashion, she purposely adopted a tool and language that for decades had been the restricted property of institutional power brokers. By using tools that have been traditionally denied to marginalized communities, Baca turned the tables on the world order ushered in by globalization. She used the strategies of the oppressor, so to speak, to empower the oppressed. A similar tactic had been used by indigenous Mexican groups like the Zapatistas in Chiapas, whose first communiqués and political manifestoes were transmitted via the Internet much before their activities were known to the mainstream press. Likewise, antiglobalization actvists who, according to Jeffrey Juris, enact various forms of "hacktivism" and "electronic civil disobedience," were also inspired by "the pioneering use of the Internet by the Zapatistas."[39] Baca tapped into a relatively recent—yet powerful—tradition of radical activists utilizing technology to further their political causes.

Digital technology also presented an opportunity for the artist to continue fortifying her alliances and collaborations with youth, whether these were at-risk adolescents or college-age students. As cyber studies scholars—such as Julian Sefton-Green, David Buckingham, and Joseph Tobin, to name a few—maintain, digital media have been increasingly associated with youth cultures, so for Baca—an artist with deep roots in the Civil Rights Movement era—adopting this technology meant renewing her praxis or work as a cultural producer. Most Chicana/o artists from her generation did not make the leap to the digital realm and, as such, their work has not been connected to innovation in the same way as have Baca's practices. Like the African American women activists discussed in the work by Anna Everett, Baca too "transformed low-tech, sixties-era mimeograph activism into high-tech, new-millennial digital news and information flows."[40] On the one hand, her adoption of digital technology was facilitated through her contact with young people who were avid digital users and, at times, even producers. On the other hand, learning the digital language gave her greater access to turn-of-the-millennium youth cultures, many of which are largely defined by their digital engagements.

The UCLA/SPARC Digital Mural Lab teaches students critical computer skills that serve them in navigating through and surviving in our increasingly globalized environment. At the same time, Baca builds upon prior knowledges that young people have of computers and digital technology, allowing their skills to be recognized and added to SPARC's arsenal, while permitting the young people to develop them further. Indeed, digital culture scholars Julian Sefton-Green and David Buckingham observed a similar phenomenon when it came to using digital technology in the classroom: "What tends to be unacknowledged here is the fact that the students will now bring with them into school a whole body of knowledge, skills, competencies and ambitions derived from their out-of-school experience of computers."[41] This new interchange dynamic in media learning and teaching is creating an increasingly interactive environment in Judy Baca's lab, where students and teachers are developing innovative relationships of cultural and intellectual exchange.

Digital Images about Youth by Youth

Baca's adoption of digital technology did not just signify a shift in her working methods, but also prompted a shift in her work's style and iconography. Now the figures populating her murals, produced in collaboration with youth, place these young people at the center of her liberatory visual narratives. Such was the case of the first initiative that came out of the UCLA/SPARC Digital Mural Lab, and of Baca's "Beyond the Mexican Mural" class, namely, the *Witness to Los Angeles History* (1996) project. *Witness* consisted of a series of digital murals created by the artist and UCLA students, with each piece representing the contributions and histories of the city's different ethnic communities. The series also came out of a collaborative effort between SPARC and the Cornerstone Theater Company in Los Angeles that, at the time, was staging the play *Birth of a Century*, a production precisely about the history of Los Angeles. The digital murals that Baca created with her students then became backdrops for the stage design. The murals were then showcased in various venues throughout Southern California, and functioned independently from the play.

Baca and the young artists who worked with her on this project rejected passive observations of social realities for enactments of more defiant forms of *witnessing*. The digital then became an ideal medium to bring active witnessing into being. Moreover, through the digital, all youthful participants of this project would intertwine the wisdom of their elders with their own ideas in order to create a far-reaching composite of these intergenerational knowledges. The imagery that was chosen by Baca and the students for *Witness to Los Angeles History* came out of what Debra Padilla described as "an intense process of negotiation"[42] between and among generations. The students were charged with selecting figures that would represent each of the city's largest ethnic populations: Native Americans, Asian Americans, African Americans, Latina/os, Filipinos, and Anglo-Americans. The images were then scanned, enhanced, and placed within a digital collage. Both the students and their mentor carried out intensive research to obtain the images, which they called "first-source material." First-sources could be family photographs, personal effects, archival material, etc. A student then submitted an image to represent one of the city's ethnicities to the larger group. The image would need to be approved by everyone else in the group before it became a part of the murals. Many of the resulting digital pieces that composed *Witness to Los Angeles History*, however, featured family photographs belonging to the students themselves and, as such, personal history became collective history for many of them. The figures in these photographs—which would then be featured in the finished mural—became both participants and witness to this counterhistory that Baca and her students were producing. It came as no surprise that three of the six resulting murals featured the figures of young people who stood to represent entire populations.

We now return to *Arnoldo's Brother* (Figure 1), the image used as an opening discussion piece of this chapter. *Arnoldo's Brother* was created to represent Los Angeles' Mexican and Chicana/o community in *Witness to Los Angeles History*. As previously described, the mural depicts a fourteen-year-old Chicano boy wearing sunglasses, standing before a digital backdrop. His glasses reflect images of the U.S.–Mexico border fence and migrant farm workers, suggesting that—in spite of his youth—he is a conscientious witness to his community's history. The background of the mural is largely composed of a graffiti gang roll call. Roll calls, often tagged throughout city spaces, are listings of the various members of any given gang or clique. Interspersed amid the graffiti text, the figures of young Chicana activists emerge in the composition, thus balancing the gender representation in the mural. The pairing of this Chicano boy with the graffiti text, however, was meant to probe the viewer's assumptions and stereotypes about Mexican youth. "People thought that it was a fourteen-year-old gang kid," Debra Padilla told us, "but in reality it's Arnoldo's brother who was a fourteen-year-old honor student."[43] Arnoldo was also the sibling of one of the participating students/artivists who brought his brother's photograph, a first-source material, before the larger group. *Arnoldo's Brother* celebrated Los Angeles' Mexican and Chicana/o heritage by putting particular emphasis on the importance of youth culture and its many dimensions.

Figure 2
Judy Baca and UCLA students, *Toyporina* (1996), digital mural. © SPARC www.sparcmurals.org.

The digital medium with which the mural was created further stressed the youth aesthetic that underpinned the entire series.

Perhaps one of the most famous digital murals from *Witness to Los Angeles History* was the piece representing the Native American population, namely, *Toyporina* (see Figure 2). In the process of carrying out research for this piece, Baca and her students encountered the historical figure of Toyporina, a twenty-four-year-old Tongva woman in the nineteenth century, who led a revolt against the San Gabriel Mission, the site where the city of Los Angeles would eventually be built.[44] The task was then to find a first-source image that could represent or stand for Toyporina. While carrying out research at the University of Southern California for another project, Baca encountered a small nineteenth-century photograph of an anonymous Tongva girl. Baca was deeply captivated by the beauty and poise of the young woman in the picture. She then took the image back to the students in her class, who would then approve her as the visual representation of Toyporina in the mural. When they scanned the photograph and projected it on a large screen, Baca had an unexpected reaction: "The first time she came up on the screen, it just knocked my eyes out. It was so bizarre to see this brown, extremely beautiful woman on the screen, a Tongva woman on the screen in the computer. Why was this so weird?"[45] Baca, in a way, was re-acting to the seemingly paradoxical melding of an indigenous *and* digital aesthetic within the same pictorial space. She was also impressed with the amazing flexibility of digital media through which she could greatly enlarge and render monumental that which is small and intimate. Further, she embraced the technology's capacity to proliferate that which has been historically marginalized and erased. Baca contends, "I could actually make [this Tongva woman] giant; I could take her from a postage stamp and into a ten-story building. I could send her over the Internet, put her on the Web, I could disseminate her. Then I really got wild in terms of thinking."[46] Digital technology allowed Baca and her students to transform and overturn the colonial discourses often attached to indigenous imagery in ways that had not been possible in the past.

The image of the Tongva young woman in *Toyporina* takes center stage in this digital mural's composition. She returns the viewer's gaze with an expression of self-confidence and resolve. Her body, however, bears the scars of colonization and conquest in the form of tattoos depicting Native peoples being hanged and burned at the stake. As such, we are reminded that indigenous women's bodies were often the site of colonization's violent assaults that usually resulted in rape. Toyporina here stands amid a group of Franciscan monks who are staring at her. According to the UCLA students working on the project, the friars represent "the constant scrutiny and dehumanization of the native people."[47] Below them, the architectural structures of the San Gabriel mission emerge as a symbol of the colonial institution that served as a foundation for the city of Los Angeles.

The following year in 1997, Baca and her students at UCLA would embark on the second part of the *Witness to Los Angeles History* project in SPARC. As a result of Baca's reputation as a public artist and the success of the digital mural pieces, the Los Angeles Public Housing Authority approached the artist and her students in the "Beyond the Mexican Mural" class to create a series of public art works in the Estrada Courts Housing Project (East Los Angeles). Estrada Courts occupied a special place in the history of Chicana/o–Latina/o Los Angeles. It is one of the oldest housing projects in Los Angeles, constructed in the early 1940s, in a place where most of its residents are of working-class Mexican and Latin American backgrounds. Estrada is also the site of a major mural initiative that took place in the 1970s, led by community artist Charles "Gato" Felix.[48] Baca and the students then sought to respond to the site's mural history in both laudatory and critical ways. The methodologies the artists used, however, were not unlike other mural projects they had carried out:

Students conducted oral history interviews with 25 Estrada families, researched US Public Housing policy and archives, and collaborated to define the issues that are represented in the imagery. Photos collected from residents' photo albums were used to depict the complex stories of immigration, teenage pregnancy, poverty and violence that embody the neighborhood's collective consciousness.[49]

The artists in this project immersed themselves in the lives of Estrada residents, using the families' first-source material to tell the counterhistories of this housing project. "The students literally adopted these families," Baca revealed; "they ate Sunday dinners with them. They listened to their stories."[50] In this process, the young artists enacted a decolonizing artivism by bridging their personal subjectivities with those of the families who lived in Estrada Courts; they realized that disenfranchisement and neocolonization can be best understood through a symbiotic connection with those who also suffer their consequences. As such, both the artists and the residents became transformed as they approached their own histories through a critical and radical lens.

Witness to Los Angeles History: Estrada Courts also counted with the crucial participation of a young Chicana artist by the name of Alma López, who was initiated into digital media through her participation in SPARC. López then went on to become a renowned and critically acclaimed digital artist in her own right, whose work combined digital aesthetics with feminist and queer subjectivities. In her mural for the Estrada Courts project entitled *Las Four*, López, together with young Chicana residents of Estrada, acted as shaman-witness artivists to a radical feminist history. They also became transformative artivists whose witnessing transformed their creative and activist experiences. López was keenly aware of the importance of Estrada Courts as a major mural site, yet fashioned her imagery as a form of feminist contestation of the predominantly masculinist aesthetics that characterized the preexisting murals there. The artist of *Las Four* was partly responding to another mural in Estrada, namely Ernesto de la Loza's *Los Cuatro Grandes* (1993), which celebrated the historical and political contributions of four male heroes, from left to right, César Chávez, Emiliano Zapata, Francisco Villa, and Mario Moreno Cantinflas, all of whom stood as prominent architects of Chicana/o–Mexican culture. López's reaction to this type of imagery forced her to reevaluate the icons of Chicana/o identity with which she and the young women at Estrada were raised:

I grew up in northeast Los Angeles . . . during the Chicano Mural Renaissance of the 1970s and early 80s. My visual world included: wall size, meticulously spray painted black, old English, graffiti lettering; bakery and market calendars of sexy Ixta draped over the lap of strong Popo; tattoos of voluptuous bare breasted women with long feathered hair; burgundy lips and raccoon eyes painted cholas; and murals mostly depicting Emiliano Zapata, Francisco Villa, and Aztec warriors. . . . To this visual world, my contribution would go beyond the sexualized images of Ixta and the tattoo women; to create images of women parallel in presence to Zapata, Villa and the Aztec warriors.[51]

So Alma and collaborators would replace Villa, Zapata, and the others with four eminent Chicana/Latina/indigenous activists whose historical significance has long been recognized by U.S. Third-World feminists: Dolores Huerta, cofounder of the United Farm Workers; Sor Juana Inés de la Cruz, a seventeenth-century Mexican nun whose poems and plays greatly shaped baroque/colonial literature; a soldadera, female soldier of the Mexican Revolution; and Rigoberta Menchú, a contemporary Guatemalan/Mayan peace activist. Behind these monumental women we find Coyolxauhqui, the Aztec moon goddess, who—according to Mexica scripture—was murdered by her brother Huitzilopochtli, god of war, thus ushering in patriarchal rule in Aztec society. Coyolxauhqui held great metaphorical meaning for López and the young Chicana artists, because they interpreted the violent act directed at her by Huitzilopochtli as that "of a brother towards his sister, as the murder of male and female duality and balance, and the violent birth of a patriarchal system."[52]

In spite of the importance that López and the Estrada participants gave to the figures of Huerta, Sor Juana, the soldadera, Menchú, and Coyolxauhqui in *Las Four*, their presence in the mural fades into the background in order to give way to a new generation of radical feminist practitioners, namely, the young working-class Chicana residents of Estrada. Their relationship to the figures in the background, explains López, is that of "spiritual leaders nourishing a future generation of young women who can claim an ancestral legacy as ancient as [that of] the pre-Columbian goddess Coyolxauhqui."[53] For López, establishing a historical and spiritual continuity between indigenous figures like Coyolxauhqui and contemporary Chicanas promotes an indigenous consciousness that is relevant to the average young Chicana living in the barrio. Learning about the story of Coyolxauhqui, in particular, helped these women understand the historical dimensions of their own gender oppression. But López's use of real-life women in her work is precisely what seems to stir controversy among the communities that see her work. Shortly after its installation in Estrada Courts, *Las Four* was vandalized and damaged by a group of young men from Estrada who knew, and apparently disliked, some of the women in the mural, thus objecting to their representation. This episode proved that images of women's empowerment and agency were still regarded as threatening, and even offensive, to some sectors of the Chicana/o community.

Shoulder to Shoulder: Uniting across Difference

In 1999, Baca and SPARC, under the auspices of the Los Angeles Human Relations Commission, organized a summer youth program geared toward easing racial tensions among the city's youth. Calling it the Shoulder to Shoulder Program, Baca—working together with UCLA students as well as artists, writers, and performers from the local area—brought 125 middle school children together, all of them fourteen years old, to participate in a series of workshops that involved the production of visual art, writing, graphic art, and theater. These children had come to SPARC from all over the city and represented the great diversity among youth in the area. What all the workshops had in common was a frank and open dialogue among the young participants around issues of racism, stereotypes, tolerance, and difference. "It was intense, we worked our butts off!" Baca recalled.[54] The goal of the project was to create a space of healing for youth of all cultural, social, and gender backgrounds. Given the highly segregated nature of the Los Angeles urban area, these workshops provided the young people with the opportunity to work together and interact with other children from different neighborhoods, kids with whom they would have no social contact otherwise. Through a decolonizing and liberatory enactment of artivist aesthetics, the young participants of the Shoulder to Shoulder Program came to the realization that race, gender, and class are largely socially constructed and maintained.

The interaction that took place among the fourteen-year-olds in the Shoulder to Shoulder Program was perhaps the most important element of the workshops. Yet the various digital banners printed on vinyl that were produced in the process speak eloquently of the powerful dialogues the young people had with one another that summer. Many of these banners, which were eventually displayed publicly in the streets of Los Angeles, depicted the children literally standing next to one another, "shoulder to shoulder," as they engaged in the social dialogue. These images were the result of sessions in which each child was paired up with a partner from a different social and/or cultural background. Excerpts from their conversations were then incorporated into the overall design of the banners. The piece entitled *Are We Both Americans?* (see Figure 3) depicts Ben and Lupe, two young participants in the project: "[Lupe's] mother was a domestic worker; she worked as a maid. Ben's father worked in the movie industry and came from great wealth," Baca explained.[55] In this image, as well as in the conversations they both had, they confronted the issue of what it meant to be an "American." When asked the question, "What are you?" Ben replied, "I am white," while Lupe responded, "I am a Latina." However, when they were asked whether they were "American," Ben replied affirmatively but Lupe answered "No, I'm a Latina." "Ben, is Lupe an American?" the organizers then asked the boy; he also replied in the negative. The exercise demonstrated how notions of citizenship and national status are deeply connected to ideas about race and class, notions that individuals internalize at a very early age. As a way to challenge these familiar expectations, the placement of the figures within the digital banner provided a counternarrative to the racial discourses that defined the lives of these two children. While the two figures are visually separated by a dark line that cuts vertically across the composition, the children, nevertheless, are speaking and interacting across that line, thus symbolically breaking social barriers. Their status is then "equalized" in the image, as their figures are rendered at the same scale and occupy the same amount of compositional space. These visual devices thus grant them both the rights and entitlements of cultural citizenship.

Many of the children who participated in the Shoulder to Shoulder Program were asked to discuss and talk to each other about the sensitive issue of racial stereotyping. In the

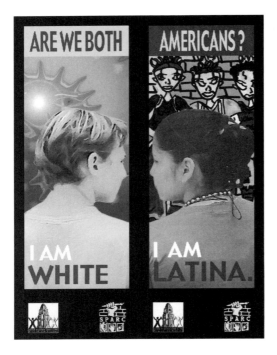

Figure 3
Judy Baca and middle school students, *Shoulder to Shoulder: Are We Both American?* (1999), digital banner.
© SPARC www.sparcmurals.org.

digital banner *See Beyond the Stereotypes* (Figure 4), an African American boy and a middle-class European American girl again touch shoulders and reveal the assumptions they held about one another: "She thought I was a frightening revolutionary," he says; "He thought I was a spoiled white girl," she responds. The fact that they both speak to each other's preconceptions, rather than making direct statements like "he is a frightening revolutionary" or "she is a spoiled white girl," further reinforces the process of dialogue involved in the creation of the banner. But dialogue was not always at the core of the visual vocabulary produced in the Shoulder to Shoulder Program, for a number of the pieces also broke with the general structure of the compositions. Many of the middle-school children in the project felt the need to make individual, and often bold, statements about racial stereotyping, and thus devote entire banners to these. When discussing the shooting tragedy at Columbine High School in 1999 near Denver (Colorado), an African American boy in the program created a piece that stirred relative controversy among the other participants and the Human Relations Commission (see Figure 5). Standing alone on the right side panel of the banner, the boy—whose figure is here rendered in a simple black-and-white drawing—appears to be uttering the words inscribed next to him: "They were white suburban kids shooting, not Black. I was relieved." On a superficial level, many held the assumption that the boy somehow felt comforted by a shooting rampage that left thirteen young people dead and dozens injured. On a realistic, or more accurate level, the underlying message was not an endorsement of the Columbine shootings, but rather a critical engagement of the criminalizing images of black youth in the public media, images that persistently and repeatedly naturalized the

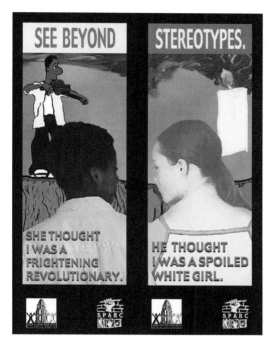

Figure 4
Judy Baca and middle school students, *Shoulder to Shoulder: See Beyond Stereotypes* (1999), digital banner.
© SPARC www.sparcmurals.org.

connection between violence and teens of color. The Columbine massacre, while terribly tragic, provided this boy with a counternarrative that disrupted and challenged the racial stereotypes that personally affected his own life. Nevertheless, this message apparently got lost in the minds of the city's public officials, who barred the image from being displayed in public; in other words, the banner was censored.

Digital technology in the Shoulder to Shoulder Program became a tool through which children can amplify and widely disseminate their social consciousness; the banners were placed in two public spaces, namely, in the streets of Los Angeles and the cyber domain of SPARC's Web site, where they still reside today. The computer also facilitated the use of various different media to create the banners. The children produced numerous hand-drawn sketches using colored pencils, markers, paint (including murals), and other materials. These sketches then became the background images to the photographs of the children featured in each banner. Digital technology thus allowed these different forms to meld together seamlessly. Most important, however, this technology offered a means by which to allow two very distinct forms of aesthetic consciousness to converge, namely, those of the adults and of the children in the project. While the participating artists, including Baca, provided a structured and organized platform for the middle-school children to express themselves around issues of race in a safe and nonthreatening environment, the kids offered an honest and refreshing form of creativity that is fairly unconcerned with issues of order and control. These two sensibilities are brought together digitally in the images themselves, where the dark framing and the digital photography epitomize the adult aesthetics, while the background drawings

Figure 5
Judy Baca, *Shoulder to Shoulder: They Were White Suburban Kids...* (1999), digital banner. © SPARC
www.sparcmurals.org.

and the dialogue text represent the youth creativity. Drawing from the concept of the "machinic assemblage" formulated by theorists Gilles Deleuze and Félix Guattari—who argue that social products are the result of machine-like convergences of disparate components through movement[56]—Jeffrey S. Juris contends that "digitally powered social movements are... 'rhizomatic'—constantly emerging, fusing together, hiving off."[57] The converging and diverging nature of these digital social movements thus allows for collectivity and autonomy to take place the same time, something that greatly facilitated the collaborative form of digital artivism taking place between children and adults in the Shoulder to Shoulder Program.

Beyond the Mexican Mural: Baca's Artivist Pedagogy at UCLA

I think [Judy Baca] is very inspirational. She has a lot of knowledge that she's picked up from years of experience. She's worked with the Chicano Movement, she has done her share of public works with the community. As a teacher she brought that in and she dialogued with us. She would talk about her experience and then she would open up the floor for us to say something. I really appreciated that because it's rare to find professors at the university level who are willing to hear the perspective of the students.[58] —UCLA Chicana/o Studies and Women's Studies undergraduate student.

A great deal of the digital artwork Baca creates with youth has been produced within her UCLA course "Beyond the Mexican Mural—Muralism and Community Development," which takes place in SPARC's Digital Mural Lab. In the class, students learn to utilize mural-ism "as a method of community education, development, and empowerment."[59] Through a series of workshops and studio sessions, students create large-scale, digitally created mural pieces with the goal of placing them in community settings. The work the students produce in this class entails a rigorous process of research, design, and work with community partic-ipants. Using much of her experience in working with youth within a public setting, in this class the artist employs a critical pedagogy that brings to the forefront every student's abil-ity to be creative, critical, and self-empowered, regardless of his or her academic, personal, and/or cultural background. Baca facilitates this process by guiding the students through the production of public artworks—namely, murals. Unlike traditional forms of public art, which are supposed to instill a sense of civic pride, and thus indoctrinate audiences with hegemonic ideologies, Baca teaches her students a type of public art that makes a critical intervention into the public space. While many mainstream types of public art are meant to articulate collective identities, Baca's students are instructed in the ways in which the personal can also be collective and even political. As such, the public artworks that come out of "Beyond the Mexican Mural" place youth voices at the center of the urban or public space, a milieu that rarely—if ever— takes into account what young people have to say.

On October 24, 2006, Baca invited us to visit and participate in one of her classes for "Beyond the Mexican Mural." We immediately encountered great enthusiasm and passion for the course material among the students, as one of them directly told us:

This is the best course I've taken at UCLA in four years because it's extended from the private classroom out into the community. Our class is also very close, we all talk, spend time together.... As a fine art student, I realized that I didn't like the gallery space, I didn't like the institution of it. So to me it's amazing to see that there is something else I can do with art, something that really is a political act, so it's a new possibility for me in my life, after I graduate.... [This course] is the perfect combination of art, activism and community.[60]

Another student approached us to tell us that this class was a parting gift of sorts for her: "I'm graduating and this is my very last class, but I wanted to take this class my whole career [in UCLA].... It's like what Cesar Chávez said, 'All education should end in service,' that's what this class is leaving me with as I finish UCLA."[61]

During this particular meeting of the course, the students were to bring their works-in-progress for a group critique. As we entered the lab—which was fitted with dozens of high-speed computers, high-definition scanners, laser printers, multimedia equipment, and a computer projector—the mood among the students, Baca, and the staff in SPARC was enthusiastic and eager (see Figure 6). Baca created a relaxed and welcoming atmo-sphere as the students were invited to help themselves to some tea or coffee from a lit-tle kitchen in the lab. Baca began the session by telling students what a group critique entails. Traditionally, group critiques in studio art classes, Baca explained to us, are in-stances in which students share their works-in-progress with their fellow classmates and instructor in the hopes of receiving meaningful and helpful feedback. These critiques, in conventional art departments, however, have been a source of great anxiety for students of color trying to get through studio art programs. Put-downs, covert racist remarks, and subtle taunting, Baca recounted, are all too often part of the critique experience for students of color:

Critiques are not meant to take someone apart although within the university systems and art schools—particularly during my period of time as an undergraduate and graduate student—that was the name of

Figure 6
UCLA students awaiting group critique. Social and Public Art Resource and Public Art Resource Center,
Venice, CA. October 24, 2006. Photograph by Guisela Latorre and Chela Sandoval.

the game. How much could you take and how could you stand up to the assaults of professors? Literally
it was like having your pants taken down, be exposed and be beaten. That doesn't help and it doesn't
give you a sense of how to improve your work.[62]

Not only did she assure her students that such behavior and exchanges would not be tol-
erated in SPARC, but she also began the session by discussing her own work in progress,
namely her Robert F. Kennedy Monument for the new school to be built on the site of the
recently demolished Ambassador Hotel in Los Angeles (see Figure 7). While, as an established artist, she no longer needed to put herself through the scrutiny of art professors, as a
public artist she continued to expose herself to the whims of patrons, art commissions, and
corporate sponsors, who often take issue with Baca's political positions. For the Ambassador
Hotel, the site of Robert F. Kennedy's fatal shooting, Baca was currently working on a piece
that illustrated the relationship between Kennedy and César Chávez, focusing on the day
Kennedy visited Chávez during the break of the UFW cofounder's famous fast in 1968. The
Gonzalez Goodale Architects, the firm in charge of designing a new school on the site of the
demolished Ambassador Hotel, argued that she was using too much "content" rather than
articulating more "universal" themes with her piece: "'Universal' has been a euphemism for
a dominant culture which is historically Anglo," Baca told the students in the classroom, "at
this particular moment 'universal' is Latina/o. I'll keep you posted as to this process but I
wanted you to know what it is like for a public artist."[63]

Indeed, as a public artist, she constantly has to put herself in a position of vulnerability
before a sometimes hostile audience. While Baca warns of the difficulties of negotiating
her position as a public artist, she actively disrupts such power dynamics in her classroom.
As such, she creates a safe space within SPARC that is both critical but also nurturing and

Figure 7
Judy Baca discussing her Robert F. Kennedy monument with students. Social and Public Art Resource and Public Art Resource Center, Venice, CA. October 24, 2006. Photograph by Guisela Latorre and Chela Sandoval.

Figure 8
UCLA/SPARC student art work. Social and Public Art Resource and Public Art Resource Center, Venice, CA. October 24, 2006. Photograph by Guisela Latorre and Chela Sandoval.

empowering. For this particular assignment, students were charged with the creation of digital mural pieces that defined their personal relationships to the urban spaces around them, in particular Los Angeles.

In Baca's pedagogy, the traditional critique utilized in art schools becomes a witness ritual where the young students/artivists stand before their works-in-progress to describe the experiences and perceptions that led them to create the images. When the students/artivists finished their explanations of the world that is exemplified in their unique images, they then asked the rest of the class to witness for them; in other words, to share with them what the images generated meant for each spectator. At that point, potential critics are transformed into active witnesses; they become themselves artivists, who describe the images from their own sets of experiences and perceptions of the world. This critique process becomes a collective learning experience for the student/artivist as creator and transformer of reality, and for the active witnesses who understand that sharing widely differing perceptions works to enrich and deepen this shared experience of reality. This kind of pedagogical ritual generates an intense learning experience that pushes artistic, emotional, spiritual, and intellectual boundaries. Each student/artivist addresses his or her relationship to the LA metropolis differently: one seeks control while another seeks liberation from a situation of hopelessness. Still another student creates a history of indigenous identification in which madness and hope express their own kind of language. For one student, the city is represented as overlaid by a network of twisted vines, while another expresses a strong sense of isolation and fear as a recent immigrant living in a hostile urban environment. In another example, a student depicts herself sitting on the sand by the ocean's edge as the city of Los Angeles is reduced to a castle at her side, while another student provides his self-portrait entangled in the city's skyline (Figure 8). In Baca's system of critique as active witnessing, each artivist teaches the others how history, life, and materiality can be expressed and experienced differently.

Conclusion

Baca's pedagogical tools have inspired young people of color for nearly three generations now. Her long-term and proven success in empowering and inspiring youth of color to express themselves through digital technology has gained her a prominent and established reputation in community, activist, and academic settings. These settings, however, do not engage systematically the one social sphere that most critically affects the lives of young people, namely the public school system. While Baca's various community projects do include the participation of elementary, middle, and high school students, these are just temporary interventions—albeit positive and meaningful ones—into the deeply problematic relationship that students of color have with the public school system. There is a great deal of research within the field of Chicana/o studies that demonstrates how young people of color are increasingly more likely to fall between the cracks of the system than are their white counterparts.[64] Much of this research faults the system for the low educational attainment of Chicana/os.

We propose that Baca's methodologies and pedagogy be incorporated into the public school system as part of students' general curriculum. Federal and public funding must be provided to encourage and advance these developments within curricular structures. The incredible pedagogical and liberatory collaborations represented through Baca/SPARC/youth artivism must be recognized by public and private institutions, for they have much to offer our nation at this pivotal juncture of digital media's increasing power and influence. The model that Baca has produced together with young people is sufficiently developed to be replicated in educational spaces across the United States. Baca's creation of digital artivism works well in areas where peoples are segregated according to race, class, and culture, for Baca's pedagogical technologies thrive on dialogue across these different spheres. However, new digital artivism cannot continue creating inroads toward social, democratic, and egalitarian change without institutional recognition, commitment, and support. Our study has demonstrated how UCLA provided the institutional means to permit Baca, SPARC, and youth of color to enact social dialogue and change by using digital technology.

Ultimately, digital artivism, like the kind practiced by Baca together with young people, depends on the ability to utilize different aesthetic forms, putting them together in innovative ways with the purpose of confronting adversity, thus arriving at more democratic and egalitarian conclusions. Digital artivism demands a new loyalty, not to any specific artistic medium, but to a committed cross-disciplinary aesthetic. But this mode of creating does not simply combine approaches for the mere sake of experimentation; Judy Baca's digital artivism utilizes all these different approaches with the purpose of constructing a brave new world of egalitarian exchange. Having said all this, we again return to the emblematic figure of *Arnoldo's Brother*; for he, like the young participants in SPARC, gazes unflinchingly at inequality and strife, looking right through them to encounter the possibilities of hope and social justice.

Notes

1. Constance Penley and Andrew Ross, eds., *Technoculture* (Minneapolis: University of Minnesota, 1991), xii–xiii.

2. Alondra Nelson, Future Texts, *Social Text* 20, no. 2 (Summer 2002): 9.

3. Gloria Anzaldúa, *Borderlands/La Frontera*, 2nd ed. (San Francisco: Aunt Lute Books, 1999), 102.

4. Anna Everett, On Cyberfeminism and Cyberwomanism: High-Tech Mediations of Feminism's Discontent, *Signs: Journal of Women in Culture and Society* 30, no. 1 (2004): 1282.

5. John Jota Leaños, The (Postcolonial) Rules of Engagement: Cultural Activism, Advertising Zones & Xican@ Digital Muralism, http://leanos.net/Rules%20of%20Engagement.htm. Retrieved August 25, 2005.

6. Michelle-Lee White, Aftrotech and Outer Spaces, *Art Journal* 60, no. 3 (Fall 2001): 90.

7. Logan Hill, Beyond Access: Race, Technology and Community, in *Technicolor: Race, Technology and Everyday Life*, ed. Alondra Nelson and Thuy Linh N. Tu, with Alicia Headlam Hines (New York and London: New York University Press, 2001), 14.

8. From SPARC Web site, http://www.sparcmurals.org.

9. Ibid.

10. Everett, On Cyberfeminism, 1282.

11. Guillermo Gómez-Peña, The Virtual Barrio @ the Other Frontier (or the Chicano Interneta), in *Technicolor: Race, Technology and Everyday Life*, ed. Alondra Nelson and Thuy Linh N. Tu, with Alicia Headlam Hines (New York and London: New York University Press, 2001), 195.

12. Jennifer Brayton, Cyberfeminism as New Theory, formerly available online from the University of New Brunswick Web site and cited in Everett, On Cyberfeminism, 1279.

13. See Anick Jesdanun, Youths No Longer Predominant at MySpace: Half of Social Networking Site's Users are 35 or Older, The Associated Press, October 5, 2006.

14. Amalia Mesa-Bains, Oral History Interview with Judith Baca in Venice, CA, August 5 and 6, 1986, *Smithsonian Institution*, Archives of American Art.

15. Joe Austin and Michael Nevin Willard, eds., *Generations of Youth: Youth Cultures and History in Twentieth-Century America* (New York: New York University Press, 1998), 1.

16. Julian Sefton-Green, ed. *Digital Diversions: Youth Culture in the Age of Multimedia* (London: UCL Press, 1998), 4.

17. Josh Kun, *MacArthur Foundation Series on Digital Media and Learning*, Open Forum Posting, October 20, 2006, http://community.macfound. org/openforum. Retrieved October 21, 2006.

18. The Tomás Rivera Institute, *Latinos and Information Technology: The Promise and the Challenge* (Claremont, CA: The IBM Hispanic Digital Divide Task Force, 2002), i.

19. The Tomás Rivera Institute, 24.

20. Ray Santisteban, A Program for Change: Chicano Media into the Next Millenium, *Aztlán* 24, no. 2 (Fall 1999): 126.

21. Ibid., 128.

22. Judith F. Baca, Birth of a Movement, in *Community, Culture and Globalization*, ed. Don Adams and Arlene Goldbard (New York: The Rockefeller Foundation, 2002), 112.

23. Ibid.

24. The connection between Haraway's "cyborg" consciousness and *mestiza/o* is substantiated by digital media scholar María Fernández: "In her famous essay 'A Manifesto for Cyborgs: Science, Technology, and Socialist Feminism in the 1980's,' Donna Haraway proposed the cyborg, 'a hybrid of machine and organism,' as a foundation for feminist politics. By basing her cyborg on the model of mestizaje, the phenomenon of racial mixing that took place during the colonial period in the New World, Haraway attempted to bridge a profound gap that had opened in the United States between white and Third World feminism." See Postcolonial Media Theory, *Art Journal* 58, no. 3 (Fall 1999): 63.

25. Donna Haraway, A Cyborg Manifesto: Science, Technology and Socialist-Feminsm in the Late Twentieth Century, in *The Cybercultures Reader*, ed. David Bell and Barbara M. Kennedy (London: Routledge, 2000), 295.

26. Chela Sandoval, New Sciences: Cyborg Feminism and the Methodology of the Oppressed, in *The Cybercultures Reader*, ed. David Bell and Barbara M. Kennedy (London: Routledge, 2000), 375.

27. Anzaldúa, *Borderlands/La Frontera*, 101.

28. Mesa-Bains, Oral History Interview with Judith Baca.

29. For more on the gendered aspects of Chicana/o muralism, see Guisela Latorre, Gender, Muralism and the Public Sphere: Chicana Muralism and Indigenist Aesthetics, in *Disciplines on the Line: Feminist Research on Spanish, Latin American, and Latina Women*, ed. Anne J. Cruz, Rosalie Hernández-Pecoraro, and Joyce Tolliver (Newark, DE: Juan de la Cuesta Hispanic Monographs), 321–356.

30. Ibid.

31. For more on Chicanas' critique of the Chicano and feminist movements, see Anna Nieto Gomez, Sexism in the Movimiento, *La Gente* (March 1976): 5–20, and Patricia Zavella, The Problematic

Relationship of Feminism and Chicana Studies, *Women's Studies: An Interdisciplinary Journal* 17, no. 1 (1989): 25–36.

32. Baca, Birth of a Movement, 117.

33. Interview with Debra Padilla by Guisela Latorre and Chela Sandoval, Social and Public Art Resource Center, Venice, CA, July 24, 2006.

34. Ernestine Jiménez, testimonial posted on the SPARC Official Web site, www.sparcmurals.org.

35. Interview with Debra Padilla.

36. Jeffrey S. Juris, The New Digital Media and Activist Networking within Anti-Corporate Globalization Movements, *The Annals of the American Academy of Political and Social Science* 597 (January 2005): 205.

37. Interview with Judy Baca by Guisela Latorre and Chela Sandoval, Social and Public Art Resource Center, Venice, CA, July 24, 2006.

38. Ibid.

39. Juris, The New Digital Media, 195.

40. Everett, On Cyberfeminism, 1283.

41. Julian Sefton-Green and David Buckingham, Children's 'Creative' Uses of Multimedia Technologies, in *Digital Diversions: Youth Culture in the Age of Multimedia* (London: UCL Press, 1998), 64.

42. Interview with Debra Padilla.

43. Ibid.

44. For a historical account of Toyporina's participation in the San Gabriel Mission, see Thomas Workman Temple II, Toypurina the Witch and the Indian Uprising at San Gabriel, *Masterkey* 32 (September–October 1958): 136–152. For an analysis of the gender and racial implication behind Toyporina's role in California's colonial history see the work of Chicana historian Antonia I. Castañeda, Sexual Violence in the Politics and Policies of Conquest: Amerindian Women and the Spanish Conquest of Alta California, in *Building with Our Hands: New Directions in Chicana Studies*, ed. Adela de la Torre and Beatríz M. Pesquera (Berkeley: University of California Press, 1993), 15–33; and Engendering the History of Alta California, 1769–1848: Gender, Sexuality and the Family, in *Contested Eden: California Before the Gold Rush*, ed. Ramón Gutiérrez and Richard J. Orsi (Berkeley: University of California Press, 1998), 230–259.

45. Interview with Judy Baca.

46. Ibid.

47. The UCLA César Chávez/SPARC Digital Mural Lab Web site, www.sparcmurals.org.

48. For more information on the Estrada Courts murals from the 1970s, see Marcos Sánchez-Tranquilino, Space, Power, and Youth Culture: Mexican American Graffiti and Chicano Murals in East Los Angeles, in *Looking High and Low: Art and Cultural Identity*, ed. Brenda Jo Bright and Liza Bakewell (Tucson: University of Arizona Press, 1995), 55–88.

49. SPARC, *Our Vision Has Come of Age*, brochure produced by the staff of the Social and Public Art Resource Center.

50. Cynthia Lee, Murals Pay Homage to History, Heritage, *UCLA Today: Connecting Staff and Faculty in the UCLA Community* (2004), the Regents of the University of California, http://www.today.ucla.edu/2000/001121murals.html. Retrieved September 1, 2006.

51. Alma López, "Las Four," http://www.almalopez.net.

52. Ibid.

53. Ibid.

54. Interview with Judy Baca by Guisela Latorre and Chela Sandoval, Social and Public Art Resource Center, Venice, CA, October 24, 2006.

55. Ibid.

56. For more on the concept of the machinic assemblage, see Gilles Deleuze and Félix Guattari, *A Thousand Plateaus* (Minneapolis: University of Minnesota Press, 1987).

57. Juris, The New Digital Media, 199.

58. Interview with anonymous former-student of Judy Baca by Guisela Latorre, September 2, 2006.

59. Department of World Arts and Cultures, UCLA, online course catalogue, http://www.registrar.ucla.edu/schedule/catalog.asp?sa=WLD+ART&funsel=3. Retrieved September 21, 2006.

60. Judy Baca, Beyond the Mexican Mural (classrooms discussions and conversations), Social and Public Art Resource Center, Venice, CA, October 24, 2006. Sessions recorded by Chela Sandoval and Guisela Latorre.

61. Ibid.

62. Ibid.

63. Ibid.

64. For general studies on the performance of Chicana/o students within the school system see, Esther Vigil, Coping with a Prejudiced Educational System, *Nuestro* 8, no. 5 (June–July 1985): 51; C. H. Arce, Chicanos in Higher Education, *Integrated Education* 14, no. 3 (1976): 14–18; Tara J. Yosso, *Critical Race Counterstories along the Chicana/Chicano Educational Pipeline* (New York: Routledge, 2006); Daniel G. Solórzano et al., *Latina Equity in Education: Gaining Access to Academic Enrichment Programs* (Los Angeles, CA: UCLA Chicano Studies Research Center, 2003).

Circling the Cross: Bridging Native America, Education, and Digital Media

Antonio López

World Bridger Media

Introduction

Here, I learn about the needs and desires of my people and my community. I learn how I can help them through remaining and participating with those I love. Thus, we will remain one house, one voice, one heart, and one mission: that mission is to strengthen the Indian way of life. . . . I learn I have learned that education and wisdom happen whenever people speak with good thoughts in a caring, supporting environment and that my teachers are all those who help me to understand the world and myself. . . . There is a larger society, a larger world in which I must learn to live and survive, but I must never forget who I am and where I came from. The past helps me to the future.

Excerpt from the Santa Fe Indian School's Mission Statement, circa 1992

Sociologist C. Wright Mills wrote many years ago, "Those who rule the management of symbols, rule the world."[1] For many Native Americans, symbols are ciphers of power, a type of symbolic "medicine." I learned this at age fifteen, when I had the rare opportunity to live in a small village on a reservation in northern Arizona that has been home to Native Americans for thousands of years.[2] My host was an elder designated by the tribe to convey its spiritual teachings to the outside world. He was someone who had had an audience with the Pope and addressed the United Nations General Assembly. What he shared during my stay more than twenty-five years ago remains with me today, and informs my approach as a digital media literacy educator working with Native Americans to promote interpreting and deconstructing symbols as a primary tool for critical digital literacy.

During my stay in the village, a community that had split in the 1900s because of tribal divisions caused by U.S. government and white cultural intervention, my host said that when his tribe first encountered Spaniards in 1540, they intuitively read the conqueror's intentions by interpreting their overarching visual symbol, the crucifix. His ancestors were interested in the cultural meaning of the symbol's shape: a grid formed by intersecting, angular lines indicating a linear mentality. As such, they correctly assessed the Europeans' intellectual agility and ingenuity; but what troubled them was a missing element in the Europeans' symbolism, which the tribe possessed: a cross enclosed by a circle that represented the unity of multiple elements: human, earthly, psychological, and spiritual. Also known as a "medicine wheel," it is a common emblem among North American tribes. The community assessed that whatever the Europeans intended to achieve, it would not be sustainable. Owing to a faulty thought process (or operating system in modern parlance), logic and reason without holism was ultimately doomed to fail. Although the Europeans successfully colonized the territory, it set in motion an ecologically destructive system that may, in the end, make the conquest a transient fact.

As an educator promoting digital media literacy, what interests me about this story is the genius and perceptibility the tribe's ancestors had regarding the cultural uses of signs, drawing on their metaphysical understanding of symbolism to perceive the practical application of differing paradigms. They were creative media deconstructionists before such a thing came into existence four hundred years later, and like most other tribes in North America, they still maintain a savvy, critically engaged perspective on the dominant power structure and its media systems. As such, this tribe's story presents us with a powerful lesson in comprehending socially constructed communication systems and their long-term impact on communities and the environment. As Hopi artist, filmmaker, educator, and activist Victor Masayesva Jr. stresses,

We are knowledgeable about obsessing on technology at the expense of life and living. We have experienced the impacts of technology beginning with control of water in our desert environment and the unequal powers created by such technologies . . . personally, I have continued to reinforce the message that the Internet is only a rumor and until the context is clear we will always be cautious about the messenger.[3]

In terms of understanding the mentalities of the circle and the cross, Native American scholar Donald L. Fixico believes, "The wars fought between Indians and the whites were more than just over land—they were wars of the minds. The American mainstream thinks in a linear fashion, which is very different from the circular fashion of traditionalists. These two are at odds when both are not realized, as by one not knowing the other one."[4] In sociological terms, we are dealing with different "subjectivities," distinctive ways of perceiving and being in the world. Thus, we can extend this discussion to a broader understanding of communication systems as mental environments, or as "media ecologies." For "the five-hundred-year relationship between America's indigenous people and Europeans and their descendents may easily be described as an unending chain of rhetorical situations."[5] Relating this concept of media ecology to a generalized view of the impact of technology and media to our interaction with the world, media scholar Neil Postman remarks:

[N]ew technologies compete with old ones—for time, attention for money, for prestige, but mostly for dominance of world-view. This competition is implicit once we acknowledge that a medium contains an ideological bias. And it is a fierce competition, as only ideological competitions can be. It is not merely a matter of tool against tool—the alphabet attacking ideographic writing, the printing press attacking the illuminated manuscript, the photograph attacking the art of painting, television attacking the printed word. When media make war against each other, it is a case of world-views in collision.[6]

One of the primary battlegrounds for "worldviews" in collision is in schools. As advocates of digital media education, we understand that it is important to be cognizant of alternate modes of engagement, and to design programming that is appropriate and sensitive to these differences, not out of a tokenistic desire for multiculturalism, but out of a real engagement of difference that is positive and constructive.

While examining the training program implicit within compulsory government education, what has been more obvious to Native Americans is the manner in which education is conventionally used as a tool for control and assimilation into the dominant society. From what I've learned by working in the public school system, I'm taking it as a given that government educational standards do not necessarily promote challenging the power grid's assumptions, but rather encourage students to reinforce the economic and political structure of our society through standards. My beliefs are echoed by former teacher and education critic John Taylor Gatto when he observes that "school, as it was built, is an essential support system for a model of social engineering that condemns most people to be subordinate stones in a pyramid that narrows as it ascends to a terminal of control. School is an artifice that makes such a pyramidical social order seem inevitable, even though such a premise is a fundamental betrayal of the American Revolution."[7]

While recognizing that there are plenty of excellent and well-meaning educators that do work in the system, it's important to recognize how Gatto's critique concurs with the manner in which Native education policy has played out. This analysis has implications for the broader social structure, for this discussion is also about the interplay between education, technology, and racism in our general society.

While we explore the issue of digital media and technology as it relates to education, youth, and Native America, we need to probe deeply into our own operating paradigm to understand fully what is required to nurture critically engaged youth that will not simply replicate the assumptions of our system, but will be engaged in culturally and locally relevant pedagogy. Ultimately we need to see this as not just a Native American issue, but one facing our broader society, for what happens in Vegas doesn't just stay there, it infects the entire grid. Given that we inhabit a world primarily of electronically delivered symbols that potentially replicate the power structure, it is necessary to develop an education strategy that is both practical and constructive, by way of supporting cultural integrity and sustainability. While the image of a broken medicine wheel is often used to describe the contemporary state of Native youth, its potential reconstruction and reestablishment literally represents healing. Through a strategy of community-based education and "glocalization" (combining the terms *global* and *local*) it is my belief, in the spirit of the story I learned twenty-five years ago, that the new electronic media environment has the potential to facilitate the bridging of the circle and cross.

A note on context: I am not a tribally affiliated Native American. Rather, I am a digital media activist and educator who has been invited by dozens of tribes across the United States to assist youth programs to develop media literacy and production projects. As a former teacher at a federally funded Native American boarding school, I have been a mediator between children, elders, school administrators, nonprofits, tribes, and government officials. I am aware that Native America is incredibly diverse, thus making it very difficult to make generalizations. My contribution here is to argue passionately that there is a value to incorporating media literacy within a community education model that honors local input as a way of balancing the issues related to new digital media and traditionally underserved communities. What follows is not meant to be a definitive solution or exhaustive definition of the situation. Rather, the subsequent discussions and recommendations are based on case studies from my own experiences that suggest best practices and effective ideas for how to rethink pedagogy. Finally, what is often lost in the discussion of Native American education is that, historically, there have been many instances in which the white culture learned and benefited from Native American knowledge and technology. We should consider this to be one of those instances, for ultimately how this issue is addressed has much greater implications for mainstream society than would generally be admitted.

The Problem with Standards and the No Child Left Behind Act

What is more important to a community: access to the Net, or the death of an elder whose knowledge, as the saying goes, is the equivalent of a library? Local knowledge is important for all communities, and it is no different for Native Americans. Although a computer can tell you the weather, it can't show you how to tell the weather. One is not exclusive of the other, but we have to understand that our cultural priorities need to be viewed within a historical and a cultural context. Is the intention of education in the Information Age (as tends to be the case with the status quo) to homogenize culture and reproduce hegemonic power structures? Is the motivation to provide tools so learners can critically engage the larger discourse of the dominant society? Or is it to empower participants to transcend their current conditions and transform themselves? As Native filmmaker and educator Jacques La Grange points out, the presence of new computer technology is

like a double edge sword . . . a sort of damn [*sic*] if we do, damn [*sic*] if we don't. Lets be honest our children need to know how to use technology. Especially if this is the only way to a better life. But do we give them the keys to the car without first showing them how to drive? . . . It is difficult enough for Native Americans to have a voice, but even harder for Native American Children to have a voice at all. If we do not nurture their ideas and give them a chance to succeed then it is we who have failed them.[8]

Usually, the discussion about technology for underserved communities begins with access, but rarely is it contextualized in terms of wisdom. For example, there are numerous programs by major computer companies that offer technology to Reservation schools and after-school programs, but they lack a pedagogy that incorporates art, ecology, or community. Part of the problem is that much digital technology programming draws on conventional thinking about education; moreover, if computers are going to government schools or institutions, their use will be subject to standards and school policies. In the context of Native American communities, it's useful to address why this is problematic.

In terms of the concept that computers empower individuals, schools have very strict filters on their computer networks, so students are often locked out of many Web sites, including chat and social networks like MySpace. More affluent students in the mainstream have computers at home that provide them with more unrestricted access; Native students, by contrast, are constrained by the policies of those who provide access and host the computer systems. This is why some of the digital divide remedies—donating computers to schools or after-school programs—don't necessarily empower students individually, because they are inhibited by institutional filters and other restrictions. Also, these remedies take decisions about access away from the families. It is reminiscent of the early days of books when Bibles were chained down in monastery libraries so that they could not be read away from the watchful eyes of proctors. This goes back to my very strong belief that technology must be accompanied by critical literacy. Students should be allowed to explore the technological world, but also must be trained to engage digital media content and production mindfully from within a community context.

In addition, with increasing emphasis on test standardization, which focuses on the core principles of pre-digital education (the so-called Three R's—reading, writing, and arithmetic), chances for teaching necessary skills for digital literacy are reduced in U.S. schools, and especially in schools that are historically underfunded. Thus it is necessary to map how educators and activists are coping with these general conditions, and how such lessons pertain to education in Native American schools, which have traditionally been devastating to Native communities.

The horrors perpetrated against Indian students at Bureau of Indian Affairs (BIA)-run schools for small transgressions, including speaking their native language, are well documented, and are beyond the scope of this chapter, but can be summarized by the articulated education policy of the 1800s: "Kill the Indian, save the man." The point is not to review the history of Native education, but to trace some of the elements related to the mental programming of alien constructs that have been imposed on Indian communities since the arrival of Columbus in 1492. Having set course for the bifurcation of our holistic sense of the world and nature, our technologies for interpreting the world, from perspective painting technique, movable type, photography, film, and TV to cyberspace have been an exponential amping-up of external stimuli that feed back on themselves. The power of mental systems as they are transmitted through the education of communications media are tools by which we pass on cultural information, which are overwhelmingly metaphysical: "Almost all Indian education studies, reports, and commissions have described, analyzed, and bemoaned a Western-inspired institution built on curriculum, methodologies, and pedagogy consistent with the Western worldview. This much-studied educational system was and, sadly, remains too often directed toward cultural assimilation into the dominant society."[9]

When in the twenty-first century Native Americans encounter media technology and education, the history of the clash of civilizations is also a collision of communication strategies and consciousness. Thus an important back-story is that "literacy" on the reservation is historically linked with control and colonization. In the United Sates, the government's primary strategy for assimilation was through boarding schools, which were instituted by Congress in 1870. By making Native Americans "literate," the intention was to "civilize" Indians by separating them from their traditional communities: "The goal of education was to 'Americanize' Indian children by teaching them to conform and obey, to speak English, and to do manual labor for a living . . . boarding schools aimed to prepare students to own private property and to become wage earners."[10] Part of our culturally biased thinking relates to an institutional attitude that considers our communication systems (including literacy) as rational, evolutionary progressions of civilization, a position that has been thoroughly debunked by anthropology. "The point is that very few people believe what anthropology teaches: that indigenous, small-scale traditional societies are not earlier (or degenerate) versions of our own. They are rather differing solutions to historical circumstances and environmental particulars that testify to the breadth of human intellectual creativity and its capacity for symbolization."[11]

Media theorist Marshal McLuhan complained that education threatened to approach new technology from a "rear-view mirror" approach; that is, our inability to comprehend the current media environment with nineteenth-century attitudes. Our multisensory "acoustic" media space is not compatible with the linearity of print literacy that is the intellectual legacy of education policy. Unfortunately, the trend toward standardized testing promoted by the No Child Left Behind Act (NCLB) is very much a rear-view-mirror orientation—it tests rote knowledge, and lacks a rubric for other types of learners, especially those who are more nonlinear in their learning styles. Native Americans, and minorities in general, tend to score below national averages on these tests, so being subjected to these standards puts them at yet another disadvantage, and sets them up for failure:

In summary, the body of research, although small, on learning styles of American Indian students presents some converging evidence that suggests common patterns of methods in the way these students come to know or understand the world. They approach tasks visually, seem to prefer to learn by careful observation preceding performance, and seem to learn in their natural settings experientially. Research with other students groups has clearly illustrated that differences in learning style (whether they be described as relational/analytical, field dependent/independent, or global/linear) can result in "academic disorientation." While it is not clear where Indian students fit on this continuum, it is clear from the research . . . that American Indian students come to learn about the world in ways that differ from those of non-Indian students.[12]

The National Indian Education Association and Center for Indian Education, in a detailed study, *Preliminary Report on No Child Left Behind in Indian Country*, concluded that:

- The statute is rigid and it tends to leave children behind.
- We need opportunity; we need resources to do that.
- (Any) Success has clearly been at the expense and diminishment of Native language and culture.
- The approach dictated by the law has created serious negative consequences.
- Schools are sending the message that if our children would just work harder they would succeed, without recognizing their own systemic failures.
- Indian children are internalizing the (school) system's failures as their personal failures.
- Children have different needs.
- It does not provide for the level of funding that we need.
- Music, art, social studies, languages—these areas are totally ignored by the law.[13]

These assessments are made, even though NCLB has instituted a special Native American initiative under Bush's Executive Order 13336. I saw on the ground how one successful Native American program that started out as a way of coping with the new digital media environment was negatively impacted by NCLB. At the Native boarding school where I worked, Intel financed an eighth-grade computer-building program, based on the company's "Journey Inside" curriculum. Over the course of the school year, students assembled and installed PCs, and if they kept up their grades at a certain level, eventually they could take the computers home. As part of the program, for two years I worked on a digital video documentary with student assistants, going into households and interviewing families who received these computers. Generally, we found that families were grateful for the computers and that multiple people used these systems in their households to meet a variety of needs.

In one case, a student's stepfather was a jeweler and used the system to book travel for trade shows. Another family used the student-built computer to research water issues. In all cases the computers were intrinsic to the academic achievement of extended family members (the PCs were shared by multiple users, inside and outside the home). The additional benefit is that students learned technical skills that would contribute to their academic achievement and economic success. Unfortunately, the program was discontinued after NCLBA was instituted, because science scores were shown to be below average for that grade level. The program was ended to teach to the standardized test, a cautionary example of an utterly disastrous application of Federal education standards insensitive to community needs.

Toward a Rez Pedagogy: Community as Text

For the sake of clarification, I submit that two very different understandings of technology are the issue. A deeply seated (metaphysically based) Western view of technology as science applied to industrial (manufacture) and commercial objectives, versus a (metaphysically based) American Indian, or rather indigenous, view of technology as practices and toolmaking to enhance our living in and with nature. The Western conception and practices of technology are bound up in essentially human-centered materialism: the doctrine that physical well-being and worldly possessions constitute the greatest good and highest value in life. Indigenous conceptions and practices of technology are embedded in a way of living life that is inclusive of spiritual, physical, emotional, and intellectual dimensions emergent in the world or, more accurately, particular places in the world.[14]

Efforts to address the needs of Native America's technological challenges should not be just educational tokenism or window-dressing for funding. A fundamental shift in pedagogy must be considered and incorporated; we shouldn't just repeat old patterns of replicating the power structure. In what they characterize as "indigenizing education," Vine Deloria and Daniel R. Wildcat propose incorporating two formulas: TC3 (technology, community, communication, and culture) plus P3 (power-and-place-equal-personality). While P3 "makes for a spatial metaphysics of experience," TC3 "is an attempt to identify the natural cultural features of human beingness."[15] The two keys to this formula are a sense of place and community.

Deloria and Wildcat remind us that "American Indians have a long history of rejecting abstract theologies and metaphysical systems in place of experiential systems properly called indigenous—indigenous in the sense that people historically and culturally connected to places can and do draw on power located in those places. Stated simply, *indigenous* means 'to be of a place.' . . . To indigenize an action or object is the act of making something of a place."[16] Other experts of Native American education echo these views: "It is not enough to focus only on students' classroom experiences; expanding the focus is a central component of the change from an Anglo-conformity orientation . . . the collective historical experiences of the community must be used as the context for all learning in the school. There are no easy formulas for implementing these changes; patience, ingenuity, and a spirit of committed experimentation are necessary."[17]

In terms of a strategy for approaching new digital media and learning, it is useful to review how popular educator Paulo Freire speaks of literacy. He makes the connection between "word and world," recognizing that the context of life is as much of a text as a book. Here he speaks of his home environment as being his first "text":

Truly, that special world presented itself to me as the arena of my perceptual activity and therefore as the world of my first reading. The *texts*, the *words*, the *letters* of that context were incarnated as in a series of things, objects and signs. In perceiving these I experienced myself, and the more I experienced myself, the more my perceptual capacity increased. I learned to understand things, objects, and signs through using them in relationship to my older brothers and sisters and my parents. . . . Part of the context of my immediate world was also the language universe of my elders, expressing their beliefs, tastes, fears, and values, which linked my world to a wider one whose existence I could not even suspect.[18]

I'm moved by this passage because it reminds me of the unique and diverse circumstances the students come from at the Southwestern Indian boarding school where I worked, and how their world is so rich with text. Among the students, there were two generally dichoto-mous and culturally distinct groups: urban and reservation, and Diné (Navajo) and Pueblo. Among the Pueblos, there are also different language groups and a general split between northern and southern tribes. What struck me was that, with the exception of the urban students, who were generally acculturated/assimilated into mainstream society (yet they re-tained many characteristics of regional identity), the youth exist in various perceptual realms simultaneously. At school, they maneuver within a mediated territory fully engaged with technology, the Internet, and the mainstream educational system, learning a curriculum necessarily accommodating of and constrained by state and federal standards.

At home on the rez, though Internet access is generally limited, like typical American teens, students consume mainstream media, such as radio, movies, and television entertain-ment. Yet many rez teens are also participants in the ongoing, traditional ceremonial prac-tices of their tribes. It was normal for students to disappear for short periods owing to tribal obligations. On occasion we'd see them dancing during one of many "feast days" throughout the school year. Such occasions were school events; the staff organized vans and buses to visit Pueblos having celebrations. As teachers, we were invited to visit the homes of administrators, staff, teachers, students, and friends. We found ourselves gorging on delicious chili stew, Jell-O cake, Navajo tacos, and Jemez enchiladas at large tables with the extended community network of our students. During these gatherings I was reminded of how much of the generous and communal spirit of the tribes remain an important aspect of contemporary cultural life.

One of the reasons community context is important can be related to the particular learning style of Native American students:

Current theorists and researchers have recognized one difference in thought of oral versus literate people. People from oral traditions contextualize their articulation of thought; they depend on shared knowledge of the people who will be listening to them and do not necessarily articulate what others already know. People from literate traditions tend to decontextualize thought, to add the context that a distant audience will need to make sense of speech or writing.[19]

Like Freire's own sense of "text" of the world, there is the essence of tradition that remains deeply engrained within the Indian students with whom we work. Moreover, spending time in student homes is critical to my own education and pedagogy, because "teachers must become participants in the community; they must observe and ask questions in a way that communicates genuine care and concern. Teachers are learners too, and must let students (and their parents) know this."[20]

By working within the context of community, it brings into stark relief the extent to which youth are mediated by technology. From watching students in both environments—on the rez and at school engaging computers and other media—my sense is that they are something like 25 percent cybernetic in that there are whole portions of their personalities that appear downloaded off the Net; or in McLuhan-esque terms, they are physically extended into the technosphere. Media theorist Douglas Rushkoff describes youth as the new human prototype, and at the Indian boarding school I felt I was seeing that manifest, for many of the attitudes and beliefs I saw students adapt at school were not coming from the home environment, but clearly through engaging the national pop culture and new digital media. This is not exclusive to Indian students, but the fact became more obvious to me because of the extreme contrast between the realms within which they were navigating.

Achieving local control is not simple in a political environment that is hostile to Native American sovereignty. At the time of my tenure at the boarding school, it was funded by the BIA, but was administered under tribal supervision. The physical campus had been designated sovereign, making it a nation within a nation (requiring its own judicial and security systems so that it could run fully autonomous from U.S. federal and municipal systems). Yet even that move is a partial fiction. The school's administrators are constantly under threat by government officials who annually bang a drum to eliminate Native sovereignty nationally, and ultimately the school is subject to the standards of federal and state funding, and therefore must comply, like all other schools that receive federal funding—such as NCLB. So, though the school makes a special effort to address the needs of its student community (drawing from over twenty-five different regional and national tribes), it also is constantly under a federal microscope that some would interpret as harassment. If it is true, as critics contend, that NCLB is an effort to push America's schools into privatization structures, then this is yet another impending threat to local control of Native American schools.[21]

As teachers, we negotiated between the concerns of youth and elders, finding that it was not unusual to hear one group say they didn't understand the other. No doubt, contrasting experiences—one coming from a reality unmediated by the torrent of mass media, the other from a digitally mediated realm—are bound to rub against each other. This needn't be the case, though, for there are approaches being made in Native communities addressing this gap, many of which are promising. One example is the boarding school's community-based model approach in which its interdisciplinary program educates students in an assortment of subjects, including tribal law and technology. Also included are courses in the use of hi-tech gear, such as global positioning systems (GPS) and global information systems (GIS) mapping, and these services are offered to the tribes that are served by the school. The goal is to connect the technology skills students are learning in school to the needs of their communities in mutually beneficial ways. For in the past the tendency was for students who succeeded in learning specialized technology skills to be hired away by companies that did not service or benefit the students' home communities. The program collaborates with communities to best harmonize the learning environment of students that is relevant and beneficial to all parties involved. For example, one of the biggest challenges confronting southwestern tribes along the Rio Grande is the remediation of the river forest ecology. As a result, students have been asked by several tribes to map with GIS various stretches of forest. Back at the school, students learn how to incorporate the data into maps. On several projects, my specific contribution was to assist students in producing digital media documentation of these programs. Here we see a positive convergence of the school working in conjunction with tribal communities to provide technical expertise and training with digital technology to service the ecological needs of the tribe, and also to promote self-sufficiency by training tribal members to utilize cutting-edge technology.

Other models are abundant. An example of how the oral tradition can be bridged by digital media is the effort by some tribes to use digital video to preserve their languages. In northern New Mexico, one tribe is attempting to have kids interview their elders in their native language on video, and then catalog the footage on DVD for their tribal library. In Oklahoma, a high school program is re-creating traditional stories spoken in the indigenous language by using stop-motion claymation that is then edited on computers. The Cherokee Nation, in particular, is making incredible advances in using digital technology to enhance their cultural heritage.[22]

Applying Media Literacy

In terms of a community-based model of digital media production and literacy, I'm interested in "internal" forms of production because, though it is important for mainstream society to be familiar with Native issues (and also simply to have Native Americans as a visible presence that affirms their lively existence in contemporary society), the flood of commercial media also threatens language, cultural integrity, and mental sovereignty, and performs an overall spiritually colonizing effect. The potentially troubling aspect of technological aesthetics and culture is its homogenizing effect, which is duly noted by a group of Native scholars who examine the subject closely:

Certainly some computer companies and Web sites are pushing the notion of "one world, one culture" (cyberculture, we suppose!). The idea, however, lacks an understanding that synthetic communication has a push-pull effect that works to push groups apart at the same time as it works to pull them together. We suspect that, with American Indians, it will remain largely the same as it has been, though other more powerful circumstances, especially economic ones, may prevail, and tend to diminish ethnic boundaries.[23]

In my view, "internal" media (productions by and for Native audiences) should have two components: mindful engagement (literacy) and self-empowerment (production). For example, many of the communities with which I have worked are using digital media as an educational tool for health issues. In terms of connecting health with digital media, the frontline of this approach comes from the national media literacy movement of nonprofits, one of the few areas in which tools of critical engagement of media—digital and analog—are actually practiced. Although the term *literacy* is problematic because of its epistemological and semantic context, we still need a word that describes the thing we are trying to do, which is to come up with a method that enables "learners" and "readers" of media to analyze, evaluate, and communicate in some form a cogent response that reflects an awareness of how media operate, and also promotes the capacity to detect the bias of media systems and their producers. I call my own methodology "media mindfulness," for at a minimum, students should be critical participants of media systems, and at best be active producers of their own content, reflecting an engaged awareness of media environments in the context of their community needs, values, and their own personal realities. I'm interested in a kind of mindful engagement with media forms that include Web sites, animations, video (music, narrative, documentary, and experimental), music, video games, and advertising.

When working within Native American communities, I also feel that media content should reflect directly upon their lived experiences and complex realities. This is a hard task, given that there are so few mainstream media samples to work with that reflect contemporary Native culture. One of the most interesting areas where technological and media savvy have practical applications is in tribal efforts to reclaim tobacco for sacred uses and for promoting smoke-free environments. Media literacy is considered a no-nonsense tool for health education because it differs from the conventional approach, which is to tell teens to stop doing something because it's bad for them. The latter technique usually produces the opposite result; but if you demonstrate how massive multinational corporations use media to manipulate their belief systems, it appeals to the students' natural sense of rebellion. Here, media literacy is not simply an abstract pedagogical tool, but also serves the practical needs of the tribe. After all, if we are dealing with education from a systems view, then the prevalence of malnutrition, drug addiction, diabetes, alcohol abuse, and domestic violence typical of impoverished communities does not suggest a positive educational environment. As such, media education, especially as it relates to commercial tobacco abuse, is literally a form of mental decolonization. Keep in mind that one of the skills Indians taught European colonizers was the "culture" of tobacco. That is, by showing them how to grow and cultivate the ceremonial plant, colonists were able to generate great wealth, so much so that tobacco leaves are featured as part of the design of the one-dollar bill. Through the deconstruction of tobacco ads and nefarious marketing practices on the Web and in film, and through the steady effort to both prevent addiction and support abatement, tribes are slowly reclaiming the power of one their most sacred plants, and reaffirming its role in their culture and society.

Because of current funding and standards implementation, there have been backdoor efforts by media educators to introduce novel approaches for digital media literacy through a variety of nontraditional education channels. In New Mexico, media literacy units have been inserted into social studies, language arts, and health education curriculum standards, but nationally these requirements are few and far between. Consequently, students are more likely to encounter media literacy in after-school or summer programs serviced by nonprofits and funded by special grants. For example, state tobacco settlement funds have been a boon for media education specialists in various regions. In New Mexico, many literacy programs were offered through state tobacco settlement grants, administered by public school system health advocacy organizations or through county and state agencies that value media literacy as an effective public health education tool for pressing health issues, such as preventing driving under the influence (DUI). But here, too, is a cautionary tale of why cultural sensitivity and community context is so important. A lot of antitobacco media literacy activists make the mistake of demonizing tobacco, and fail to distinguish the sacred relationship of the plant with Native Americans and its abuse by commercial cigarette and other enterprises. One well-meaning program was banned from a Native-run school for this very reason. Without making the distinction between religious and commercial uses, the nonprofit conducted a survey that asked students if they used tobacco in the previous month. The unusually high percentage that said "yes" were confused because many of the students carry tobacco with them as part of their religious practice. In another misstep by a different program, a public service announcement (PSA) about DUI was made depicting Native students drinking in their car. Even though the script was written by Native students, depicting images that are already strongly embedded in the national consciousness, in particular those of Indian alcoholics, is of dubious benefit.

Native American health advocacy programs operated by tribal governments outside of schools have taken a special interest in media literacy. I have attended numerous commercial tobacco prevention conferences and "wellness" camps led by tribal health agencies to train adults and youth in media literacy strategies, and to produce grassroots, community-based PSAs for their communities. In my opinion, campaigns that have focused on producing media for insertion into mainstream media have not had nearly as much impact as those programs featuring youth designed and produced PSAs at community events that offer food and celebration. Unless you are as well funded as the antismoking Truth campaign to build a brand, I liken PSAs in mainstream media to throwing a glass of water into a waterfall. As youth media producers become peer educators, they inspire the wider community to produce culturally specific and community-targeted messages. Community events have tremendous power because they incorporate traditional and modern storytelling techniques in a way that brings people together, rather than isolating them. Likewise, when students at the Indian boarding school make PowerPoint presentations to their communities summarizing their fieldwork and findings, these are very important events that dignify and empower the students and their audiences. Finally, when I was working at the boarding school, we started having "film festivals" to showcase student work to the school and community.

Because of the nature of funding (which is typically based on advocacy), my methodology begins with an activist approach informed by deconstruction, and other analysis-based techniques promoting media literacy. But then I also incorporate "reconstruction" projects that enable students to enter into dialog with and respond to mass media by using digital media tools, thereby engaging its form. Part of the problem of commonly used media literacy techniques is that kids are pitted against "bad" media, and are forced to make a "with us or against us" choice, rather than being offered an alternate route. Experimental film, music videos, flash, animation, and video games are all ways to expose students to positive uses of media. Media literacy should celebrate the environment that youth occupy, while offering tools for them to engage critically with their digital world. This is the best way to inspire them to challenge the credibility of media-generated information, because it encourages their natural rebellion and desire to "question authority" (to borrow an old punk and hippie term) as they pass through adolescence and on to adulthood as individual, knowing subjects. But also keep in mind that some tribes do not consider rebelliousness as appropriate behavior for youths, because traditionally, individuality is considered contrary to community harmony. Ultimately, in my experience, demonizing media backfires because it ultimately challenges the veracity of a world that kids find very real. If you focus on the likely intent or potential benefits of media producers (such as commercial tobacco or alcohol), you get a much better response.

Connecting Ecology with Digital Media Literacy

Deloria and Wildcat quote an elder who said, "If you don't know where you are going, any road will get you there."[24] Such can be said of the so-called information highway. Information for information's sake can get us somewhere if we don't know where we are going; but without wisdom, what sort of destination are we heading toward? What is the point of data if they have no useful meanings? What are they in terms of human experience? Many tribal people still believe in and respect the limits of digital media's inevitability (such as giving it "rumor" status). As Okanagan activist Jeannette Armstrong puts it, "I see the thrust of technology into our daily lives, and I see the ways we subvert emotional ties to people by the use of communications that serve to depersonalize. I see how television, radio, telephone, and how computer networks create ways to promote depersonalized communication."[25] By contrast, "In a healthy whole community, the people interact with each other in shared emotional response."[26]

Although it's true that one of the more demeaning stereotypes of Native Americans is that of the "noble savage" and "natural ecologist,"[27] of the tribes that I have worked with the most pressing issues for their communities, aside from sovereignty, are ecological or health related, both of which are intimately linked to poverty and all its attendant social ills. One way of mending this broken medicine wheel (thereby uniting the circle and the cross) and giving new digital media useful "meaning" is to ensure that there is a holistic discussion of technology that incorporates an ecological perspective. Digital technology is intrinsically a feedback system; not to broaden the concept of feedback to the greater system of production and consumption is looking only at the "angles" of the digital media environment. Consequently, one of the least discussed issues in our country is the impact energy policy and technological research exert on Indian Reservations. I would be remiss not to reflect on the fact that what we are talking about is encouraging the use of electronic devices that are powered by the consumption of extractive resources, such as coal, fossil fuels, and water. Some also believe that engaging computers intensifies this process. Jerry Mander, one of the most vociferous critics of technology and globalization, observes, "The advance of computers is contributing to a loss of ecological sensitivity and understanding, since the very process of using computers, particularly educating through computers effectively excludes an entire set of ideas and experiences that heretofore had been building blocks for developing connection with the earth . . . computers alter the pathways of children's cognition."[28]

However, under local control and proper pedagogy, this is a limited perspective. Take, for example, the following scenario, which is rather complex and contains a number of gray areas. Los Alamos National Laboratory (LANL), and other weapons programs across the United States, impact tribes through the production of toxic waste and contamination of tribal lands. LANL, in particular, where the first atomic weapons were developed and built, is literally constructed on the ancestral grounds of a tribe that currently lives down from the lab's watershed. The lab itself is surrounded by four tribes, and all of them are impacted by the lab's emissions. These tribes also receive federal assistance, which ironically is how technological needs are met on some of these reservations—a bargain not taken lightly.[29]

A few years ago, this relationship also produced an interesting program that served both the technological and ecological needs of a tribe. A reservation bordering the lab was given a FEMA grant because a major fire damaged its lands in year 2000, which also destroyed a huge part of the town of Los Alamos. The tribe's governor committed a portion of the grant to create a summer youth employment program that was run by teachers from the boarding school where I worked, and by tribal employees. The nature of our project was twofold. One was to generate a baseline study of biological species along the Rio Grande River's cottonwood forest spanning tribal lands; the other was to do a similar study in a canyon where discharge from the town of White Rock and LANL facilities was released into the Rio Grande's watershed. The bosque (Spanish colloquial term for *woods*) study was necessary because of an overgrowth of "introduced" or "invasive" species—tamarisks (salt cedar) and Russian olive trees—were salinating the river's forest ecosystem and crowding out the cottonwoods. The tamarisks were originally planted by the Army Corps of Engineers to reduce flooding, and had been part of a fifty-year project to reengineer the river's entire system through dams, dredging, and the introduction of exotic plant species. Tribes up and down the river are in the process of repairing the river's ecology through removal of these exotic species and inducing floods to stimulate the growth of new cottonwood trees, without which the vital old-growth tree stands will die out. Our job was to document what was along the river before the exotics removal commenced, which is a very complex and disruptive process for the river's ecology. It was important to have a baseline study for before and after the procedure, to see if the ecological remediation is effective, and also to measure the program's ultimate impact on the river ecosystem, documenting in time the natural biodiversity of the local system.

The students, all paid tribal members aged 14 to 19, cordoned off sections of the forest and used GPS, GIS, and digital cameras, combined with field notes and computers, to log and document biological species (animals, plants, and insects). On alternating days, we also traveled to a canyon below the labs to test soil for contaminants and to count species there. My job was to lead a small crew of students to do video documentation of the program, and later to edit a piece for presentation in Washington, DC.

One of the most telling moments occurred that summer when we were winding up the narrow road that leads up to the sage-covered mesa where Los Alamos and its weapons laboratory reside. We stopped at an overlook from which one can observe across a canyon ancient cavates in the cliffs that sheltered the tribe's ancestors. In the shallow valley below, it is possible to see among bark beetle–ravaged pine trees the outlines of a long-abandoned pueblo that was also once the ancestral home of the tribe with which we were working. Lining the mesa ridge above are rows of desert lawn-adorned McMansions that house weapons lab administrators and staff. We framed a digital photo juxtaposing the ancient and modern lodging for input into a PowerPoint presentation we were to do a month later in DC for our state's senator and other Washington officials whose departments contributed to our program's funding. Later on, as we prepared the slide show in our DC hotel, my colleague asked the tribal governor what to title the image of the caves and mansions. Without missing a beat, he told us in a deep, grave tone, "Temporary Housing."

The governor's remark demonstrates awareness of the self-destructive logic, and ultimately cyclical nature, of empire and technology. My colleague and I were also conscious of the other subtext of our project: we both recognized that our study of invasive species had greater implications than the biological realm we were cataloging. As educators of European descent, we too were an "invasive species." Yet we were also bridges; we possessed the technological know-how of GIS, GPS, computers, and media. The tribe's governor reminded the youth at the beginning of the summer program that there was a world beyond the cattle guard at the reservation's edge, and that they would be wise to learn as much as possible about that world, so as to better survive it. Our job was to be guides within that realm.

Conclusions/Leapfrog

Language is a part of our identity. Deeply embedded in our Native languages are philosophical ideas that skip across centuries to the center of our Native universes. Governments tried to silence us, but still we make our voices heard. Today, we use every means available to pass our languages to the next generation. We can see films made in Seneca, Zaporo, Hopi, and Inupuit; checkout websites in Quechua, Aymara, Lakota, and Cherokee; download songs in Cree Shuar, and Hawaiian. Art is a visual language and when contemporary Native artists use the vocabulary of tradition, they, too, are keeping a language alive. When they use that vocabulary in a new way, they show that we can innovate yet remain connected to our Native identity. Embracing change, while holding onto our philosophical center, is survivance.[30]

Recalling the broader debate concerning "globalization" and that of indigenous people from across the world, the frontline nations in the struggle between education, media, environment, and culture are those of indigenous people. This was brought into stark relief during the campus Apartheid debates of the 1980s, when students demanded that educational institutions divest from South Africa. Many of us felt that it was important to remind our country that the Reservations system in the United States also represented a kind of domestic apartheid. At the time (1985) there was (and remains to this day) an ongoing struggle in the Four-Corners region of the U.S. Southwest, in which tribes are pitted against each other in a struggle over land and natural resources. Although triggered by a historical quarrel between the tribes that pre-dates the intrusion by the U.S. government, the conflict is now exploited and exacerbated by corporate and government interests to extract coal from the region.[31] We invited a Diné activist to visit our campus and to build a hexagonal-shaped hogan (traditional Diné home) among the shanties constructed by students to protest Apartheid. Upon arrival, he commented that it was his first flight, and that during it he had an epiphany. "No wonder you white people are so messed-up," he said. "You all live in squares!"

  From the onset of relations with the European immigrants, Native Americans have not been self-defined, but constructed as a negative in relation to the white or European protagonists of written and mediated history. Thus Native Americans have the contention of dealing with the insidious construct of being an "Other" in relation to the development and creation of a national identity in the United States. And as outsiders from Indian culture, whether we like it or not, we are part of a what Edward Said calls "communities of interpretation." Said warns that much of what we understand about other cultures, such as Arabs (who have been subjected to the same Wild West myths as Native Americans), is through our second-hand worlds that filter and source information from outside our daily experience: "Between consciousness and existence stand meaning and designs and communication which other men have passed on—first, in human speech itself, and later, by the management of symbols. Symbols focus experience; meaning organizes knowledge, guiding the surface perceptions of an instant no less than aspirations of a lifetime."[32] Accordingly, it is vital that Native American communities be the ones defining and determining the symbols representing their world: "Ending the digital divide in Indian country requires allowing tribal communities to craft their own solutions based on their unique environments and needs. . . . Indian people will achieve equal opportunity for the first time when they participate in shaping their own destiny by getting involved in the leading edge of technological development."[33] But ultimately, because of the level by which new media infuse our lives, I don't believe there is a pure culture in isolation of the greater society, and the reality on the ground with the kinds of kids with whom I've worked is that they live in a hybridized mode of perception; it is not possible to call it living in two worlds, since each world, in itself, is its own conglomeration of realities. I'm reminded of Néstor García Canclini's observation, from his vantage point of the hybridization of Latin American culture, that all cultures are border cultures.[34]

Also of relevance is Gerald Vizner's discussion of "survivance." In short, Vizner argues, "survivance, in the sense of native survivance, is more than survival, more than endurance or mere response; the stories of survivance are an active presence."[35] Survivance is a concept that appears often in new literature about the contemporary state of Native America. It adds a dimension of resistance to the mere concept of survival and "victimry"; it affirms that Native Americans are rather ingenious in their ability to respond to the dominant culture. For example, despite the colonizing effects of education and literacy, it should be strongly noted that Native Americans have a very rich tradition of indigenous literature and media production. Their ability to transform the tools of mental colonization and oppression into empowering acts of literature and art is distinctive, demonstrating "the truism that in situations of extreme oppression, the oppressed of necessity know more about the oppressors' ways than the oppressors understand the ways of those whom they oppress."[36]

As has been demonstrated by the resourceful harnessing of media by Australian Aborigines, communications technology should ultimately be in the service of self-determination, sovereignty, and empowerment. Anthropologist and indigenous media scholar Faye Ginsburg concludes from her work in Australia,

that the social relations built out of indigenous media practices are helping to develop support and sensibilities of indigenous actions for self-determination. Self-representation in media is seen as a crucial part of this process. Indigenous media productions and the activities around them are rendering visible indigenous cultural and historical realities to themselves and the broader societies that have stereotyped or denied them. The transitional social relations built out of these media practices are creating new arenas of cooperation, locally, nationally, and internationally.[37]

Consequently, Native Americans may actually be poised to take great advantage of new communications technologies. Of all the cultural groups I've worked with across the United States, I've noticed that Native Americans get digital media literacy in ways that I believe are unique to their history and culture. It is my sense that, because Native Americans are generationally closer to an oral tradition and have been less conditioned by print literacy than European societies have been, they have the potential to leapfrog us in terms of harnessing digital media. It is increasingly clear from studies of knowledge work that the beneficiaries of new modes of engagement will be those who are most adept at "symbol management." If it's true that the mentality best suited for this activity belongs to those who are visual and spatial thinkers, then it's possible that Native Americans may fare better as future operators of new media systems than those conditioned by print. "This provides us with the intriguing but perhaps no longer so unusual situation of a people's moving rapidly from 'oral' to electronic society, but bypassing print literacy. Attention to the particulars of both the traditional system and accommodation to the imposed one offers insights into the limitations of our unexamined theories of unilineal media evolution."[38] The emergent potential of the social Web (Web 2.0) based on communities and relationships could represent the most positive development of new digital technology for Native Americans and the greater society, enabling a process of organic, self-organizing affinities to develop beyond the traditional power structure:

> Internet, with its particular reliance on visual imagery to be effective, is such that it is not so far removed from traditional forms of Indigenous communication—the sense of community is immediate, given without interpretation by non-Indigenous peoples, except as technicians and facilitators where needed. This may well be one of its main strengths, and the imperative to communicate, grounded in traditions of oral and visual forms of communication may, in fact, be one thing underlying the rapidity with which Indigenous peoples in First World nations have adopted the new technologies.[39]

In closing, I am reminded of what I learned in Kentucky when I was working with white mountain people typically labeled derogatorily as "hillbillies." Although they are not indigenous, I think they experienced something that Native Americans often have had to endure from mainstream society. The Kentuckian's term for do-gooders is *brain eaters*—the social workers, sociologists, and outsiders who are engaged in social engineering that began with Lyndon Johnson's Great Society program, which was designed to lift people out of poverty, but was also very paternalistic. The potential threat of the greater social agenda of digital media education is to produce yet another set of brain eaters without being sensitive to the very real needs of Native American communities, which are still confronting the legacy of colonialism. By taking our cue from the Native insight on the use of cultural symbols, we could also learn to draw a circle around our cultural cross. For we would be remiss not to learn their valuable insight that technology without holism has disastrous consequences. By the way, in a strange twist of fate, the emblem of the circle enclosing the cross also happens to be the astronomical symbol for planet Earth.

Notes

1. Charles Wright Mills, The Cultural Apparatus, in *Power, Politics, and People*, ed. I. L. Horowitz (New York: Oxford University Press, 1963), 405–406.

2. For the purposes of this chapter I am omitting the names of tribes, specific locations, and in some cases the names of tribal officials out of a desire to focus on ideas and to avoid intervening in the delicate political reality of the specific Native American groups with which I have worked. I do this with some trepidation because, on the one hand, there is a tendency of outside scholars to dehumanize Native Americans by not identifying the living beings they write about. On the other hand, inevitably when outsiders intervene, they can generate conflict. Colonized peoples live in divided and conflicted societies. In many cases, there are numerous views, opinions, and factions dealing with the outside world. My goal in this chapter is to focus on concepts without dredging up preexisting political conflicts with specific tribes. I apologize in advance if this approach is offensive to anyone, but in the interest of describing some general ideas, I feel this is the best approach.

3. Victor Masayesva, 6 – RE: Question 2: How Can Young People of Color Balance or Incorporate New Media Technology within Traditional, Urban and Rural Community Contexts? Online posting, October 23, 2006, http://community.macfound.org/openforum. Retrieved October 23, 2006.

4. Donald L. Fixico, *The American Indian Mind in a Linear World* (New York: Routledge, 2003), 15.

5. Ernest Stromberg, Rhetoric and American Indians, in *American Indian Rhetorics of Survivance: Word Medicine, Word Magic*, ed. Ernest Stromberg (Pittsburgh: University of Pittsburgh Press, 2006), 5.

6. Neil Postman, *Technopoly: The Surrender of Culture to Technology* (New York: Vintage Books, 1993), 16.

7. John Taylor Gatto, *Dumbing Us Down: The Hidden Curriculum of Compulsory School* (Gabriola Island: New Society Publishers, 2005), 13.

8. Jacques La Grange, "50 - RE: Do We Need To Be Concerned About How Young People Encounter and Interact With Race and Ethnicity Issues Online and in Other Digital Media Technologies? And What Do Our Histories Teach Us?" Retrieved October 26, 2006. http://community.macfound.org/openforum.

9. Vine Deloria Jr. and Daniel Wildcat, *Power and Place: Indian Education in America* (Golden, CO: Fulcrum Resources, 2001), 19.

10. Sally Hyer, *One House, One Voice, One Heart: Native American Education at the Santa Fe Indian School* (Albuquerque, NM: Museum of New Mexico Press, 1990), 4.

11. Eric Michaels, *Bad Aboriginal Art: Tradition, Media and Technological Horizons* (Minneapolis: University of Minnesota Press, 1994), 82.

12. Karen Swisher and Donna Deyhle, Adapting Instruction to Culture, in *Teaching American Indian Students*, ed. Jon Reyhner (Norman: University of Oklahoma Press, 1994) 86–87.

13. National Indian Education Association and Center for Indian Education, *Preliminary Report on No Child Left Behind in Indian Country*, 2005, 7–8, http://www.niea.org/sa/uploads/policyissues/29.23.NIEANCLBreport_final2.pdf.

14. Deloria and Wildcat, *Power and Place*, 70.

15. Ibid., 75.

16. Ibid., 31–32.

17. Jim Cummins, The Empowerment of Indian Students, in *Teaching American Indian Students*, ed. Jon Reyhner (Norman: University of Oklahoma Press, 1994), 7.

18. Paulo Freire and Donaldo Macedo, *Literacy: Reading the Word & the World* (Westport, CT: Bergin & Garvey, 1987), 30–31.

19. Linda Miller Cleary and Thomas D. Peacock, *Collected Wisdom: American Indian Education* (Boston: Allyn & Bacon, 1998), 188.

20. Swisher and Deyhle, Adapting Instruction to Culture, 86–87.

21. Jon Reyhner and Jeanne Eder, *American Indian Education: A History* (Norman: University of Oklahoma Press, 2004), 322.

22. See Angela M. Haas, Making Online Spaces More Native American to Native American Indians: A Digital Diversity Recommendation, *Computers and Composition Online*, http://www.bgsu.edu/cconline/Haas/index.htm. Retrieved October 30, 2006.

23. Larry J. Zimmerman, Karen P. Zimmerman, and Leonard R. Bruguier, Cyberspace Smoke Signals: New Technologies and Native American Ethnicity, in *Indigenous Cultures in an Interconnected World*, ed. Claire Smith and Graeme K. Ward (Vancouver: University of British Columbia Press, 2000), 86.

24. Deloria and Wildcat, *Power and Place*, 29.

25. Jeanette Armstrong, "Sharing One Skin: Okanagan Community," in *The Case Against the Global Economy*, ed. Jerry Mander and Edward Goldsmith (San Francisco: Sierra Club Books, 1996), 468.

26. Ibid., 469.

27. Jacquelyn Kilpatrick, *Celluloid Indians* (Lincoln: University of Nebraska Press, 1999), xviii.

28. Jerry Mander, Technologies of Globalization, in *The Case against the Global Economy*, ed. Jerry Mander and Edward Goldsmith (San Francisco: Sierra Club Books, 1996), 356–57.

29. I am aware of this relationship because I have been involved with tribal programs that were funded by the Department of Defense and FEMA, but out of respect for the privacy of the tribes involved, they will remain anonymous.

30. Jolene Richard and Gabrielle Tayac, on a placard from the "Our Lives" exhibition at the National Museum of the Native American, Summer 2006.

31. Winona LaDuke, *Recovering the Sacred* (Cambridge, MA: South End Press, 2005).

32. Edward Said, *Covering Islam* (New York: Vintage Books, 1997), 46–47.

33. Thomas Davis and Mark Trebian, Shaping the Destiny of Native People by Ending the Digital Divide, *Educause* (January/February 2001): 46.

34. Nestor García Canclini, *Hybrid Cultures: Strategies for Entering and Leaving Modernity* (Minneapolis: University of Minnesota Press, 1995), 206–63

35. Gerald Vizner, *Fugitive Poses* (Lincoln: University of Nebraska Press, 2000), 15.

36. Stromberg, *Rhetoric and American Indians*, 6.

37. Faye Ginsburg, Embedded Aesthetics: Creating a Discursive Space for Indigenous Media, *Cultural Anthropology* 9, no. 3 (August 1994): 365–82.

38. Michaels, *Bad Aboriginal Art*, 84.

39. Claire Smith, Heather Burke, and Graeme K. Ward, Globalization and Indigenous Peoples: Threat or Empowerment, in *Indigenous Cultures in an Interconnected World*, ed. Claire Smith and Graeme K. Ward (Vancouver: University of British Columbia Press, 2000), 18.

PART III: NEW DIGITAL ARCHETYPES: CYBER HATE, ONLINE GAMING, AND E-HEALTH

Race, Civil Rights, and Hate Speech in the Digital Era

Jessie Daniels

City University of New York—Hunter College, Urban Public Health and Sociology

Introduction

The emergence of the digital era has had unintended consequences for race, civil rights, and hate speech. The notion prevalent in the early days of new media, either that race does not exist on the Internet or that cyberspace represents some sort of halcyon realm of "colorblindness," is a myth. At the same time MCI was airing its infamous commercial proclaiming "there is no race" on the Internet,[1] some were already practiced at adapting white supremacy to the new online environment, creating Web sites that showcase hate speech along with more sophisticated Web sites that intentionally disguise their hateful purpose. Yet, there has been relatively little academic attention focused on racism in cyberspace.[2] Here I take up the issue of racism and white supremacy online with the goal of offering a more nuanced understanding of both racism and digital media, particularly as they relate to youth. Specifically, I address two broad categories of white supremacy online: (1) *overt* hate Web sites that target individuals or groups, showcase racist propaganda, or offer online community for white supremacists; and (2) *cloaked* Web sites that intentionally seek to deceive the casual Web user. I then explore the implications for youth who are, increasingly, growing up immersed in digital media.

Overt hate speech includes the kind of racial epithets and explicitly racist language that are widely regarded as unacceptable public expressions of racism in the contemporary political climate in the United States and throughout much of the world.[3] Cloaked Web sites, on the other hand, are those published by individuals or groups who deliberately disguise a hidden political agenda.[4] With regard to race, cloaked Web sites contain virulent anti-Semitism and hate propaganda not usually explicit or expressly on the surface. But they do reveal their racism several page-layers down, or they provide links to such information. And while arguing intent can be problematic, it is the case that these Web sites intentionally conceal their racism either on the entry page or throughout the Web site. While the two forms of online hate speech (overt and cloaked) may seem disparate, they are both grounded in an epistemology of white supremacy, which seeks to undermine hard-won political battles for racial and ethnic equality by rearticulating an essentialist notion of white racial purity, and an attitude of entitled privilege based on this notion. Most striking is these Web sites' audacious deployment of the rhetoric of civil rights.

At the same time, the epistemology of white supremacy is, as philosopher Charles W. Mills has noted, "an inverted epistemology, an epistemology of ignorance," which produces the ironic outcome that whites in general are "unable to understand the world that they themselves have made."[5] The presence of white supremacy online reinforces this episte-mology of white supremacy offline by allowing whites to retreat from civic engagement and into a whites-only chimera. Thus, the early emergence and persistent presence of white supremacy online calls for multiple literacies: a literacy of digital media and new literacies not merely of "tolerance," but literacies of social justice that offer a depth of understanding about race, racism, and multiple intersecting forms of oppression.

For young people today, there is nothing "new" about digital media; for them, digital media have always existed. According to a July 2005 report by researchers at the Pew Internet & American Life Project, 87 percent of youth aged 12–17 now use the Internet, which amounts to nearly 21 million youth.[6] A report by the Kaiser Family Foundation concerning eight-to eighteen-year-olds released the same year found that "Generation M" (for media), makes extensive and overlapping use of all kinds of media, spending six to six-and-a-half hours a day engaged in some kind of media use.[7] Whether accessing the Internet through a desktop computer or connecting through short message services (SMS) via mobile phones, digital media are ubiquitous in many young people's lives. Futurist and Internet pioneer Howard Rheingold has observed that "search engines have replaced libraries" for young people in the digital age, and indeed they have.[8] This has real consequences for race, civil rights, and hate speech, because it means that the first, perhaps the *only*, place that young people go to "do research" about race is the Internet. Whether youth of color are looking for information about the history and political struggles connected to their racial and ethnic heritages, or white youth are looking to find out more about diverse "others," or youth of whatever ethnicity are searching out clues about how to craft their own identities, often the first and only information destination is to a search engine to look for information online. Guiding young people's development of a new set of literacy skills to evaluate this pervasive digital environment critically is a key challenge facing parents, educators, scholars, and activists in the twenty-first century. However, youth's acquisition of digital media literacy alone is not sufficient for addressing the new white supremacy online; it is also necessary to help young people develop critical thinking about racism in digital media environments.

White supremacy in the United States, as I use the term here, is a central organizing prin-ciple of culture, politics, and the economy rather than merely an isolated social movement.[9] In previous research, I noted that there are striking similarities between extremist rhetoric and more mainstream expressions of white supremacy,[10] and research by others has con-firmed this.[11] Joe Feagin has written extensively about this and what he calls "the white racist frame."[12] In response to a query about the connection between new media and his concept of the "white racist frame" during a recent MacArthur Foundation–sponsored online forum, Feagin's comments were instructive and bear quoting at length:

This framing of society goes back to at least the 1600s. It is nearly four centuries old now. This nation was founded in extensive slavery, and those whites that founded it soon rationalized that racial oppression (enslavement of Africans and killing of Indians) with this well-developed white racial frame. That frame, then and now, is full of racist stereotypes (such as lazy and dumb African Americans, uncivilized Indians, white culture is civilized and superior, etc), prejudices, and emotions that have been perpetuated by all forms of mass media since the first century of slavery. (We had 246 years of slavery in our first 258 years after the founding of Jamestown. VA in 1607; this was followed by nearly 100 years of legal segregation from 1870s to late 1960s). Thus, we have only been an officially "free" country that is free of legal racial apartheid, since the last civil rights law went into effect in 1969. About 90 percent of our history has been one of overt and extreme racial oppression. Ten percent has been free. The early mass media spreading the white racist frame (which was and is white supremacist in many ways) included ministers speaking from pulpits and early pamphlets and newspapers. Later on in the 1900s many new magazines came in, then radio in the 1920s, and television by the 1950s. Then, the email system and the Internet [emerged] in the 1990s. Each new technology has mostly just extended the ability of those, mostly whites, interested in spreading that white racist frame to more people. It has not changed the white racist frame itself.[13]

If most adult whites are not aware of this long history of white supremacy embedded in the institutions of the United States; what, then, can we expect of their children? If they think of racism at all, many whites think of racism as a social problem rooted in a distant past, and located mostly in the South. They regard the post–Civil Rights era of colorblindness as a period in which the United States solved the issue of racism, led by enlightened white Northerners who battled ignorant white Southerners in order to liberate poor blacks. Today, too many white liberals embrace the belief that any lingering racial differences and racist consequences are rooted in economic class, and therefore are "not really" about racism. However, people of color have a very different experience of racism and white supremacy. For most people of color, regardless of class background or position, living with everyday racism is a shared group experience that is part of the toll society extracted from living in a white-dominated society. Examples of these dissimilar experiences with race abound, but perhaps the arena of criminal justice highlights this duality most aptly. Between 1992 and 2001, police brutality complaints in New York City rose 62 percent; approximately 80–97 percent of these victims were people of color, while the overwhelming majority of the officers involved were white. In addition, in 75 percent of the cases where the police killed someone, the person killed was unarmed.[14] And these alarming experiences result in very different contexts of race and racism. So when I use the term *white supremacy* here, I mean a kind of tenacious white supremacy that is cemented in the very architecture of the culture and political structures of the United States. Given this level of structural, systemic white supremacy, it should not be surprising that overt racism, especially racist speech, has found both an ease of expression and a broader audience in the United States via the Internet.

Overt Hate Speech Online and Youth

Hate speech is easiest to see and examine online in its most overt forms. In the following section, I sketch the contours of three distinct articulations of overt hate speech online and the consequences for youth. First, I explore an instance of a woman who was targeted by a white supremacist hate site. Second, I discuss Don Black's long-running Stormfront.org; then I turn to the tactics of committed extremists who use both the public features of the Web to showcase hate, and the quasi-private features of the Internet for what Michael Whine refers to as "communication, command and control."[15] Finally, I take up the issue of cloaked Web sites.

Hate Speech OL, Hate IRL
Hate speech online (OL) can have very real consequences in real life (IRL). In fact, it "offers a new way to harass women and people of color, including youth of color."[16] Take, for example, the illustrative case of Bonnie Jouhari, a white mother of a biracial child who was harassed, forced from her home, stalked, and terrorized for years by a white supremacist. Jouhari, an employee of a fair housing organization in the United States, worked to fulfill the mission of the housing organization and advocated for nondiscriminatory housing practices;

this apparently enraged a white supremacist. In March of 1998, a white supremacist Web site in the United States began posting pictures of Jouhari's workplace exploding amid animated .gif flames. The Web site featuring Jouhari was modified a few months later to include hate speech attacking Jouhari's child, describing her as a "mongrel." Soon after, a car began regularly following Jouhari home, she received harassing phone calls at work and at home, and she has moved several times to get away from this ongoing threat to her life and the life of her child.[17]

The hate-filled targeting of an individual as in this instance is not unique. Similarly, Fred Phelps' hate site (www.godhatesfags.com) features animated .gif flames surrounding a picture of murdered hate-crime victim Matthew Shepard, with a daily counter marking Matthew's "number of days in hell." While the Web site in this case appeared after Shepard's murder and so did not contribute directly to his death, Phelps' rhetoric serves to justify similar hate crimes, and is certainly a source of ongoing harassment for Dennis and Judy Shepard, Matthew's surviving parents. The Web site threatening Bonnie Jouhari and her daughter received over 97,000 visits in a three-year time period. Thus, the Internet in both these instances functions as a mechanism of harassment and as a force multiplier, expanding the reach of that harassment.[18] If Jouhari's case had occurred in any one of a number of European nations—say, Germany or Norway—she would have had legal recourse under antiracism laws.

In 2002, a Norwegian citizen was sentenced to prison for posting racist and anti-Semitic propaganda on a Web site, even though the server for the Web site was outside Norway.[19] Since her case happened in the United States, which has no comparable antiracism statutes, Jouhari's attempts to obtain assistance from local, state, and federal law enforcement and other agencies have proven futile. Jouhari and her daughter have moved several times, including cross-country, and continue to be the target of these online threats and offline harassment.[20] The experience of Bonnie Jouhari is distressing on two fronts. First, it illustrates the way hate speech online can—and does—have real consequences for peoples' lives. Her position as a relatively powerless member of society (a woman and a mother of a biracial child) disadvantages her both as one who is a vulnerable target for hate speech and as one whose attempts to get protection from the legal system has proven ineffective. Second, Jouhari's inability to get legal protection from online hate speech illustrates the frustrations with and consequences of a judicial system that, by upholding First Amendment protections, also functions to sustain and extend white supremacy.

Fortunately, it seems that most youth online today do not face the kind of targeted harassment that Bonnie Jouhari and her daughter faced. However, there is growing apprehension about the all-too-common practice of schoolyard bullying moving online. In what some have termed "cyberbullying,"[21] bullies target other young people for online harassment based on physical characteristics (like size, disability, or age) or social identities (such as gender, sexuality, race, or ethnicity). While the initial research in this area suggests that the targets of harassment are most often women and girls,[22] the fact is that the perpetrators of cyberbullying tend to be *white males*, both kids and adults. Similarly, in both the Shepard and Jouhari cases, the online harassers are white males.

Don Black's Stormfront.org
One of the earliest and longest continually published Web sites of any kind is Don Black's www.Stormfront.org. With its tagline "White Pride World Wide," the site has been a portal for online white supremacist activity since 1999 (see Figure 1). Don Black is a former Grand

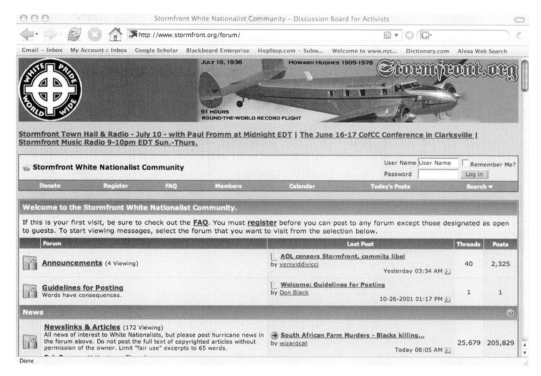

Figure 1
Don Black's "White Pride World Wide," www.stormfront.org.

Wizard of the Ku Klux Klan, and spent time in federal prison for an armed attack. Using job training he received in prison, Black has worked since his release primarily as a computer software engineer based in West Palm Beach, Florida. A follower of David Duke (and actually married to Duke's ex-wife, Chloe), Black has long been an advocate for "mainstreaming" the white supremacist movement, and the Internet is his preferred medium for doing so.[23] His first and primary online presence is Stormfront.org, and it has long been organized primarily as a discussion forum with multiple thematic message boards. The boards make it possible for members to post, read, and respond to others. This feature distinguishes Stormfront.org in significant and qualitative ways from sites that function as one-way transfers of information, such as the site that targeted Jouhari and her child.

While the possibility of white supremacists posting on message boards may suggest an onslaught of racist slurs, this is not the case at Stormfront.org. The tone of the rhetoric is quite muted; members are warned against using racial epithets or slurs, and are specifically prohibited from describing anything illegal or posting violent threats. Strategies like these, along with other rather standard online community-building tactics, have proven quite effective for Stormfront.org. As T. K. Kim puts it, writing for Southern Poverty Law Center's *Intelligence Report*:

Using everything from good manners to "white scholarships" to such catchy gimmicks as highlighting its members' birthdays, . . . [Don Black has] built something that very few people on the entire Internet have—a genuine and very large cyber-community.[24]

Further evidence of Black's savvy with online community building can be seen in a few of the relevant statistics on the site's registered users. In January 2002, Stormfront.org had 5,000 registered users. A year later, the number of users reached 11,000; and a year after that, in early 2004, there were 23,000 registered users. By January 2005, the number of registered users hit about 42,000, and it topped 52,566 in June of that year (the latest date for which numbers are available). Traffic to the site estimated by Alexa (the Web monitoring service) ranked Stormfront.org in June 2005 as the 8,682nd most visited site on the Internet—a rank well above that of most civil rights sites.[25]

Even though this sort of online community building can create and sustain life-affirming rituals,[26] it also offers the possibility of community rituals that affirm white identity and white supremacy.[27] As many online community experts will attest, it is no small accomplishment to sustain a community this large for this length of time. One of the first rules of operation is having a precision about what type of community this is to be, why it is being built, and for whom it is being built.[28] Don Black has exercised this sort of clarity of vision about his online community building in that he has constructed Stormfront.org as a community with the explicit purpose of "defending the white race," primarily *for* white men who feel disaffected *as white men*.[29] This form of community building relies on "a virtual tribal identity of white masculinity to attract white men," who define themselves and their online community by their vocal opposition to minorities, particularly Jews.[30] It is certainly not the case that white women are any less racist or any less implicated in the system of white supremacy than white men.[31] However, given the overlapping hierarchies of gender and race which convey cultural messages that code technology as a "male" domain of expertise[32] and an economic system in which whites hold disproportionate access to technological resources,[33] the net result is that white men have been at the forefront of establishing white supremacy online.

Not Just One "Web": Showcasing Hate in Public and C³ in Private

For committed extremists, the Internet has been useful for showcasing racist propaganda and for what Michael Whine refers to as "communication, command and control" (C³).[34] The distinction here between the capacity for public showcasing and the ability to communicate in quasi-private ways through chat rooms, e-mail lists, and encrypted and/or password-protected Web spaces highlights what many commentators have noted are the limitations of using monolithic terms like "the Internet" or "the Web," or even "cyberspace."[35] In fact, there is not just one "Web," but rather multiple forms of communication media contained under that umbrella term, some of them public and some of them quasi-private or anonymous.[36]

Using the public Web to showcase racist propaganda has certainly been the most common application of digital media by extremists. Many of the old-school white supremacist groups that were active before the emergence of the digital era have simply moved their rhetoric virtually unaltered from print-based newsletters to Web sites. A prime example of this shift is Tom Metzger, a former Ku Klux Klan leader, a television repairman by trade, and a one-time candidate for Congress.[37] After a falling out with the Klan about political ideology, Metzger broke with the KKK and created his own hate group, "WAR," an acronym for "White Aryan Resistance." WAR featured a more radical analysis of political economy than the KKK, and dropped all references to Christianity. To spread the message of WAR, Metzger created both print and broadcast vehicles: a newsletter, entitled *WAR*, a cable access television show called "Race and Reason," and a radio broadcast.[38] All these media are now showcased and available via Metzger's Web site, "The Insurgent" located at the URL www.resist.com (see Figure 2).

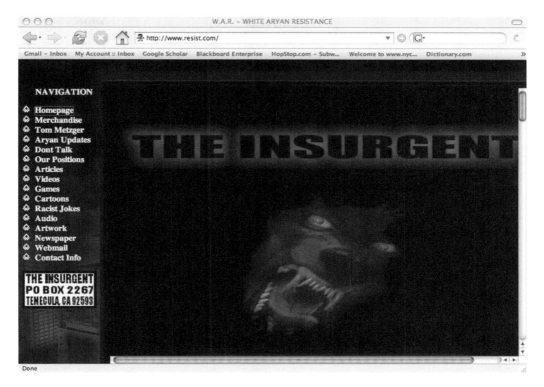

Figure 2
Tom Metzger's "The Insurgent," www.resist.com.

The Web site includes position statements about a variety of topics, including immigration, international conflicts (most often involving Israel), homosexuality, and women. Prominently featured on the Web site is a link to purchase Aryan-branded merchandise (t-shirts, caps, key chains). The merchandise page includes the use of some forms that require a user login, but to actually place an order, the end user has to print out and mail in an order form with a check or money order. Aside from these forms, most of the features on the Web site are primarily static, and function as one-way transfers of information.

One of the noteworthy features on Metzger's Web site—because it is unique to the digital media environment intended to appeal to youth, and was not available during the print-era—is the selection of hate-filled computer games like *Drive By 2*, where players can experience *What It Is Like in the Ghetto*, *African Detroit Cop*, *Watch Out Behind You Hunter*, a game where players are instructed to "shoot the fags before they rape you," and a game called *Border Patrol*, with the tag line, "Don't let those Spics cross our border" (see Figure 3). The games allow individual users to download and play the games on their desktop PCs. In addition to being violently racist and homophobic, the computer games are also deeply gendered in ways that are consistent with more mainstream games; that is, the games socialize boys into misogyny and exclude girls from all but the most stereotypical roles.[39] Research clearly demonstrates that adolescents are more likely to play computer games than adults; among adolescents, boys are more likely than girls to be gamers.[40] Adolescents are also

Figure 3
Metzger's hate-filled computer games.

significantly more likely than adults to say that violence is their favorite part of gaming.[41] Metzger has included these computer games on his Web site to appeal to his core audience: young white males. However, Metzger's computer games are crude bits of gaming code that barely adhere to standards in gaming[42] and seem unlikely to meet the minimum demands of sophisticated gamers who have grown up playing *Everquest*, *Mortal Kombat*, and *Grand Theft Auto*. Without an evaluation of his internal Web site statistics, it is impossible to know how effective Metzger's racist games are, but there are indications these games have been unsuccessful in reaching a wider audience, since he recently removed them from the site.

Visitors to the site are invited to sign up for a listserv and to get an e-mail address with an "@resist.com" suffix, hosted by Metzger himself. This type of feature points to the quasi-private Web technology of e-mail listservs, password-protected Web spaces, and encrypted communications. These are only "quasi-private" because the privacy used in these sorts of communication tools is easily breached; and, I use this term to distinguish these modes of Internet-facilitated communication from the World Wide Web. It is this use of encrypted Internet technology that Michael Whine intends when he refers to "communication, command, and control" used by extremists and terrorists.[43] The capacity of the Internet to facilitate relatively inexpensive means of communication between and among people in dispersed geographic regions of the world is certainly one of the primary benefits white supremacists see in the medium. Further, the fact that this communication can be encrypted and anonymous is appealing for many white supremacists,[44] although certainly not all, such as Metzger, who clearly relishes the spotlight.[45] Ironically, at the same time that anonymity is appealing for some, networked communication also reinforces what Back has referred to as a *translocal whiteness*[46]; that is, a form of white identity not tied to a specific location, but reimagined as an identity that transcends geography and is linked via a global network.

The idea of "command and control" is based on a military style of leadership in which a designated authority-figure "commands and controls" troops or followers. While encrypted communications provide the capacity for using the communication technology for command and control purposes, the reality is that this potentiality is mitigated against in some very real ways by fissures in the movement along ideological, often religious, lines.[47] Metzger's split from the KKK over religion was no small matter within the movement, and religion is still a hotly contested issue that countervails the power of the communication technology.[48] The "command and control" model is further weakened by the strategy of leaderless resistance advocated by other white supremacists. Metzger describes the philosophy behind "The Insurgent" in this way:

THE INSURGENT is a NETWORK of highly motivated White Racists. Each person is an individual leader in his or her own right. THE INSURGENT promotes the Lone Wolf tactical concept. Made up of individuals and small cells. Each INSURGENT associate serves the Idea that what's good for the White European Race is the highest virtue. Whatever is bad for the White European Race is the ultimate Evil. Each Associate works at whatever his or her talents allow.[12]

The notion of a "leaderless resistance," in which small, covert cells acting independently work toward one shared political goal, has been popularized by another white supremacist, Louis Beam, and widely adopted within the movement.[49] The presence of quasi-private hate speech online, and the sort of overt hate speech that Metzger showcases, is disturbing because of the potential for translating into, or justifying, violence; however, the connection between hate speech and hate crimes is far from clearly established. Perhaps more germane for those interested in youth and digital media is the possibility that young people might stumble upon this sort of hate speech.

The threat of inadvertent exposure to overt hate speech is a misplaced cause for apprehension, but one that gets reiterated often. This statement is typical of this sort of alarm: "Millions of people are being exposed to virulent anti-Semitism and hate propaganda at the flick of a switch on their computers."[50] This sort of assessment misjudges the harm of hate speech online. In a critique of this assertion, Best writes:

Who are these millions of people who are somehow running accidentally into "virulent anti-Semitism and hate propaganda?" I have been online since the 1980s and have never seen such hate material on the net. I am quite certain I can seek it out. But it does not come at the "flick of a switch." I would view this material only because I actively sought it.[51]

Best makes a number of excellent points here. First, it is highly improbable that a casual Web user would stumble upon the kind of virulent anti-Semitism, racism, and homophobia of Metzger's Resist.com or even Black's Stormfront.org. The "flick of a switch" metaphor suggests a misapprehension of the way the Web works; the only "switch" flicked is the one to turn on a computer, and most of these are now buttons to be pressed rather than switches to be flicked. It also belies the presence of quasi-private Web spaces that are nearly impossible to stumble upon inadvertently. Beyond that, the notion that a young person could stumble upon such hate speech fails to take into account that there are a number of steps required to find information online, usually involving a search engine with specific search terms typed in. Best's assessment that he is "certain" he could seek out hate speech is a more accurate reference to how one encounters this material online. A few keystrokes in any search engine can yield hundreds of results for hate speech. However, I want to suggest a reevaluation of Best's claim that he would view this material "only because I actively sought it." This statement, like the "flip of a switch" metaphor, suggests a misunderstanding about the way white supremacist rhetoric operates online. There is credible evidence to suggest that the unsuspecting Web user may actually happen upon white supremacist Web sites when looking specifically for legitimate civil rights information. Again, the implications for youth have a special pertinence here.

Covert Hate Speech: Cloaked Web Sites

Unsuspecting Internet users looking for civil rights information online may inadvertently encounter white supremacist rhetoric through *cloaked* Web sites. Indeed, a number of these sites deliberately seek to disguise the racist motives of the Web site's author by using carefully chosen domain names, deceptive graphic user interface (GUI) and language that is less strident than what appears in overt hate speech online. One example of a cloaked site is www.AmericanCivilRightsReview.com, a Web site owned and operated by Frank Weltner, a member of the National Alliance, a neo-Nazi organization. Weltner also maintains the hate Web site www.Jewwatch.com.[52] The animated .gifs and crude graphic design of AmericanCivilRightsReview.com give this site away as a first-generation Web site (featuring unappealing background colors and default font settings that were characteristic of early Web sites of 1993–1995) created by an amateur, but the racism and anti-Semitism of the site are cloaked in fairly sophisticated ways. For instance, on an interior page image-linked through a reproduction of a Currier & Ives painting, the author describes the "high self-esteem for many slaves" and goes on to make an argument for slavery as an "idyllic" social system. The argument in favor of slavery is not new, but the sophistication comes in the way Weltner chooses to make this argument, which is to draw on oral histories of former slaves recorded by WPA workers in the 1930s. He then compiles selectively chosen excerpts on a page entitled "Forgotten Black Voices," such as this quote from Adeline, 91: "I wants to be in heaven with all my white folks, just to wait on them and love them, and serve them, sorta like I did in slavery time." With this site, Weltner is one good graphic designer away from having a much more pernicious Web site for, while the annoying audio file and rudimentary graphic design betray the amateur origins, the racism is harder to discern when it is cloaked by a recondite, if sinister, use of oral history source material.

Another example of a cloaked site is IHR.org, the online home of the Institute for Historical Review. Here, the GUI is much more polished than on Weltner's site and there are no audio files or animated .gifs. The rhetoric on the site is presented, at first glance, as dedicated to exploring "truth and free speech." There are books and tapes available for sale on the left and right sides of the page, and down the center is a list of brief, paragraph-long descriptions of various news stories, each accompanied by a hyperlink and a photo. Across the top is a row of links to other pages on the site. The structure, graphic design, and text on this page look completely benign; of course, they are not. IHR.org, as critically aware readers will know, is an organization that seeks to deny the existence of the Holocaust and is published by Mark Weber out of Orange County, California. IHR.org touts itself as a source of scholarly

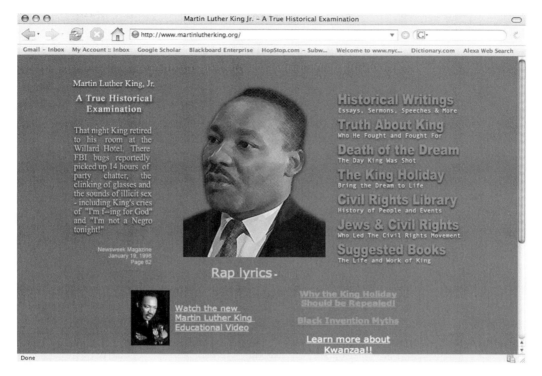

Figure 4
Cloaked Web site, www.martinlutherking.org.

information and claims that "countless scholars, researchers and journalists have turned to the IHR for solid and reliable information" (http://www.ihr.org/main/about.shtml). The Web users who are already aware of the mission and deceptive nature of the Institute for Historical Review will not be misled by the cloaked Web site but, for the uninitiated and many youths, it is very likely that the combination of professional-looking graphic design and non–extremist-sounding rhetoric can be disarming and delusory.

Don Black, the white supremacist discussed above who maintains Stormfront.org, also publishes a number of cloaked sites, including one with the URL www.martinlutherking.org (see Figure 4). At first glance, this Web site appears to be a tribute site to Dr. Martin Luther King Jr., albeit one intended for a younger audience as indicated by the link at the top, "Attention Students: Try our MLK Pop Quiz," and the one further down the page indicating "Rap Lyrics." Using a standard search engine and the search terms "Martin Luther King" this Web site regularly appears third or fourth in the results returned by Google. Before even viewing the content of this site, the URL makes it appear to be legitimate, in part because the main Web reference is made up of only the domain name "martinlutherking," and the URL ends with the suffix ".org." There are a number of clues that something is amiss. The first clue is the description of the Web site that appears in the search engine returns and on the Web site itself: "A True Historical Examination"; the use of the word "true" here suggests an "uncovering" of a heretofore untold truth about Dr. King.

Once on the Web site, there are a number of additional indications as to the source of the information, including a link in the right margin that reads "Jews and Civil Rights," which is suggestive of anti-Semitism.[53] Clicking on that link leads to a page that more than suggests anti-Semitism, as it includes a chapter called "Jews, Communism and Civil Rights" from white supremacist David Duke's book *My Awakening*. For the astute Web user, this is a giveaway about the ideological orientation of the Web site's author. Still, for many younger or less experienced Web users, as well as those unfamiliar with recent U.S. racial political history, the name "David Duke" may have no resonance. Going back to the first page, there is one more clue if a casual Web user wanted to know the origin of this "True Historical Examination." Scrolling down to the very bottom of the first page, there is a link that reads "Hosted by Stormfront," and clicking on that link takes the user to Don Black's "White Pride World Wide" at Stormfront.org. Although these clues may seem fairly obvious to some Web users (such as readers of this volume), others can easily miss them. Thus, unsuspecting visitors to the site who have little Web experience but are aware of how white supremacy works in the United States, may very well be familiar with "David Duke" or be suspicious of language referring to "Jews and Civil Rights," and therefore understand that the site is not actually intended as a tribute to Dr. King but rather aims to undermine the civil rights cause.

The presence of cloaked sites raises important questions about youth and digital media; one of these questions has to do with whether someone could "stumble upon" virulent anti-Semitism or racism online. It is not only possible, but also likely that casual or novice Web users could inadvertently come across white supremacist rhetoric while looking for legitimate civil rights information. The cloaked site www.martinlutherking.org is a case in point. Using the Web monitoring service Alexa, I charted the traffic of this cloaked site (see Figure 5) and to the legitimate civil rights Web site for The King Center, run by the King family in Atlanta (see Figure 6). I also charted them comparatively (see Figure 7). The estimated traffic for both sites is in the tens of millions in terms of number of hits; and, the traffic patterns for the two sites are strikingly similar. Not surprisingly, traffic to both sites peaks annually around the time of Martin Luther King Day (toward the end of January), and during Black History Month (February). There is also one noticeable difference in traffic between the two sites and this is evident when looking at the graphs side-by-side. Here, there is evidence of a spike in traffic to the King Center site (the legitimate site) on January 31, 2005, the day Mrs. King died. Other than this one, rather dramatic, difference the traffic patterns for the two sites are remarkably comparable. The patterns are so similar, in fact, that it suggests that Web users who are looking for legitimate civil rights information may very well be ending up at the cloaked white supremacist site.

Once at these cloaked sites, it is possible that unsuspecting Web users will find this disorienting. In a series of experiments and interviews, when asked to search for information on Martin Luther King, I discovered that even high-achieving and Internet-savvy adolescents had difficulty deciphering whether this cloaked Web site was a trustworthy source of information about Dr. King.[54] For example, one seventeen-year-old respondent woman had this to say when asked to evaluate the cloaked site:

It looks good to me. I mean this is just about how people tried to undermine him (referring to a quote on the first page). And, this (referring to the links to the right of the page) just look like his writings, but I can't tell if these are *his* writings or writings *about* him. Oh, and this looks good (clicking on the link, "King's Dissertation"). I like this because it's got primary sources. (Interview, January, 2006)

As this young woman browsed the cloaked Web site, she displayed a number of advanced skills associated with long hours spent surfing, including quick use of the mouse button

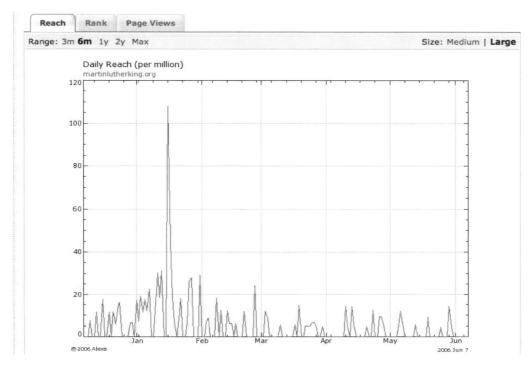

Figure 5
Estimated reach in millions for www.martinlutherking.org. Source: Alexa, Web Trafficking Service (www.alexa.com).

and a deft ability with the right click button. And, as a high school junior, she did know that primary sources are important. However, she did not recognize this site as something published by a white supremacist, but instead read it as a legitimate source of information about Dr. King. The link to "King's Dissertation" is not, in fact, a link to a primary source for King's writing, but is, instead, a rehashing of the charge that he plagiarized parts of his dissertation. When asked to refer to the page containing information on David Duke's book *My Awakening*, she replied that Duke did not look familiar, but his (vanity) press "Free Speech Press, does sound familiar" (Interview, January, 2006). This young woman, like other adolescents in this same study, was largely unable to evaluate critically or to distinguish between cloaked sites when they were paired with legitimate civil rights Web sites. What this makes clear is that it takes either a familiarity with white supremacy or a fairly experienced, critically engaged Web user (or both) to recognize cloaked Web sites quickly and distinguish them from legitimate ones.

New White Supremacy Online

Given the presence of white supremacy online, many parents and other adults involved with youth express trepidation about the dangers of the new white supremacy online for youth engaged with digital media.[55] Primarily, there are two questions that are most commonly

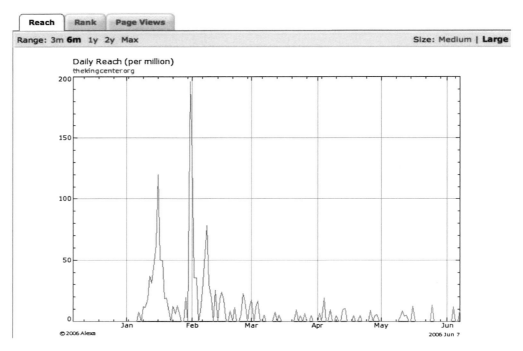

Figure 6
Estimated reach in millions for www.thekingcenter.org. Source: Alexa, Web Trafficking Service (www.alexa.com).

raised with regard to white supremacy online. The first has to do with political mobilization: Can neofascist organizations like white supremacists use the Internet to mobilize a large, viable political threat to our democracy? The second, related to the first, is this: Can people, particularly young people, be persuaded to join white supremacist movements via the Internet?

New digital media—like blogs, wikis, and such mobile computing technology as SMS—have made formerly obscure activist subcultures more accessible and created new avenues of political participation for those who are looking for such avenues.[56] When it comes to political mobilization, the Internet has demonstrated just how powerfully it works as an amplifier of many messages, values, and ideas. People who are interested in particular ideas can connect using the Internet and, in this way, the Internet "amplifies" those connections and strengthens networks of like-minded people.[57] For extremist white supremacists, like others in obscure subcultures, the Internet provides a relatively inexpensive venue for widespread communication without gatekeepers.[58] Whether or not this wider availability of white supremacy online will facilitate greater political mobilization for strengthening the movement remains a question under investigation. Among those who have taken up this question, the assessment of Jeffery Kaplan and his colleagues comes closest to posing an answer:

Internet or no Internet, barring some cataclysmic development, WAR, [and similar organizations] ...currently seeking to take advantage of the new technology are unlikely to become serious

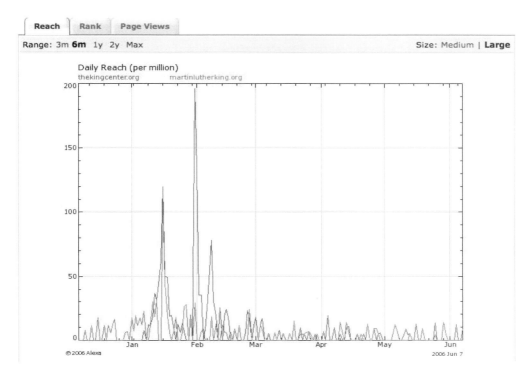

Figure 7

Comparative reach in millions for the cloaked and the legitimate sites. Source: Alexa Web Service (www.alexa.com).

political contestants. Nevertheless, the Internet does furnish them with a link, a way of circumventing the gatekeepers of the other channels of mass communication.[59]

A serious consequence of participatory media is its accessibility and availability to specialist and nonspecialist users alike. And as a result of this open system, some with nefarious goals and agendas will join in and create their own suspect content. In analyzing what this means for digital media learning and youth, it is important to parse the actual harm from the potential threat. The likelihood that Don Black's or Tom Metzger's organization could become a serious political contender is, in my view, remote. However, the issue of communicating without gatekeepers is significant for the epistemology of white supremacy online and a topic to which I will return. For the moment, let me continue addressing the issue of why the possibility of a larger political mobilization by white supremacists remains distant, but a concern nevertheless.

To effect change, social movement organizations must mobilize resources, such as attracting financial backing, garnering media coverage, establishing organizational structure, and forming political alliances with those in power.[60] The Internet is an important new tool for mobilizing these resources, because it increases the speed at which resources can be mobilized and then dispersed for accomplishing movement goals.[61] Adopting a resource mobilization framework, Hara and Estrada compared the use of the Web by Stormfront.org and MoveOn.org, a Web site for liberal-to-progressive political activity.[62] Their findings

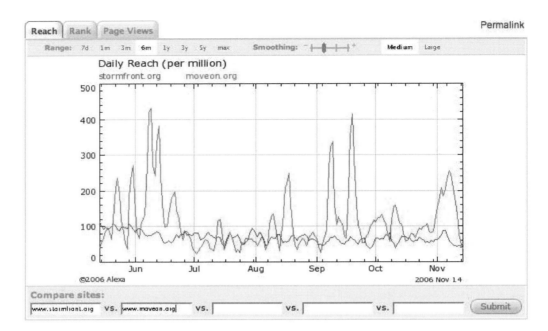

Figure 8
Comparative reach in millions for Stormfront and MoveOn. Source: Alexa Web Service (www.alexa.com).

suggest that while there are some similarities between these two Web sites in terms of attempts at political mobilization, they are not equally effective. They find that MoveOn.org is more popular and more effective than Stormfront.org for a variety of reasons. For example, they point to the use of other media, such as print journalism and network news, to drive traffic to the Web sites and garner support for the respective movements. Both Stormfront.org and MoveOn.org have been featured in mainstream media reports, yet MoveOn.org has been much more aggressive in seeking out this media attention and, Hara and Estrada argue, it is this strategy, rather than content alone, which has enabled MoveOn to sustain a broad-based political mobilization that Stormfront has been unable to achieve.[63] The broader appeal of MoveOn.org is borne out using other data (see Figure 8).

Comparing the Web traffic to the two sites,[64] the figures confirm Hara's and Estrada's analysis of MoveOn.org as having a broader appeal than Stormfront.org. As alarming as the 52,000+ registered users at Stormfront are, the fact that MoveOn remains consistently more popular than Stormfront should be heartening for those who are committed to democratic ideals. However, the fact that there are that many people interested enough in white supremacy to register at Stormfront should give those interested in social justice great pause to consider which civil rights goals have been achieved and which goals remain unfilled. But what of those 52,000+ registered users? Are these people being recruited into the white supremacist movement?

To better understand the issue of recruitment into white supremacist groups via the Internet, it is important to distinguish between "supporters" and "members" in social movement organizations. Unlike traditional groups that have formal organizational structures including "leaders" and "members," sociologists have conceptualized new social movements as consisting not of members, but of more informal, loosely organized social networks of "supporters." This is an important distinction for talking about the sort of peripheral involvement of many people in social movements online. For example, in a well-grounded quantitative study of both online and offline environmental activists in the Netherlands, researchers found that online actions were more popular among those who did not take part in any traditional street actions, and thus they suggest that online activism may be an "easy entry point" for more peripheral participants.[65] Whether or not peripheral online participants inevitably, or eventually, become supporters or more involved activists and what the mechanisms of that evolution might be remain unclear. Online communities rather famously suffer from "participation inequality," in which an estimated 90 percent of those in any given community do not actively participate, but instead "lurk" (or read without posting).[66] In terms of the 52,000+ registered users at Stormfront.org, it is useful to think of a certain percentage of these users variously as "devoted members," "supporters," "peripheral participants," and "lurkers."[67] While I do not want to diminish the importance of those 52,000 registered users, I think that regarding them as movement members who have been "recruited" is to reverse the online dynamic. The underlying issue, and the much more troublesome one, is not that Don Black is necessarily "recruiting," but that people are *seeking out* Stormfront and the message of "White Pride World Wide." This speaks to the existence of an embedded and internal white supremacy that is built into the culture, rather than an extremist one external to the core culture. The fact that some fifty years after the civil rights movement there are 52,000+ registered users at Stormfront suggests that the message of white supremacy, far from being an anachronism, still resonates.

While a number of writers have asserted that the Internet is a *potential* site for recruiting young people to join white supremacist groups, these claims are largely unsupported by empirical evidence, and instead play on parents' fears about their children's online activities. For example, in an article for the *Psychiatric News*, Lynne Lamberg writes: "Hate Web sites aggressively pursue impressionable children and teenagers."[68] And, tying this fear to another, she adds: "Surveys show parents worry most about children's access to Internet sex sites and that many parents know little about hate Web sites."[69] The handful of research studies that do take up the empirical question of whether, and precisely how, white supremacists might recruit young people online find little data to support the claim of the Internet as a recruiting tool.[70] For example, in their important study of the effects of "persuasive storytelling" of hate sites on adolescents, Lee and Leets found only minimal effects on adolescents who were infrequently exposed to explicit hate messages.[71] By design, their research did not explore the effects on adolescents who might have repeated exposure to such messages, nor how adolescents might become exposed to these messages on the Internet in the first place.

In his seven-year ethnography of white supremacist groups in the Pacific Northwest region of the United States, Blazak found that in face-to-face interactions the groups used "red flags of strain to guide recruiting activity."[72] Among these "red flags" are four main areas of strain: racial/ethnic (shifts to multicultural curricula), gender (feminist activist groups), heterosexuality (gay pride events), and economic (factory layoffs).[73] Youths, most often young white males, experiencing cultural alienation or anomie[74] because shifts in any of these areas of strain are susceptible to recruitment and targeted by white supremacist groups. As Blazak describes it, this is a years-long process that happens almost entirely offline, in face-to-face social gatherings. The transformation from "white boys" to "terrorist men" also makes clear the ways gender and sexuality, and specifically heteronormative masculinity, are central to white supremacist discourse and recruitment.[75] This kind of young, white male alienation predates the advent of digital media; and to locate the harm in this, we need look no further than to the 168 people killed at the Murrah Federal Building in Oklahoma City.

For those concerned about youth and digital media, there is a very real possibility that alienated young white men may direct their frustration at those perceived to be "others," whether based on race, gender, sexual orientation, or the combination of one or more of these identities. The potential harm in the presence of white supremacy *online* is that it is easier for already-alienated young white males to seek out validation for their discontent. For youth of color, for women and girls, for gays and lesbians, the potential harm is in real life, just as it was (and is) for Bonnie Jouhari and her child. The key factors that trigger this kind of alienation, including the introduction of multicultural curricula, feminist or gay/lesbian groups organizing, as well as economic changes such as layoffs, develop separately from digital media, but may be amplified by it, and suggest that the root cause lies in the epistemology of white supremacy. This inverted epistemology of ignorance produces the ironic outcome that whites, in general, are "unable to understand the world that they themselves have made."[76] Thus, the small number of straight white men who create hate speech online, and the many thousands more who actively seek it out, constitute a privileged population sector in terms of race, gender, sexuality, and class (certainly within a global context); yet, these privileged white men end up identifying as an oppressed minority group. This is the very essence of the epistemology of white supremacy.

Epistemology of White Supremacy and Hate Speech Online

Epistemologies of race, how we know what we say we know about race and racism, are rooted in profoundly different experiences for whites and for people of color, wherein some experience everyday racism while others enjoy the privilege of ignoring it on a daily basis. Added to this bifurcated experiential epistemology, digital media is creating a shift in how knowledge beyond one's own experience of the world is sought, acquired, evaluated, and retained. The shift from libraries to search engines as the primary source of information for young people raises important questions about how we understand race, hate speech, and civil rights in a knowledge environment without traditional gatekeepers of editors, publishers, and peer reviewers. The same search engine and browser window that serves up the United Nations Web site, the *New York Times*, DailyKos, MoveOn, and the King Center also delivers Resist.com and MartinLutherKing.org. The increasing need for critical literacy to distinguish effectively between these sites is a task left to the user. In my view, a much more likely, and more pernicious risk to young people from hate speech online than either mobilizing or recruiting them into extremist white supremacist groups, is an epistemological vulnerability. The epistemological peril of white supremacy online lies in its ability to change how we know what we say we know about issues that have been politically hard won, issues such as civil rights.

Both forms of online hate speech discussed here, overt and cloaked, are grounded in an epistemology of white supremacy. The presence of overt hate speech online reinforces this epistemology of white supremacy by allowing white racists to retreat from civic engagement and into a whites-only fantasy of superiority or victimhood. For those who create overt hate speech, the Internet provides a forum for amplifying racist propaganda. For those who seek it out, overt hate speech online validates an essentialist notion of white racial purity, privilege, and entitlement by rearticulating white supremacy using the rhetoric of civil rights. Such a rearticulation rests on a disavowal of everyday racism and blindness to the myriad ways in which whites are privileged by race. Within a context filled with like-minded individuals and absent gatekeepers, these rearticulations set up an infinite loop within the technology, reinforcing white supremacy by design. Even for nonracist whites, the Internet and white supremacy work as reinforcing mechanisms. For well-meaning white liberals, extremists often represent an "Other" who signifies racism and undermines any examination of the ways white supremacy is embedded in the culture and institutions of the United States.[77] For some white liberals, hate speech online is a reliable target for focusing attention on issues of racism, because it is easy to point to vast differences that distinguish liberals from extremists; yet, this focus often obfuscates the more difficult investigation into the ways that white supremacy is built into the mechanisms of the dominant culture, institutions, even the technology itself, administered by those with no ties to extremist groups.

As for cloaked Web sites, they shift the terrain of racial politics to domain name registration and GUI. The decision to register the URL "martinlutherking.org" in 1999, relatively early in the evolution of the Web, was a prescient and opportune move for advocates of white supremacy; failure to do likewise was a lost opportunity for advocates of civil rights. Recognizing that domain name registration is now a political battleground, a number of civil rights organizations have begun to reserve domain names to prevent them from being used by opponents of racial justice. For example, the NAACP registered six domain names that include the word "nigger"[78] and the ADL registered a similar number of domain names with the word "kike."[79] However, registering offensive epithets is only a small part of the struggle. The move by opponents to register the esteemed symbols of civil rights as domain names, such as Martin Luther King, and to use them to undermine racial justice, is one that was clearly unanticipated by civil rights organizations. To be effective, cloaked domain names such as www.martinlutherking.org and www.AmericanCivilRightsReview.org rely on the naïveté of their target audiences, those whites who fail to understand this practice and the world that they, themselves, have made. The vulnerability of these cloaked sites, however, lies in their inexpert GUI and rudimentary designs, which makes them easier to spot. The problem is that poor graphic design and Web layout are technological bugs that are easy enough to fix, and when that happens, reliance on these visual elements will not be enough to discern cloaked sites. Instead, people will need to parse the rhetorics of white supremacist ideology and progressive racial politics based on the content of the sites, rather than the color of their graphics, so to speak.

Obviously, unsuspecting white people are not the only ones who read these cloaked sites; people of color, particularly youth of color, read these sites also. For youth of color, reading cloaked sites means having their own cultures and histories distorted in the retelling, and this is characteristic of the epistemology of white supremacy. This, however, is not new or unique to digital media. For people of color have had their cultures and histories distorted by whites, both those with and without good intentions, for many centuries. Black feminist epistemology, an alternative epistemology suggested by Patricia Hill Collins[80] and others, may hold some keys for understanding these sites. Collins' epistemological stance places an emphasis on lived experience as a criterion of meaning, and suggests that ideas cannot be divorced from the individuals who create and share them. This is where youth of color may have an advantage in critically evaluating these sites. If they draw on lived experience of everyday racism and do the critical work of evaluating which individuals are creating the ideas contained in cloaked Web sites, then they may have an advantage over those steeped in the epistemology of white supremacy that reinforces illiteracy about racism.

Digital media is neither a panacea for eliminating racial inequality, nor is it a dangerous lure for young people drawing them inexorably toward hate groups. A more nuanced understanding of both racism and digital media suggests that new white supremacy online looks, in many ways, like the old white supremacy, and our culture and institutions are steeped in it. Analogously, young people who are immersed in digital media do not, somehow, speak with a pure voice when it comes to matters of race and racism, but rather speak with an inflected voice that both mirrors and shapes the culture and institutions in which they grow up. Within the United States, the culture and institutions were originally formed by slave-owning elites (see, e.g., Thomas Jefferson's *Notes on the State of Virginia*),[81] and this legacy of white supremacy endures. Young people, depending on their lived experience offline, may use digital media to resist or to reinscribe white supremacy, and engaged adults can influence which of these paths they choose. Trying to understand hate speech online exclusively in terms of extremists, without taking into account the context of white supremacy from which it emerges, is to replay the epistemological error that Mills describes. In her work on race and digital media, Tara McPherson calls for an examination of "the ways in which race may be embedded in the very root structures of American technology, functioning as a kind of ever-present ghost in the machine."[82] Similarly, what I mean to suggest with this discussion of epistemology is that white supremacy is constitutive of digital media, particularly in the United States, and not merely added on to digital media. The early, persistent, and durable presence of white supremacy online calls for different kinds of literacies: a literacy of digital media, to be sure, and new literacies not merely of "tolerance," but literacies of social justice that offer a depth of understanding about race, racism, and multiple, intersecting forms of oppression. At stake in this shifting digital terrain is our vision for racial and social justice.

Multiple Literacies: Digital Media, Anti-racism, and Social Justice

One of the ways that digital media has sparked innovation is by opening people's minds to new possibilities and reminding us that we are, in fact, designers of our own social futures.[83] New ways of thinking and learning have emerged, and among those leading the way in thinking about these issues are Richard Kahn and Douglas Kellner, who have called for a *multiple literacies* approach.[84] A multiple literacies approach combines traditional print literacy with critical media literacy and new forms of literacies about how to access, navigate, create, and participate in digital media.[85] Digital media also poses new challenges and opportunities for parents, educators, activists, and scholars for understanding racism, antiracism, and social justice.

Ten years into the digital media revolution, our initial ways of educating young people about digital media literacy seem ineffectual at best, and misleading at worst. For example, one strategy widely used in Internet literacy curricula is instructing students to "look at the URL," and especially at the three-letter suffix (.com, .edu, .org). In the case of the cloaked Web sites, following this advice only serves to make the cloaked site appear *more* legitimate, rather than less so. Another response popular with some parents and youth-oriented organizations is "hate filters," software programs designed to "filter" hate sites encountered through search engines. These filters are woefully inadequate at addressing anything but the most overt forms of hate speech online, and even when they work as intended, they disable the critical thinking that is central to what is needed in our approach to digital media literacy.

The direction that digital media literacy needs to take is promoting the ability to read text closely and carefully, as well as developing skills necessary to "read" critically the visual imagery and graphic design. Along with visual and textual literacy, the critical thinking skills required to decipher Web authorship, intended audience, and cloaked political agendas in making knowledge claims must be combined with at least some understanding of how domain name registration works. At a minimum, this is what is required to be a fully engaged, thoughtful user of the Web. Important in this effort is for young people to become content creators actively engaged in creating their own digital media, which helps demystify the medium in significant ways. And, introducing young people to the regular use of a range of free, online tools for Web analysis is important as well. Technology such as the "Who Is Registry" (www.internic.net/whois.html) can sometimes help determine who the author of a Web site is in the absence of clear information. The Alexa (www.alexa.com) Web trafficking service can help young people see how many visitors a particular site gets, and provide some analysis about how that site relates to other sites. The free software Touch Graph (www.touchgraph.com) uses a Java applet to display visually the relationship between links leading to and from a site. Even though youth are immersed in the use of digital media, they are not necessarily adept at thinking critically about digital media, and this is where adults—whether parents, teachers, activists, or scholars—can play a role in connecting them to technology that facilitates this critical thinking. Technological literacy alone, however, is not enough for addressing the challenges of white supremacy online.

Among the advantages of incorporating principles of critical media literacy into a multiple literacies approach required for digital media is that it calls for valuing young people's voices as well as deconstructing images produced by corporate-owned media. Furthermore, critical media literacy calls for understanding multiple perspectives. Understanding multiple perspectives is an important corrective to the racism, sexism, and homophobia generated by corporate-owned media outlets; and, as Henry Jenkins has rightly pointed out, this is a vital contribution of participatory media.[86] However, I want to add a small but significant corrective to the idea of valuing multiple perspectives, by suggesting that not all perspectives are to be valued equally. If "valuing multiple perspectives" is our only standard, then we have no basis on which to critically distinguish between a cloaked Web site and a legitimate civil rights Web site, no way to evaluate the content generated by The King Center over that produced at www.martinlutherking.org. The usual approach within critical media literacy of "understanding multiple perspectives" is simply not enough for understanding the epistemology of white supremacy online. If new media literacy merely advocates valuing multiple perspectives without regard to content, then there is no way to distinguish between different perspectives, no basis for a vision of social justice. So, in addition to understanding digital media, youth need to be well versed in literacies of racism, antiracism, and social justice. And, of course, this is one of the places where adults (provided they have this knowledge themselves) can become involved. Young people of all racial and ethnic backgrounds need to read histories of the United States that include critical race perspectives. Youth of color need critical consciousness to go with lived experiences of everyday racism; and white youth need to begin the lifelong process of unlearning the epistemology of white supremacy. Bringing these multiple literacies together—visual and textual literacy, critical media literacy, and a literacy of antiracism and social justice—will empower young people not to be seduced by white supremacy, whether overt or cloaked, whether in online in digital media or offline, in culture and institutions. The shifting terrain of race, civil rights, and hate speech online compels us to think critically about how we make and evaluate knowledge claims within digital media. How we develop and teach new literacy skills, and how we articulate a vision for social justice will determine whether we will carry forward hard-won civil rights victories, or relinquish them and the Internet to a new era of white supremacy.

Notes

1. Anna Everett, Introduction, this volume.

2. The rare exceptions that prove this point include the two most frequently cited volumes on race and the Internet: Beth Kolko, Lisa Nakamura, and Gilbert B. Rodman, eds., *Race and Cyberspace* (New York: Routledge, 2000); and Lisa Nakamura, *Cybertypes: Race, Ethnicity, and Identity on the Internet* (New York: Routledge, 2002).

3. Joe R. Feagin and Hernan Vera, *White Racism* (New York: Routledge, 1996).

4. The term *cloak* to refer to a Web site appeared for the first time, as far as I know, in Ray and Marsh's 2001 article to refer to www.martinlutherking.org. I am using the term *cloaked Web site* in a similar way, and expanding it to include other types of cloaked sites. These can include political sites, such as www.whitehouse.com, which is intended as satire, or Web sites connected to sexual politics, such as www.teenbreaks.com, which appears to be a reproductive health Web site but is, in fact, a showcase for pro-life propaganda.

5. Charles W. Mills, *The Racial Contract* (Ithaca, NY: Cornell University Press, 1997.

6. Amanda Lenhart, Mary Madden, and Paul Hitlin, *Teens and Technology: Youth Are Leading the Transition to a Fully Wired and Mobile Nation* (Washington, DC: Pew Internet & American Life Project, 2005).

7. Donald F. Roberts, Ulla G. Foehr, and Victoria Rideout, *Generation M: Media in the Lives of 8-18 Year-Olds; A Kaiser Family Foundation Study* (Menlo Park, CA: Kaiser Family Foundation, 2005).

8. Howard Rheingold, Keynote Speech, NMC Online Conference, 2006.

9. For similar uses of the term *white supremacy*, see Derrick Bell, *Faces at the Bottom of the Well: The Permanence of Racism* (New York: Basic Books, 1993); Joe R. Feagin, *Systemic Racism: A Theory of Oppression* (New York: Routledge, 2006); and Cornel West, *Race Matters* (New York: Vintage, 1993).

10. Jessie Daniels, *White Lies: Race, Class, Gender and Sexuality in White Supremacist Discourse* (New York: Routledge, 1997).

11. Abby Ferber, *White Man Falling: Race, Gender and White Supremacy* (Lanham, MD: Rowman & Littlefield, 1998); Abby Ferber, ed., *Home Grown Hate: Gender and Organized Racism* (New York: Routledge, 2003).

12. Feagin, *Systemic Racism.*

13. A read-only record of this discussion is available online at http://community.macfound.org/openforum.

14. Tim Wise, Everyday Racism, White Liberals & the Limits of Tolerance, http://www.raceandhistory.com/historicalviews/18062001.htm (accessed June 18, 2007).

15. Michael Whine, Cyberspace: A New Medium for Communication, Command and Control by Extremists, *Studies In Conflict and Terrorism* 22 (1999): 231–45.

16. Comments made by Catherine Smith in the MacArthur Foundation-sponsored online discussion. A read-only record of this discussion is available online at http://community.macfound.org/openforum.

17. For more on this, see Catherine E. Smith, Intentional Infliction of Emotional Distress: An Old Arrow Targets the New Head of the Hate Hydra, *Denver University Law Review* 80, no. 1 (2002); Brian Marcus, *Hacking and Hate: Virtual Attacks with Real Consequences* (Boston, MA: HateWatch.org, 2000).

18. Comments made by Catherine E. Smith in the MacArthur Foundation-sponsored online discussion. A read-only record of this discussion is available online at http://community.macfound.org/openforum.

19. Rare Case Has Norwegian Man Convicted of Racism on the Web, 2002, April 24, Associated Press, http://www.law.com (accessed June 10, 2005).

20. Smith, Intentional Infliction of Emotional Distress; Marcus, *Hacking and Hate.*

21. Qing Li, Gender and CMC: A Review on Conflict and Harassment, *Australasian Journal of Educational Technology* 21, no. 3 (2005): 382–406; Justin W. Patchin and Sameer Hinduja, Bullies Move Beyond the Schoolyard: A Preliminary Look at Cyberbullying, *Youth Violence and Juvenile Justice* 4, no. 2 (2006): 148–69.

22. Paul Bocij and Leroy McFarlane, Cyberstalking: The Technology of Hate, *International Journal of Police Science and Management* 76, no. 3 (2003): 204–21.

23. T. K. Kim, Electronic Storm: Stormfront Grows into Thriving Neo-Nazi Community, *Intelligence Report*, Southern Poverty Law Center, http://www.splcenter.org/intel/intelreport/article.jsp?aid=515 (accessed June 18, 2007).

24. Ibid.

25. Ibid.

26. Howard Rheingold, *The Virtual Community: Homesteading on the Electronic Frontier* (Reading, PA: Addison-Wesley, 1993).

27. See, e.g., Todd J. Schroer, White Nationalists' Media-Constructed Rituals, and Michael R. Ball, Evil and the American Dream, in *American Ritual Tapestry: Social Rules and Cultural Meanings, Contributions in Sociology*, ed. Mary Jo Deegan (Westport, CT: Greenwood, 1998).

28. Amy Jo Kim, *Community Building on the Web: Secret Strategies for Successful Online Communities* (Berkeley, CA: Peachpit, 2000).

29. Kim, Electronic Storm.

30. Ibid.

31. See Kathleen Blee's work for evidence of the racism of white women, *Inside Organized Racism: Women in the Hate Movement* (Berkeley: University of California Press, 2003); Becoming a Racist: Women in Contemporary Ku Klux Klan and Neo-Nazi Groups, *Gender & Society* 10, no. 6 (1996): 680–702; *Women of the Klan: Racism and Gender in the 1920s* (Berkeley: University of California Press, 1991).

32. See, e.g., Maria Lohan and Wendy Faulkner, Masculinities and Technologies, *Men & Masculinities* 6, no. 4 (2004): 319–29.

33. See, e.g., Richard Dyer, *White* (New York: Routledge, 1997); David Skinner and Paul Rosen, Opening the White Box: The Politics of Racialised Science and Technology, *Science as Culture* 10, no. 3 (2001): 285–300.

34. Whine, Cyberspace, 231–45.

35. See, e.g., Philip E. Agre, Introduction: The Limits of Cyberspace, *Science as Culture* 11 (2002): 150–53; Jodi Dean, Why the Net Is Not a Public Sphere, *Constellations* 10 (2003): 85–112; Gordon Hull, Thoughts

on the Fetishization of Cyberspeech and the Turn from "Public" to "Private" Law, *Constellations* 10, no. 1 (2003): 113–34.

36. Barry Wellman, The Three Ages of Internet Studies: Ten, Five and Zero Years Ago, *New Media and Society* 6 (2004): 123–29.

37. In 1979, Metzger won 43,000 votes in a losing bid for a Democratic congressional seat in a San Diego primary.

38. Morris Dees and Steve Fiffer, *Hate on Trial: The Case against America's Most Dangerous Neo-Nazi* (New York: Villard, 1993).

39. Justine Cassell and Henry Jenkins, *From Barbie(R) to Mortal Kombat: Gender and Computer Games* (Cambridge, MA: MIT Press, 2000).

40. Ibid.

41. M. D. Griffiths, N. O. Mark, and Darren Chappell, Online Computer Gaming: A Comparison of Adolescent and Adult Gamers, *Journal of Adolescence* 27 (2004): 87–96.

42. Katie Salen and Eric Zimmerman, *Rules of Play: Game Design Fundamentals* (Cambridge, MA: MIT Press, 2004).

43. Whine, Cyberspace, 231–45.

44. Ibid.

45. Denise M. Bostdorff, The Internet Rhetoric of the Ku Klux Klan: A Case Study of Community Building Run Amok, *Communication Studies* 55 (Summer 2004): 340–61; Lynn Thiesmeyer, Racism on the Web: Its Rhetoric and Marketing, *Ethics and Information Technology* 1 (1999): 117–25.

46. Les Back, Wagner and Power Chords: Skinheadism, White Power Music and the Internet, in *Out of Whiteness: Color, Politics and Culture*, ed. Vron Ware and Les Back (Chicago: University of Chicago Press, 2001), 94–132.

47. The literature on the divisions within the white supremacist movement is vast. Some notable work in this area include the following: Michael Barkun, *Religion and the Racist Right: The Origins of the Christian Identity Movement* (Chapel Hill: University of North Carolina Press, 1997); Betty A. Dobratz, The Role of Religion in the Collective Identity of the White Racialist Movement, *Journal for the Scientific Study of Religion* 40, no. 2 (2001): 287–302; Betty A. Dobratz and Stephanie L. Shanks-Meile, Conflict in the White Supremacist/Racialist Movement in the U.S., *International Journal of Group Tensions* 25, no. 1 (1995): 57–75.

48. Jeffrey Kaplan, Leonard Weinberg, and Ted Oleson, Dreams and Realities in Cyberspace: White Aryan Resistance and the World Church of the Creator, *Patterns of Prejudice* 37 (2003): 139–55.

49. The strategy of "leaderless resistance" has been wildly popular among extremists beyond white supremacists, including extremist environmentalists and Islamic jihadists. The actions of Timothy McVeigh, the white supremacist who bombed the Murrah Federal Building in Oklahoma City, is perhaps the most well-known example of this in the movement.

50. Karen Mock, Hate on the Internet, in *Human Rights and the Internet*, ed. Steven Hicks, Edward F. Halpin, and Eric Hoskins (New York: Palgrave Macmillan, 2000), 200.

51. Michael R. Best, Can the Internet Be a Human Right? *Human Rights and Human Welfare* 4 (2004): 27.

52. Weltner also created several cloaked sites in the aftermath of the Katrina disaster, with URLs such as http://www.InternetDonations.org, to scam people interested in helping out the victims. A judge in St. Louis, where Weltner is based, issued a permanent restraining order against the scam Web sites;

there is no such injunction against http://www.JewWatch.com. In 2004 there was a grassroots effort to convince Google to remove the site from its search engine, but these efforts failed.

53. Here I mean to suggest that the word *Jews* rather than *Jewish people* suggests anti-Semitism. The word *Jew* is not, in of itself, an epithet but when used in certain contexts and by those who are not Jewish, it raises concerns.

54. Jessie Daniels, Finding Civil Rights in Cyberspace: A Study of Adolescents' Internet Use (paper presented at the Eastern Sociological Association Meetings, Boston, MA, 2006).

55. Lynne Lamberg, Hate-Group Sites Target Children, Teens, *Psychiatric News* 36, no. 3 (2001): 26.

56. Phillip E. Agre, Real-Time Politics: The Internet and the Political Process, *Information Society* 18, no. 5 (2002): 311–31; Alex Campbell, The Search for Authenticity: An Exploration of an Online Skinhead Newsgroup, *New Media and Society* 8, no. 2 (2006): 269–94; Richard Kahn and Douglas Kellner, Internet Subcultures and Oppositional Politics, in *The Post-Subcultures Reader*, ed. David Muggleton and Rupert Weinzierl (London: Berg, 2003), 299–314.

57. Jennifer Earl and Alan Schussman, The New Site of Activism: On-Line Organizations, Movement Entrepreneurs, and the Changing Location of Social Movement Decision Making, *Research in Social Movements* 24 (2003): 155–87.

58. Brian Levin, Cyberhate: A Legal and Historical Analysis of Extremists' Use of Computer Networks in America, *American Behavioral Scientist* 45 (2002): 958–88; Thiesmeyer, Racism on the Web, 117–25.

59. Kaplan, Weinberg, and Oleson, Dreams and Realities in Cyberspace, 155.

60. J. McCarthy and M. Zald, Resource Mobilization and Social Movements: A Partial Theory, *American Journal of Sociology* 82, no. 6 (1977): 1212–41.

61. Richard Kahn and Douglas Kellner, New Media and Internet Activism: From the "Battle of Seattle" to Blogging, *New Media and Society* 6, no. 1 (2004): 87–95.

62. Noriko Hara and Zilia Estrada, Hate and Peace in a Connected World: Comparing Moveon and Stormfront, *First Monday* 8, no. 12 (2003), http://www.firstmonday.org/issues/issue8_12/hara/index.html (accessed June 18, 2007).

63. Ibid.

64. Using Alexa, a Web trafficking service (http://www.alexa.com).

65. Suzanne Brunsting and Tom Postmes, Social Movement Participation in the Digital Age: Predicting Offline and Online Collective Action, *Small Group Research* 33 (2002): 525–54.

66. See Jakob Nielsen's research on this, such as Jakob Nielsen, Participation Inequality: Encouraging More Users to Contribute, 2006, http://www.useit.com/alertbox/participation_inequality.html (accessed June 18, 2007). Other research confirms this, such as Blair Nonnecke and Jenny Preece, Lurker Demographics: Counting the Silent (paper presented at the Proceedings of CHI, The Hague, 2000).

67. An additional category might be "observers" or "researchers" to include those who log in from monitoring organizations such as SPLC or ADL, or those who log on the site conducting research.

68. Lamberg, Hate-Group Sites Target Children, Teens, 26.

69. Ibid.

70. Beverly Ray and George E. Marsh, Recruitment by Extremist Groups on the Internet, Review of Reviewed Item, *First Monday* 6, no. 2 (2001), http://www.firstmonday.org/issues/issue6_2/ray/index.html (accessed June 18, 2007).

71. Elissa Lee and Laura Leets, Persuasive Storytelling by Hate Groups Online: Examining Its Effects on Adolescents, *American Behavioral Scientist* 45 (2002): 927–57.

72. Randy Blazak, White Boys to Terrorist Men: Target Recruitment of Nazi Skinheads, *American Behavioral Scientist* 44 (2001): 982–1000.

73. Ibid.

74. *Anomie* is a term developed by sociologist Emile Durkheim and refers to a sense of normlessness in which one no longer knows what the rules, or "norms," for acceptable behavior are. In extreme cases, Durkheim theorized, this condition can lead to anomic suicide.

75. Blazak, White Boys to Terrorist Men, 982–1000.

76. Mills, *The Racial Contract*, 18.

77. Wise, Everyday Racism; see also Eduardo Bonilla-Silva, *White Supremacy and Racism in the Post-Civil Rights Era* (Boulder, CO: Lynne Rienner, 2001).

78. I understand that this language is offensive and that is the reason I include the racial epithets in this section in quotation marks, to signal the reader that I neither agree with nor condone such language. However, I do not see how it is possible to engage in a sustained and specific criticism of the particular use of these terms in domain name registration without using the very language I find objectionable.

79. Paul Festa, Controversial Domains Go to Civil Rights Groups, *c|net News.com* (2002), http://news.com.com/Controversial+domains+go+to+civil+rights+groups/2100-1023_3-210803.html (accessed June 18, 2007).

80. Patricia Hill Collins, *Black Feminist Thought: Knowledge, Consciousness, and the Politics of Empowerment* (New York: Routledge, 1990).

81. Jefferson's essay was originally published in 1781, and is available in Adrienne Koch and William Peden, eds., *The Life and Selected Writing of Thomas Jefferson* (New York: The Modern Library, 1998).

82. Tara McPherson, *Digital Possibilities: Re-Imagining Politics, Place, and the Body* (forthcoming).

83. B. Cope and M. Kalantzis, eds., *Multiliteracies: Literacy, Learning and Social Futures* (South Yarra: Macmillan, 2000).

84. Richard Kahn and Douglas Kellner, Reconstructing Technoliteracy: A Multiple Literacies Approach, *E-Learning* 2, no. 3 (2005): 238–51.

85. Ibid.

86. Henry Jenkins, *Confronting the Challenges of Participatory Culture: Media Education for the 21st Century* (Chicago, IL: MacArthur Foundation, 2006).

KPK, Inc.: Race, Nation, and Emergent Culture in Online Games

Douglas Thomas

University of Southern California, Annenberg School for Communication

Digital media and learning pose a set of central problems for research and educational practices. As digital media environments—such as games and virtual worlds—become increasingly social and participatory, they form a complex social and cultural matrix that both draws from and contributes to discussions about social and cultural issues. Games, like many other new media, crossed a crucial threshold when they began to provide a social context for learning and interaction. Accordingly, it has become difficult, if not impossible, to limit our understanding of digital media and learning to the text or even the experience of particular new media technologies. What happens in the context of a game or Web site can be as important as the content of the game or site itself.

Learning, then, occurs through the experiences of interactivity in virtual spaces as much as it does in the broader context of personal or face-to-face social and cultural interaction for which these spaces serve as a shared reference point. Accordingly, one of the ways to understand the intersection of digital media and learning is to explore the practices, such as message forums, wikis, and other forms of participation that happen at the borders and boundaries of the media we examine.[1]

In the case of race and ethnicity, the issues of borders and boundaries are compounded by a variety of forces that shape our understanding of the world and our place in it. This chapter is an effort to contextualize questions of race and ethnicity within game worlds, and with gamer culture more broadly, by examining a particular set of conflicts that emerged within the game *Diablo II* shortly after its release in Korea in 2003. The conflict that arose illustrates one of the ways in which notions of race and ethnicity are constructed, defined, and contextualized in virtual spaces. It also provides some insight into how notions of privilege and investment in economic and social power relationships of the physical world are mimicked and intensified in the context of virtual spaces.

Race and Cyberspace

When one considers the complexities of race and ethnicity inside virtual worlds, the already difficult questions of what constitutes race in real worlds are magnified. The temptation and tendency, as Beth Kolko has illustrated in the case of text-based multiuser domains (MUDs),[2] is to erase the category completely. As Kali Tal wrote to the readers of *Wired*, "I have long suspected that the much vaunted 'freedom' to shed the 'limiting' markers of race and gender on the Internet is illusory, and that in fact it masks a more disturbing phenomenon—the whitinizing of cyberspace."[3]

Both Kolko and Tal point to the presumed disappearance of race as a signature of the whiteness of cyberspace. This chapter examines the question of race and ethnicity from a distinctly different point of view, attempting to understand how race and ethnicity are, in fact, marked by geography, language, and specific cultural practices within virtual worlds and multiplayer game spaces, and how those markers might provide insight into the way race functions in cyberspace as well as in the cultural imagination of those who inhabit these worlds.

As George Lipsitz argues, race in American culture is often a matter of "possessive investment," suggesting that those who have power are invested in the privileges that accompany whiteness in society. Lipsitz's goal is to "stress the relationship between whiteness and asset accumulation to connect attitudes to interests" and "to demonstrate that white supremacy is usually less a matter of direct, referential, and snarling contempt and more a system of protecting the privileges of whites by denying communities of color opportunities of asset accumulation and upward mobility."[4] Following Lipsitz, this chapter addresses some of the ways in which cyberspace culture, generally, and gamer culture, more specifically, participate in cultures of racism through strategies of denial, refusal, and equivocation in an effort to maintain the status of white privilege. While racism exists in gaming culture in many explicit forms, some of which I will articulate below, it is important to understand the ways in which participating in discourses which deny racism are equally important and serve as a foundational discourse for learning in the context of digital media.

This chapter, then, looks both at the forms of direct, hostile racism and at the ways in which racist discourse often engages in acts of possessive investment in whiteness through strategies of disavowal. This chapter provides a reading of the discourse of gamers confronting issues of racial, geographic, and ethnic differences, and it suggests some insight into the events that have triggered the rise of certain racist practices in one particular game. This discussion also aims to understand the process by which some American youth process notions of race and ethnicity in virtual spaces, and the various entitlements and possessive investments they feel in relation to the virtual world of gameplay.[5]

While significant discussion about the impact of games has focused attention on violence and explicit sexual content, very little attention has been paid to the more subtle forms of learning that occur in and around the spaces of games.[6] By broadening the scope and boundaries of games and play, we can begin to understand how various cultural forms and productions emerge that can help us better understand issues of race and ethnicity in games and culture.

Gamer Culture, Nation, and Race: KPK, Inc., and the "Korean Problem"

In the past decade, massively multiplayer online games (MMOGs) have emerged as a central form of youth entertainment in the digital age. MMOGs are fundamentally social environments wherein players create and name personal avatars, interact with other's characters through gameplay and chat, and create and negotiate meaning in the game world through social, economic, and cultural exchanges and interactions. The games represent a fusion of the logics of text-based MUDs (the text-based forerunner of MMOGs), which were heavily social in nature and allowed players to construct identities creatively through textual, literary production, and graphical adventure games, which provided for game interactivity in a primarily graphical nonmodifiable context. This combination preserved the flexibility of complex identity play from MUDs with fast-paced game-play and interactivity more characteristic of adventure and first-person shooter games. As a result, the blend of these two types of worlds has produced a new—and arguably revolutionary—framework for play that is both social and individualistic, and grounded in the game mechanics of player advancement, combat, and acquisition of items, treasure, and money. While much attention has been focused on traditional questions of media effects (e.g., the relationship between games and violence), little attention has been paid to the emerging intercultural dynamics of this new medium and its unforeseen consequences, especially regarding matters of race and ethnicity. Because MMOGs function as microcosms of larger social configurations, the ways they can be used, and the communities of practice that they spawn, can be complex and culturally rich.[7] Most important, because these online games are spaces in which cultural meanings are both created and negotiated, they help us understand the ways in which the cultural imagination of players is being shaped outside of issues they confront in their daily lives.

MMOGs have become a worldwide phenomenon, with extensive player bases throughout North and South America, Europe, and Asia.[8] Because the games are Internet based, young players from different countries and diverse racial and ethnic backgrounds are able to inter-act and play together with relatively few problems. Consequently, it is not uncommon in these spaces to see from England, Sweden, Germany, America, Canada, Korea, and Japan all playing the same game on a single server. Among American gamers, such interactions may be their first, and in many cases only, interaction with citizens of other nations, which is quite significant in and of itself. In many cases, these interactions can be positive and fruit-ful learning experiences.[9] In others they can create and foster racist attitudes that promote stereotyping. I am interested, therefore, in examining some surprising and disturbing out-comes of the transnational adoption of these games within the context of one such MMOG, *Diablo II*, and in examining the fallout of the game's adoption in Korea (especially in relation to player groups, such as KPK, Inc.). What makes this group a significant case study for our purposes is the fact that it is a group formed outside of the game-space with the expressed purpose of eliminating Korean players from the U.S. game-space (KPK stands for "Korean player killers").

Diablo II

On June 28, 2000, Blizzard Entertainment released *Diablo II*, a follow-up to its enormously popular 1997 *Diablo* game. By July 17, *Diablo II* had sold more than one million copies, making it the fastest-selling video game at that time in PC history.[10] Within six months, *Diablo II* had sold more than two million copies and had been named "Game of the Year" by a host of gaming magazines and Web sites, marking it as one of the most successful PC games of all time.

As Blizzard describes it, *Diablo II* is set in the context of an "eternal struggle to decide the fate of all Creation," which has "now come to the Mortal Realm. . . . After possessing the body of the hero who defeated him, Diablo resumes his nefarious scheme to shackle humanity into unholy slavery by joining forces with the other Prime Evils, Mephisto and Baal. Only you will be able to determine the outcome of this final encounter." The game is set in a "world of dark fantasy," where players play "one of five distinct character types, explore the world of Diablo II—journey across distant lands, fight new villains, discover new treasures, and uncover ancient mysteries, all in the quest to stop the Lord of Terror, once and for all."[11] *Diablo II* follows the lore of the earlier game and is set in a fictional world and time, which has no identifiable geographic or temporal connection to the present-day world.

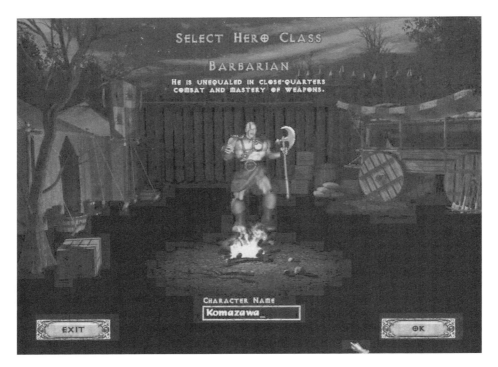

Figure 1
Diablo II character screen illustrating a generic class avatar for Barbarians.

Players are able to select from among five possible characters: Amazon, Sorceress, Barbarian, Paladin, and Necromancer. The Amazon and Sorceress characters are female, while the Barbarian, Paladin, and Necromancer characters are male. Avatars, the players' graphical representations in the game, are not modifiable, resulting in significant attention being paid to naming conventions for the purposes of identity (see Figure 1). Unlike more recent MMOGs that allow significant customization of the players' avatars, each character class in *Diablo II* was represented by a particular piece of game art, which meant that every player playing a barbarian, for example, would have an identical in-game appearance. In that sense, the only way a player can differentiate himself or herself from the other players in the game is by choosing a name.

The other point of differentiation was in the armor and weapons the characters used, which were significant parts of their characters' identities, and which determined—in large part—how successful the characters could be in the game. These items, which were treasures received from slaying monsters, were the primary resources for the game, and were seen as barometers of a player's skill and status.

The game consists of five primary areas, with each containing a number of "boss" monsters who randomly drop magical items that can be used to enhance a particular gamer's character, or that can be traded to other gamers' characters in exchange for items or gold. Each of the five areas can be played at three different levels of difficulty (normal, nightmare, and hell), with the values of items increasing along with the levels of difficulty in game-play. As difficulty levels increase, the monsters that players battle remain the same, but the monsters gain more

Figure 2
A typical *Diablo II* game-space after killing a boss monster, English UI.

hit points and resistances, making them exceptional adversaries that are much harder to kill.

While it was possible to play *Diablo II* as a single-player game, its popularity (and the profitability of its sales) was due in large part to Blizzard's free online gaming network, battle.net, which allowed anyone who purchased the game to play in an interactive multiuser environment. Anyone who purchased the game could connect to battle.net through the Internet and play cooperatively or competitively with other players who were also logged on at the time.

One of the primary goals of battle.net was to provide a setting for players to compete with one another and test their skills in a competitive environment (see Figure 2). As a result, Blizzard had to ensure that *Diablo II* could not be hacked or modified by players to give them unfair advantages in game-play. To this end, *Diablo II* game designers created a client/server model, in which all of the important information and valuable assets—such as player inventory, gold, skills, and player levels—would be stored on Blizzard's servers, while key game-play data—such as results of battles, animations, and art—would be run on the player's machine. This practice allowed Blizzard to maintain a high degree of security over crucial pieces of information needed to maintain fairness in game-play. In earlier online games, cheating had been rampant, mainly as a result of players being able to hack key files on their own machines to provide their characters with unlimited resources or improved weapons. One of the main selling points of Blizzard's battle.net system was that it ensured a level of fair play and balance for the player base. This would also be the central friction point that would animate much of the discourse about race and ethnicity in and around the game.

To do this, Blizzard assigned each player in battle.net to a "realm," a closed server that stored and secured the data for the player. Players could interact and trade with other players on their realms, but not with players on other realms. Players could choose to create characters on any of the four realms, "U.S. West," "U.S. East," "Asia," and "Europe." The realms were named geographically to accommodate player interaction based on time zone, so that each realm would have "heavy" and "light" times based on when the majority of players would log in. Heavy times on U.S. East would be 4:00 p.m. to 11:00 p.m. EST, while U.S. West would typically have a similar load three hours earlier.

Like most online multiplayer games, *Diablo II* created its own economic system. Players traded valuable items, exchanged gold and loot, and even developed a system of currency built around a game item called the "Stone of Jordan." The "Realm" system that Blizzard used kept each system closed and independent, meaning that players could not trade between realms or play with or against players on other servers, and that if a player found an exceptionally rare item on the U.S. East realm and wanted to trade it (say, for gold or for several other items that might benefit one's character more), the player could only trade with other players on the U.S. East realm. This system was designed to make the economic system of *Diablo II* more secure and less prone to cheating, item and gold duplication, and hacking. It also provided a guarantee that virtual items would have value, setting up the possibility of a genuine economic system that could be maintained outside the game-world itself in venues such as eBay.[12]

Early on in the game, the U.S. West realm gained a reputation as being "more serious" among players, signaling that many of the most devoted players (and, therefore, those likely to have the best items for trade) were playing there. Because items couldn't be traded between servers, the economies of U.S. East and U.S. West grew at different rates and created different markets, based on scarcity. Over time, this created an imbalance that greatly favored U.S. West. With more players, U.S. West saw an increase in both the diversity and number of items available, increasing the chance of acquiring needed items, while simultaneously driving prices down.

As the game grew in international popularity, players from all over the world began to converge on the U.S. West server, oftentimes overloading it and causing game-play to slowdown or "lag." At times, when lag becomes excessive, it can interfere with game-play, cause players' avatars to die, and even cause players to lose items or equipment. The problem became particularly acute when international gamers discovered a large U.S. market for *Diablo II* game items and began to farm them and sell them to (predominantly) U.S. players.

Diablo II Goes Global

The problems of lag and trade imbalances became particularly acute when the game was released a year later in Korea. By 2003, *Diablo II* was one of the top-selling titles in Korea, producing a massive influx of new players to the game. Unlike a significant portion of North American players' styles, the culture of gaming in Korea was highly competitive, resulting in an immediate source of tension. Moreover, Korean players were easily identified as "non-American" based upon language differences, which included several common, easily identifiable Korean gaming phrases, such as "Huk" (which roughly translates to "Go") and, more important, by their nonresponsiveness to questions or comments in English.

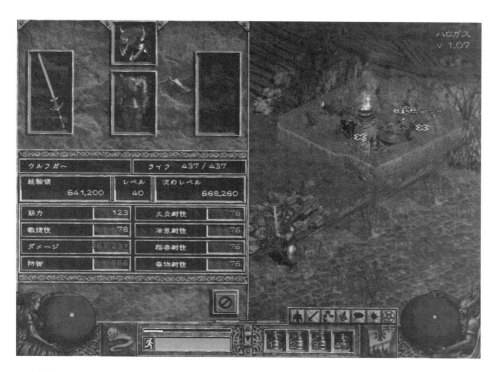

Figure 3
Player inventory interface illustrating differences in text and layout, Korean UI.

One significant barrier to international communication between these players was grounded in the differences in interfaces. The Korean version of *Diablo II* was different from the English version, both in the way that it communicated information and the ways that it facilitated game-play among Koreans (see Figure 3).

The difference in language constituted a unique barrier to communication for Korean players (see Figure 4). Localizations into other (particularly European) languages allowed for a shared vocabulary of game items (the name "Stone of Jordan" is recognizable in French, German, and English, e.g., but not in Korean). Those differences provided not only a language barrier, but also an interface barrier, in many cases making basic cross-cultural communication not just difficult, but impossible. Korean players, however, were able to create and sustain their own communities around systems of "farming," that is, creating games to farm repetitively the best areas for rare items that could be sold on third-party sites such as eBay. Many of these players were able to generate significant income based on the demand from U.S. players for rare or high quality items in the game. Unlike U.S. gamers, who routinely traded items with each other, Korean gamers were selling items for profit and real dollars in what emerged as a black market. (Selling items was against the terms of service for the game).

Within a few weeks of its release, 300,000 copies of *Diablo II* were sold in Korea, making it far and away Blizzard's most profitable overseas market. Because of the competitive nature of Korean game culture, most Korean players opted not to play on the sparsely populated Asia realm, but instead chose to create characters on the U.S. West realm, which had a large and

Figure 4
Korean Interface for game-play (illustrative of language barrier, due to ideographic text).

established player base and trade network, as well as the best market for selling and trading items.

One of the primary motives for Koreans to play on U.S. servers was economic. The economy of *Diablo II* found its most dramatic expression on eBay, where items were frequently bought and sold, even though the game's end user license agreement strictly prohibited such acts. Items that were "hot" on the realms could be bought and sold for real money on eBay and the process became so lucrative, with items often selling for hundreds of dollars, that a cadre of "professional" *Diablo II* game players emerged who spent their days playing the game and item hunting, posting their items each day for auction. At the height of the game's popularity, a professional game player could make $200 to $300 a day. A significant portion of those professional gamers were Koreans, who recognized and exploited a significant American market for these virtual goods. While some American players did engage in "black market" selling of virtual goods, the primary market that emerged was one in which Korean sellers sold items to U.S. buyers.

Accordingly, to be a successful trader (Korean or Western), one needed to have access to the realms where Americans played. As the process of trading became more and more lucrative, the number of players on the U.S. West realm increased dramatically, the demand driven not by a Korean desire to flood the American servers, but by the American demand for "black market" items sold on eBay. While a significant number of players did buy goods from eBay, the majority did not, setting up a complicated dynamic that was at odds with the basic design of Blizzard's system. Most players saw the "closed realm" system as a way to eliminate outside intervention in game-play, and many considered the purchasing of virtual goods to be cheating. Regardless, the demand for these good remained high, providing ample motivation for Korean farmers to continue to play on the U.S. servers, creating a clear division of "turf" that would soon erupt into open conflict.

Geographies of Race and the Invention of "The Korean Problem"

As the popularity of the game began to put stress on the servers, often slowing them to a crawl, a significant portion of the American players across the globe began to racialize the problem, suggesting that it was Korean players (with whom they had difficulty communicating in the game-world due to language barriers) who were causing the slowdown. While the sheer volume of players did affect the speed of the game, there was nothing particular about Korean players that increased the latency of the network. Put more simply, this latency is a measure of the delay between a user's computer and the game's server. High latency (or "lag") can cause players to miss out on valuable loot or to have their characters die as a result of being unable to respond to attacks. The game's popularity had simply overwhelmed the hardware and the network's ability to manage simultaneous connections.

As a result of these dynamics, U.S. game players began to think of the fictional game-world as a nation-space, with an accompanying sense of entitlement to the U.S. West server domain. In the context of U.S. culture, many of the youth playing in *Diablo II* would have relatively little or no direct contact with foreign national cultures. Accordingly, notions of nation and nation-space, with little understanding of trade and international exchange, were codified and discussed by these groups based on the physical location of resources (such as servers and Blizzard itself) and bodies (the physical locations from which the players connected). In that sense, the physicality and geography of nation represented not only a claim to ownership, but also a possessive investment in the resources of the game as well.

In the context of the virtual world, geography becomes a marker with which youth can tie the physical body to a virtual space, especially when the physical traits of the population are markedly different, such as is the case with Asia. In that sense, Koreans provided a "target" for online racism because both their physical location and their physicality served as markers of difference. Players who were openly racist toward Korean players would have had difficulty justifying their opposition if either the markers of location or racial difference had been removed. For example, an American player connecting from Korea would be perceived as sharing a possessive investment in the virtual nation-space based on racial affinity, while a Korean, connecting from the United States, would be seen as having a possessive claim based on geography. It was only the combination of both location and race that challenged issues of white Americans' possessive investment in the game.

In Benedict Anderson's terms, the kind of nationalism that is produced by this combination of factors is typical of all notions of imagined communities, perhaps even more so when dealing with Asia.[13] As Edward Said has illustrated, the desire to define the Other in terms of Eastern and Western epistemological frames is "an elaboration not only of a basic geographical distinction, but also of a whole set of interests, which it not only creates but maintains."[14] Said is describing, in powerful ways, the desire not only to define, but also to control the space of racial and geographical difference, the essence of what Lipsitz defines as a "possessive investment in whiteness."[15] One of the most fundamental ways of defining

Korean players was by demonstrating their Otherness and then framing their interests as alien as a result. Doing so allowed U.S. players to make claims about entitlement based solely on questions of geography, allowing them to both create and mask other interests which defined the relations between and among players of different races, ethnicities, and nationalities.

Given the enormous potential for intercultural exchange signified by the game's early international reach, that possessive investment signifies something important about U.S. West players' sense of national entitlement as an understanding of both game-based and commerce-based relations. U.S. players began a campaign against Korean players—both inside the game-space and outside on Web sites and forums. They used tropes of national borders and boundaries, and framed Korean players as "illegal immigrants" and "invaders." Players began joining games with Korean players with the sole intention of disrupting game-play and literally chasing them off of the servers. Some players adopted racist or anti-Korean names. At one point, a bug was discovered that allowed players to send a string of characters to the screen that would crash the Korean version of the game (a simple line of periods) and eject any Korean players from the game, forcing them to restart the game. As a result, they would be removed from the original game in which they were playing and be put into a queue to join other newly formed games. During the height of the conflict, it was common to see players enter a game and send the string to the screen to clear the game of any Korean players. This simple act illustrates the desire to recolonize the space by removing Koreans and staking a claim to the available resources at any given time. Perhaps most important, while the impetus for such interaction was, at base, economic (Koreans playing on U.S. West to sell items), the conflict was not. U.S. players were in no way competing with Koreans in the marketplace.

Within the rhetoric of KPK groups, there are five recurring themes that serve as common-places among these groups: conventions of naming designed to depersonalize and dehumanize Korean players, espousing the Western manifest destiny over the game space, the identification of Korean player behaviors as "savage" or "barbaric," attempts to distinguish "proper" and "improper" domains for the discussion of race, and explicit disavowals of racism.

When taken together, these five themes result in the creation of space that is defined by a dichotomy of purity and impurity, in which any contamination is unacceptable. The space of the Western servers is implicitly defined as a white, western space and explicitly characterized as a space of "innocence."

Players of the KPK, Inc., cast themselves in the role of enforcement, as agents undertaking a mission of policing the server's space. Accordingly, KPK, Inc., created a "Most Wanted List," where players could post the names of Korean players to be hunted for "offensive behavior." The two most frequent offenses being "Clogging up the public chat rooms" and creating "Korean-only games."

A Case Study: KPK, Inc.

As Kye Leung observed in an analysis of the game, "Sporting names such as KKA (Korean Killers of America) and FukForeigners, they blame foreigners for slowing down the US servers. These racists are usually Americans/Canadians and white. In the chat rooms they openly admit their racist beliefs and spam the channels with words like *chink* and *gook*, and that all foreigners, especially Koreans, need to go home."[16]

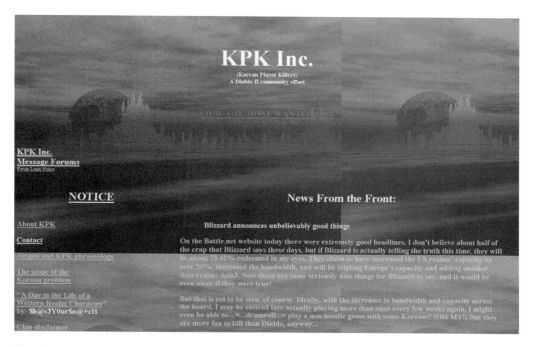

Figure 5
KPK, Inc. main Web site.

Typical of this kind of group was KPK, Inc., or Korean Player Killers Incorporated, a self-described "*Diablo II* Community Effort"[17] (see Figure 5). The group, which was active from 2001 to 2003, blamed Koreans for server instability, excessively long wait times to join games, international video piracy, creating a sense of "excessive paranoia," and filling chat rooms with "nonsense and numbers." Korean players, they argued, sought to disrupt their enjoyment of the game. As they describe the problem: "It is also all too common for a normal, peaceful, public chatroom to be instantly filled with meaningless dribble by Koreans who desire only to piss off the Western realm users."[18]

The KPK Web site, which was used by a group of players both to organize Korean player killing sessions and, more important, to justify their actions, provides a wealth of insight into how (predominately) U.S. players constructed Koreans in the cultural imagination. In Benedict Anderson's terms, they formed not only their own "imagined community," but also brought with it the inherent impulses of nationalism that have "made it possible, over the past two centuries, for so many millions of people, not so much to kill, as willingly to die for such limited imaginings."[19]

Both of these impulses are alive and well within KPK, Inc. There is not only the recognition that its members are "player killers," but also that they are putting themselves at risk (the Korean players are as likely, or even more likely, to kill them than vice versa). The fact that the possibility of sacrifice, having one's character die, goes unmentioned on the Web site is interesting, but not surprising. To portray the act of killing Koreans as risky, or admitting to the possibility of failure, would serve to undercut KPK, Inc.'s assertion of mastery over the server space.

The KPK Lexicon, or "You Are What You Eat"

Perhaps the most direct and immediate sense of the KPK's imagined sense of race comes from the vocabulary its members develop (in their terms "special words and jargon which may or may not be confusing to the uninitiated") to frame their relationships to the server space, other western players, and Korean players. Perhaps most revealing is the way they code themselves. For KPK members, the term they use to reference themselves is "Fed" or "Agent." Those terms themselves suggest a notion of authority grounded in the state making them "Federal Agents," working on behalf of a broader imagined national interest, policing the borders of cyberspace and nation spaces—a legitimating discourse in their imaginations. Furthermore, it is a chance for youth to play at positions of adult authority.

Interestingly, however, one's agency as a KPK Fed is not grounded in authority, but instead in a willingness to act. The very definition of a Fed, according to KPK, conflates the act of killing Koreans with a sense of legitimate authority. They write, a Fed or Agent is

[a]nyone acting on behalf of KPK Inc. in the interest of ridding the Diablo II Western Battle.net Realms of the FoK and other highly obnoxious players or groups. A Fed can be anybody: you, me, a few clan members who are bored and want to go Korean hunting (from any clan, KPK is not a clan), or anybody else who wants to take part in KPK.[20]

The explicit reference to KPK not being a clan is intended to distinguish it from groups that have regularly planned activities and formal membership requirements. In contrast to a clan, one becomes a member of KPK, Inc. simply by killing Korean players.

Of particular note is the reversal of the traditional relationship between authority and action. Agents, particularly working on behalf of governments, are traditionally given sanction to act by the state in ways that would be illegal in other contexts, such as detaining or killing people. In the case of the KPK, acting in such ways (in the service of what they see as the greater good) is performative, in the sense that the act of killing Koreans conveys, automatically, the authority to do so. As a result, "anybody who wants to take part" (presumably as long as they are not Korean themselves) is already a member.

The labeling of Koreans themselves is much more straightforward. According to the KPK "Jargon and Phraseology," Korean players can be identified with the following designations (all taken verbatim from the KPK, Inc. Web page):

- FoK (Forces of Kimchi). Kimchi is a special Korean food. This is used to refer to one or many Koreans (as in: "that FoK" or "the FoK came after me again!").

- WOA (Way Out of Area). This term should be obvious. These are the Koreans who clog up the Battle.net realms outside of the Asia net.

- CEA (Cabbage Eaters Anonymous). Similar in usage to "FoK."

- I-Plz. This term refers to one single Korean player. It is short for "Item plz!!!!!!" which is something any B.net player is all too familiar with seeing. It seems the only English that they have learned is "Item Plz!!!" "English, Japan FUCK FUCK !" and "Give me money!!!" I haven't a clue where "gogo" comes from, but it sure is annoying when the whole screen fills up with it.

- Gogo. Another singular term for a Korean player. Again, anybody who has played on Battle.net must be familiar with this, as they write it everywhere possible for totally inexplicable reasons. (KPK Web site)

The use of food in racial slurs is quite common (even whiteness is signified by "white bread" and "crackers"), so it is hardly surprising to find food as a marker for race. Kimchi, especially, is a designation that metonymically marks the nation of Korea as a kind of national cuisine. In that sense, it is both localized in a nation-space and fundamentally excluded from the "proper" space of U.S. Western culture. In that sense, consumption of a particular food is read as both alien and obsessive. Koreans do not merely eat Kimchi, they are defined by the practice of eating it such that it is read as fuel (Forces of Kimchi) as well as an obsession that requires treatment (Cabbage Eaters Anonymous). It is an effort both to depersonalize and to dehumanize the players as alien others with strange (and possibly dangerous) obsessions with things we don't understand while disempowering them through characterizations that have no power within the context of the game.

The corollary to game behavior functions in similar ways, demarcating behaviors which are to be read as pathological: being "way out of area," and hence occupying spaces that are inappropriate, making no effort to learn the language of the national-linguistic space they occupy, and being either crazy and/or inscrutable, obsessively spouting "Gogo" for "totally inexplicable reasons."

As a result, Korean players are never seen as players at all, but instead as noise in the system that cannot be understood rationally, cannot be reasoned or communicated with, and who have no proper place within the game-world. In short, it is an effort to call forth the Derridian principle, "tout autre est tout autre," that every bit of them is every bit other.[21]

Such arguments bear a striking similarly to the discourse on race and racism that permeate U.S. culture with respect to issues of illegal immigration, where people are reduced to food ("beaners") or practices ("wetbacks") and are seen as criminal, irrational, or other to such a degree that the only understanding of them that is possible is their identification as wholly and completely other to the American norm.

Manifest Destiny

The primary arguments that KPK, Inc., makes to justify player killing reflects a belief in a kind of manifest destiny, with Blizzard, the developers of *Diablo II*, cast in the role of the divine creator. For KPK, Inc., the question of realm ownership, rights and privileges is clear-cut. Its members' use of racist terms, they claim, is not designed to offend, but instead to make clear to people who does and, more important, does not belong in realm server space. As they submit,

These phrases, while somewhat derogatory in nature, are intended only as a slang means of expression that can be generally accepted by everyone in an effort not to offend or incite, and are not aimed at Korea or Koreans as a whole. They are intended solely to label the Korean players who are WOA (Way Out of Area) and are annoying to the point of spoiling the game for countless innocent Western players whom the US West, US East, and Europe Realms were designed explicitly for.[22]

It is clear to members of KPK, Inc., that they have a certain entitlement to server space and that their language, while "somewhat" derogatory in nature, is not meant to offend, but to label. The primary objection is not about player behavior but, instead, is about presence. It is the very fact that they are on the server ("Way Out of Area") that KPK, Inc., finds objectionable. Thus, KPK, Inc., develops a strategy for marking those who are "spoiling the game" for "innocent Western players."

What gets conflated in this notion, however, is the idea that presence itself constitutes "bad behavior." If you are recognizably Korean and you have a presence on one of these servers, regardless of what you do, you are ruining the experience for others. Moreover, for KPK, Inc., the issue is a foundational one: being Korean violates the design principle. As a result, what is to be banned is not any particular act, but rather the performance of an identity.

The question at stake is one of manifest destiny: not only who owns the space, but who owns the *rights* to the space. KPK, Inc., embodies a kind of American exceptionalism that its members use to justify their extremism. As the voice that can be "generally accepted by everyone," they speak from a position of generality and authority, echoing earlier incarnations of manifest destiny and engaging in external aggressiveness characteristic of "race patriotism," the theory that more "civilized" cultures have a right to expand, and that race, in this case whiteness, often serves as a marker of what Takaki called "political fitness."[23]

Ultimately, the goal of KPK, Inc.'s vitriolic rhetoric is to establish a dichotomy between Western and Korean players that would enable what Reginald Horsman describes as two of the most powerful connectors between race and manifest destiny: making victims responsible for their own destruction and creating an overarching rationalization that makes the group, rather than the individual, responsible for racist—and potentially genocidal—behavior.[24]

Savage Behavior

A significant portion of the KPK, Inc., Web site is used to label, mark, and describe the behavior of Korean players, in an effort to categorize them as "other." In doing so, KPK, Inc., replicates the cultural logic of imperialism. Aware that the initial perception may cause concern, KPK, Inc., wrote several documents defending its rationale for Korean player killing. "For anyone not familiar with playing Diablo II on Battle.net in the Western Realms," the document begins, "a Web site dedicated to PKing Korean players on the grounds that they are out of their area or are simply an annoyance may seem a bit extreme, or even plain mean."[25]

What follows is a set of distinctions designed to separate the proper from the improper, and that distinction relies exclusively—in the KPK, Inc., rhetoric—on notions and understandings of place. While physical markers of race and ethnicity are absent in the virtual world, cultural and geographical markers abound. Not surprisingly, many twentieth- and twenty-first-century American sources of racism have been about place as well. From Rosa Parks refusing to sit in the back of the bus, to disallowing illegal immigrants entry to hospitals and schools in California's Pop 187, racism in America has had as much to do with the physical location of people's bodies as it has to do with other factors.

The primary argument that KPK proffers in defense of killing is that Koreans are, quite simply, out of their place. "The Koreans who are playing outside of Asia" it argues, "are by no means nice, reasonable or in any way fun to play with (with a very few notable exceptions)." Their behaviors, according to KPK, are one-dimensional and well-known: "As all Diablo II players know all too well, they are famous for trying to ransom items that you accidentally drop, filling up the screen with repeated calls for "Item plz!" while you are heavily engaged in battle, not allowing you to talk to NPCs in a high-lag game by following you around and trying to trade incessantly (only to have nothing to trade nor anything to say once the trading screen comes up accept [*sic*] "Item plz!" or "Gold!!!")."[26]

The point of such descriptions is not to argue that the behavior itself is problematic, but that it reflects a savage temperament, which further marks Korean players as out of place. They lack propriety and, as a result, should be excluded from having a place.

It is not merely the interaction that is a problem for KPK, Inc. Its members are also disturbed by Korean players' isolation.

Korean players are also famous for starting private, 1 player games for a few minutes, leaving, and starting a new game. Why would that hurt anybody? Well, all the legitimate *indigenous* players on the Western Realms are having to wait up to 20 minutes in a game-creation que [*sic*] just to play! It also contributes to server splits.[27]

Of course, one cannot help but notice the deployment of the term *indigenous* to describe the players of the U.S. West realm. It is a term that connotes both an historical claim and a geographic/spatial connection to the space in question. Most important, as a location of privilege, the notion of being a native (as the word itself suggests), conveys a *birth right*, something to which U.S. players have no more claim than any other player who is "born" on that server.

Finally, KPK, Inc., offers what its members regard as the ultimate solution, which is the virtual extermination of Korean players. By repeatedly killing them, and thereby interfering with their game-play (in essence doing precisely what they accuse Koreans of doing to them), KPK, Inc., members want to drive Koreans back to what they see as the Korean's *proper* place: the Asian realms. "All we want to do," the site explains, "is PK [player-kill] them enough times in a row that they are convinced to stop playing outside of Asia."[28]

The right, they claim, is geographically based: "Within the Asia realm, we Westerners are the intruders and must abide by their rules. When they are in our realms, they must abide by our guidelines and rules of decency." And this right is dependent on players to enforce. While Blizzard could have easily set an IP address filter to distribute players geographically to regional servers, it allowed players to connect to any realm. Doing so facilitated players connecting with friends or other players in different time zones or in other parts of the world.

One of the primary motives for Koreans to play on U.S. servers was economic. The economy of *Diablo II* found its most dramatic expression on eBay, where items were frequently bought and sold, even though the game's end user license agreement strictly prohibited such acts. Items that were "hot" on the realms could be bought and sold for real money on eBay and the process became so lucrative, with items often selling for hundreds of dollars, that a cadre of "professional" *Diablo II* game players emerged who spent their days playing the game and item-hunting, posting their items each day for auction. At the height of the game's popularity, a professional game player could make $200 to $300 a day. A significant portion of those professional gamers were Koreans, who recognized and exploited a significant American market for these virtual goods.[29]

Accordingly, to be a successful trader, one needed to have access to the realms where Americans played. As the process of trading became more and more lucrative, increasing numbers of Korean players began playing on U.S. servers. The conflict between U.S. and Korean players was framed differently for Blizzard than it was for KPK, Inc., and other players who shared their beliefs.

While players could easily have petitioned Blizzard to shut down accounts that were violating the terms of service for the game by selling items on eBay, they chose a different tactic, preferring instead to take matters into their own hands. As the KPK Web site explains it, "Blizzard has, of course, anticipated all of these problems and arguments about realms, jurisdiction, etc. and has decided to stay out of the arguments and disputes between and amongst players. Therefore, it is fully fair and decent within the rules of the game and the game world of Diablo II for us to band together to fend off the irritating, offending players."

Because Blizzard had opted to stay out of the conflict, players not only felt the need to take matters into their own hands, they felt perfectly justified in doing so within the framework of the game itself. Blizzard, they felt, had provided them with the necessary tools to defend their borders as they had constructed them in their own imaginations. By implication, if they were simply following the "rules of the game" and being "fair and decent," it would be impossible to accuse them of being racist, without implicating both Blizzard and the mechanics of the game itself in their racism. Doing so marks the first step in the strategy of disavowal, which is designed both to avoid charges of racism and ensure the maintenance of a possessive investment in white privilege and white-dominated game-play.

Race, Place, and Disavowal

KPK, Inc., members are clearly aware that their words, actions, and rhetoric will be read as racist. Accordingly, they go to great lengths to explain what racism is and why their discourse should not be read as racist. Central to their discussion is the formulation of racism as an "all-or-nothing" proposition. Racism, they contend, has a certain absolutist quality, which must be both "open" and "100% derogatory." Such conditionality provides a space for disavowal through possessive investment. Racism is no longer defined either by the content of the discourse or the effect that such language or actions may have on others. Instead, racism is defined, or rather negated and erased, by uses of counterexamples. To prove one is *not* racist, all one must do, according to KPK, Inc., is to provide a counterexample to what its members consider racism.

As the KPK, Inc., Web site warns visitors:

As was stated on the NOTICE page, this site is not racist, nor do we condone open racism. Your personal views are your own, of course, and nobody can stop you from feeling or thinking whatever way that you do. However, on this site, we do not and will not condone the use of openly racial slurs which are popularly recognized as being 100% derogatory. Please refrain from the use of words such as: Gook, Dog-Eater, Frog-Head, and Slant-Eyes. They imply much more than annoying B.net behavior and also indicate a distaste for all Asians, not just Koreans.

Let's not miss the point here, we are only concerned with Diablo II on Battle.net, not world issues or race. Also, please remember that it is within KPK Inc. policy to place a non-Korean on the Most Wanted List, and really, this site is all about PKing the most annoying bastards on B.net who try to spoil the fun for the rest of us. It just so happens to be that 99% of them are Koreans, thus KPK.

The "notice" they provide reads like a primer in how to avoid *accusations* of racism, while outlining permissible permutations of racist discourse. In fact, the only prohibition explicitly stated is against *open* racism, adding that, "of course, nobody can stop you from feeling or thinking whatever way you want to do." One may not use "openly racial slurs which are popularly recognized as being 100% derogatory," but one must instead target racial slurs more specifically to Koreans.

For youth in a digital learning environment, such statements may well be taken as normative assessments of what is and is not valid as racism or racist thinking. The KPK Web site is, in essence, defining not only race, but the practice of racism itself.

The "notice" is designed to reinforce the two central arguments that KPK, Inc., has put forward in defense of racism: the specificity of Koreans who are "out of place," and the notion of "savage behavior." To return to Lipsitz's notion of possessive investment, it is important to note how preemption and disavowal function in unison to redefine notions of social relations as they are constructed around race. Here KPK, Inc., offers a series of disavowals that reflect three distinct strategies: disavowal by example, disavowal by circumstance, and disavowal by denial.

The rhetorical strategy of argument by example takes what the site's author believes is compelling evidence that logically precludes KPK members from being racist. Often this kind of disavowal will center around acquaintances or friendships, or their connection to people of color offering "proof" that they are not racist; after all, how could a true racist count a black, Latino, or Asian person as a friend?

The head of KPK, Inc., extends the logic one step farther in arguing that "KPK Inc. is in no way racist, nor do we support racism. [the site owner] has absolutely no problem with Asians in general and is, in fact, married to one." While the connection between friendship and marriage on one hand, and cultural attitudes toward race on the other, are tenuous at best and non sequiturs at the worst.

The second argument suggests a broader social or cultural context that provides a rationale for racist behavior. It is a "racism happens" argument, the result of conflict, emotion, and lack of effective borders:

As people from different cultures, backgrounds, social castes, races, and religions have come into contact with each other throughout history, there has always been an element of distrust and conflict. It is only natural that this same situation would exist on the Internet where there are no effective borders, and especially in the online gaming world where the very games we play against each other direct us to compete and fight some way. Generally speaking, people of like backgrounds tend to stick together, and in these games the situation is no different. Unfortunately, the emotions present in the game world sometimes surpass those that were intended by the game designers, and it is possible for these heightened emotions to take the form of open racism.[30]

Again, the Web site performs a didactic function, educating the reader about the historical context (and, in this case, acceptability and inevitability) of racism. As a pedagogical strategy, the site deploys techniques familiar to youth, particularly those in their midteens, who would encounter the contexts of history as a legitimate learning context.

Finally, the site owner's disavowal is completed through denial (in the double sense of the word): "Here at KPK Inc. we absolutely do not support, condone, or acquiesce to any strictly racist views. Of course, each and every individual is welcome to his view of the world, but expressions of pure racism are not permissible and are, in the end, truly counterproductive."[31]

Conclusions

The case of *Diablo II* is, in some respects, a familiar performance of national and racial adherence, employing classic tropes and forms now mapped onto an unusual, but still rather literal, representation of space and territory. And yet the strangeness of the circumstances brings out this episode's formal character—the need for an identity principle that can define the in-group ("people of like backgrounds tend to stick together, and in these games the situation is no different") despite the manifest difficulty of knowing who one's compatriots are. There is the overproduction of racialized injury on an extremely thin basis of social contact. On the one hand, the formal character of identity is testimony to the portability of the race–nation discourse: it should come as no surprise that it can be asserted in virtual spaces, or that investments in virtual lives should give rise to real senses of injury. On the other hand, the formal character is suggestive of the way these events come to resemble a game within the game—with rules, a narrative, forms of action, and arguably less of a requirement that the racist overflow be integrated into a larger racist worldview, with outside-the-game implications. Such games within the game develop through the processes of player-constructed meaning and action that always surround the game-space, no matter how scripted. If this margin around the game is responsible for a great outpouring of new roles and forms of cultural engagement—of playful interventions—it should come as no surprise that it also produces playful hatreds.

As massively multiplayer online games advance, so have the arguments about notions of nation, space, and race. Games such as *Lineage* and *Lineage II* have produced heated conflict over race, nationality and playstyles,[32] and most recently *World of Warcraft* has responded to player complaints of Chinese players' "gold farming" by banning hundreds of thousands of accounts from the game. Many of the arguments proffered in support of killing Korean players in *Diablo II* have found their way into the gamer lexicon and have been applied to Chinese players working for companies that farm items and gold in most of the larger multiplayer games.

Throughout this essay, my chief claim has been that we should look to issues of power, privilege, and investment as markers of race in cyberspace, and that often these issues are manifested in strategies of denial and disavowal, rather than explicit racism. All too often, our temptation is to look for the physical markers of race and ethnicity, markers that are easily erased or submerged within the nonphysical space of virtual worlds. That does not mean that race, ethnicity, or racism have disappeared, but rather that each has been transformed, and in some cases radically altered, within the context of the net. As we examine these issues, we need to pay careful attention not only to the representations of race and ethnicity as they appear on the surface, but also to the emergent cultures that spawn around these images and representations. Doing so can help us to understand not only what is being learned in the context of new media, but how issues of race and ethnicity are being woven into the fabric of culture through the language and practices that people use in their responses to difference and change.

Notes

1. Douglas Thomas and John Seely Brown, The Play of Imagination, *Games & Culture* 2, no. 2 (2007): 149–172.

2. Beth Kolko, Erasing @race: Going White in the (Inter)face, in *Race in Cyberspace*, eds. Beth E. Kolko, Lisa Nakamura, and Gilbert B. Rodman (New York: Routledge, 2000), 213–32.

3. Kali Tal, Life Behind the Screen, *Wired* 4, no. 10 (1996): 134–6.

4. George Lipsitz, *The Possessive Investment in Whiteness: How White People Profit from Identity Politics* (Philadelphia: Temple University Press, 2006), viii.

5. See, e.g., Ellen Seiter's *The Internet Playground: Children's Access, Entertainment, and Mis-Education* (New York: Peter Lang, 2005).

6. For a discussion of the need for this research see, David Leonard, Not a Hater, Just Keepin' It Real: The Importance of Race- and Gender-based Game Studies, *Games & Culture* 1, no. 1 (2006): 83–88; and Anna Everett, Serious Play: Playing with Race in Contemporary Gaming Culture, in *Handbook of Computer Game Studies*, ed. Joost Raessens and Jeffrey Goldstein (Cambridge, MA: MIT Press, 2005), 311–26.

7. For an extensive reading of one such game culture, see T. L. Taylor's *Play Between Worlds: Exploring Online Game Culture* (Cambridge, MA: MIT Press, 2006).

8. See Bruce Sterling Woodcock's "An Analysis of MMOG Subscription Growth—Version 21.0" at http://www.mmogchart.com. Retrieved June 17, 2007.

9. See, e.g., recent work done on gaming in international contexts.

10. See http://www.bluesnews.com/cgi-bin/articles.pl?show=44. Retrieved June 17, 2007. Sales figures are quoted from PC Data, the industry standard for monitoring and tracking PC games sales figures.

11. See Diablo II, http://www.blizzard.com/diablo2/.

12. See Edward Castronova, *Synthetic Worlds: The Business and Culture of Online Games* (Chicago: Chicago University Press, 2005); and Julian Dibbell, *Play Money: Or, How I Quit My Day Job and Made Millions Trading Virtual Loot* (New York: Basic Books, 2006).

13. Benedict Anderson, *Imagined Communities: Reflections on the Origin and Spread of Nationalism* (New York: Verso, 1991), 7.

14. Edward Said, *Orientalism* (New York: Vintage, 1973), 12.

15. Lipsitz, *The Possessive Investment in Whiteness,* viii.

16. Kye Leung, Asians and Asian Americans Face Racism in Online Game, *Azine.* http://www.aamovement.net/art_culture/games/diablo2.html. Retrieved June 17, 2007.

17. See http://www.kpk.250x.com. All references to the KPK are from this Web site. Retrieved June 17, 2007.

18. Ibid.

19. Anderson, *Imagined Communities,* 7.

20. See http://www.kpk.250x.com.

21. Jacques Derrida, *The Gift of Death* (Chicago: Chicago University Press, 1996), 68.

22. See the KPK, Inc., Web site.

23. Ronald Takaki, *Iron Cages: Race and Culture in 19th Century America* (New York: Oxford University Press, 1990), 269.

24. Reginald Horsman, *Race and Manifest Destiny: Origins of American Racial Anglo-Saxonism* (Cambridge, MA: Harvard University Press, 1981).

25. See the KPK, Inc., Web site.

26. Ibid.

27. Ibid.

28. Ibid.

29. See, e.g., Ted Castronova's analysis of this phenomenon in *Synthetic Worlds,* 122.

30. See the KPK, Inc., Web site.

31. KPK, "Racism and Multiplayer NetGames." http://www.kpk.250x.com/race.htm. Retrieved June 17, 2007.

32. Constance Steinkuehler, The Mangle of Play, *Games & Culture* 1, no. 3 (2006): 1–14.

Health Disparity and the Racial Divide among the Nation's Youth: Internet as a Site for Change?

Mohan J. Dutta, Graham D. Bodie, and Ambar Basu

Purdue University, Department of Communication

Some of the most positive consequences of the Internet have been demonstrated in the realm of health benefits for children and youth.[1] Approximately 21 million youths used the Internet in 2005, up from 17 million in 2000.[2] One of the fastest-developing uses of the Internet among the youth is to obtain health information, with this category seeing a growth of 47 percent between 2000 and 2005.[3] Furthermore, 44 percent of eighteen- to twenty-four-year-olds using the Internet do so to search for information about sensitive topics such as pregnancy, birth control, and AIDS, and 39 percent of these young online health information seekers have changed their personal behaviors because of information obtained online. With respect to the youth, online health information offers an effective means of (a) communicating with doctors, (b) managing chronic heath problems online, (c) learning health information, and (d) participating in online prevention campaigns.[4] Ultimately, online health information seeking impacts the health outcomes of the nation's youth.

In this chapter, we interrogate the link between the distribution of communication technologies among youth and the race-based health disparities that exist among the nation's youth. Several lines of work explore the intersections between the research areas of the digital divide and health disparities, suggesting that the distribution of health disparities mirrors the distribution of communication technologies. In other words, the racially marginalized sectors of the nation's youth are doubly disadvantaged by their lack of access to health care technologies and communication technologies. We suggest mechanisms through which lack of access to health care technologies among youth influences health outcomes. To do so we present an integrative model of online health information seeking that incorporates individual motivation and ability to use the Internet for health purposes. Through this model, we suggest that race-based disparities among the nation's youth are manifested in individual-level differences in the motivation to seek out health information, the perceived ability to search for health information, and the perceived efficacy to use new media technologies such as the Internet owing to deep-seated biases in the traditional communication infrastructures and limited educational opportunities for the underserved. These differences in the motivation and ability to seek out health information and participate in online technologies are situated within structural disparities and, in turn, influence the extent to which individuals search for online health information. We suggest further that the disparities in the social structures that constrain and limit the offline opportunities available to ethnic minorities also constrain the opportunities for online health.

In proposing an agenda for new media applications in health care directed at minority youth, we argue for the importance of (a) ensuring access to online technologies,

(b) developing educational programs that emphasize "how-to" knowledge that builds health information efficacy and technology efficacy in underserved populations, (c) developing culture-centered health care technologies that are organized around the communication needs of underserved youth, and (d) harnessing the dialogic potential of online media for fostering health care activism among the marginalized youth such that they can go about challenging the dominant structures that constrain their lives. We conclude the chapter with a sense of hope, drawing from an example of participation in new media technologies among minority youth,[5] thus demonstrating the ways in which minority youth enact their agency in new media platforms that empower them and challenge dominant structures that constrain or restrict their lives.

Health Disparities among Young Adults

The health care disparities that plague minority youth in the United States narrate a story of structural deprivation where racial and ethnic minority youths have lower access to health care services and preventive choices as compared to middle-class Caucasian youth. If the central goal of eliminating health disparities between ethnic and racial groups within the United States is to be achieved, as proposed by the Healthy People 2010,[6] there is an urgent need to devise policies and strategies that address the race-based structural injustices that plague youth in the United States.[7] The term *health disparities* is defined as the circumstantial result of ongoing experiences of unfairness or injustice in access to, utilization of, and quality of care, health status, or other health outcomes.[8] Williams conceptualized health disparity as being enmeshed within the social context of everyday life.[9] He refers to the importance of factors like race, ethnicity, gender, and social class, and their interactions in the impact on the health and well-being of citizens. Race and ethnicity, often interchangeably used terms, have had a distinct influence on the distribution of and access to health resources in the United States.

In addition to having limited access to basic health care resources, the Institute of Medicine[10] reports that racial and ethnic minorities in the United States still receive a lower quality of care than whites, after accounting for differential access to care. In other words, even within similar socioeconomic classes or when comparing minorities and whites with equal structural access (e.g., availability of hospitals and doctors in the area), minorities receive lower-quality treatment in medical settings. In examining the roots of these disparities, the IoM reported factors such as clinical uncertainty, stereotypical behaviors of providers (physicians and nurses), and conscious bias among health care professionals. The findings of the Commonwealth Fund's 2001 Health Care Quality Survey also demonstrate that minority Americans do not fare as well as whites on a wide range of measures of the quality of health care services they receive because of biases in the health care systems and prejudiced attitudes of providers.[11]

Race can be described as a politically designated term that has been used to explain legitimized inequality of power and opportunity.[12] Historically, race-based differences in U.S. society have resulted in differential/restricted access to socioeconomic resources like educational and employment opportunities. This segregation has meant general lower levels of income in minority families, and lower socioeconomic status. Unhealthy living conditions and limited access to structural resources like transportation, food, medicine, and insurance are all products of this race-based social differential and, in turn, exert a considerable impact on the health and well-being of minorities. Therefore, no one should be surprised that low socioeconomic status, adverse health behaviors, and lack of health insurance have been identified as the primary pathways through which racial disparities are played out in the realm of health.[13]

Several studies have depicted just how race-based differences cause disparities in access to medical care. Williams notes that there is a large body of evidence which indicates that even after adjustment for socioeconomic status, health insurance, and clinical status, whites are more likely than blacks to receive a broad range of specific medical procedures.[14] Among Medicare inpatients, Williams says, blacks were less likely than whites to receive all of the sixteen most common procedures.[15] This demonstrates the prevalence of prejudiced treatments in health care within the United States, even after controlling for social class.

In looking at the disparate health status in minority youth, it is important to draw attention to the structural racism that impedes the opportunities presented to them as well. The systematic absence of support for structural resources is evident in health care policies that continue to ignore issues of redistributive justice, social inequality, and structural violence. The social and cultural environments within which minority youth find themselves are often devoid of the opportunities that are essential to their health. Studies reveal that racial and ethnic minorities are less likely to have access to health care and more likely to be impacted by and die from most major diseases as compared to white youth (e.g., cancer, diabetes).[16]

The per capita health expenditure among white adolescents is $1,180, compared to Hispanics ($627) and African Americans ($439).[17] A sizeable proportion of American youth/children who do not have health insurance are minorities. There are approximately 11 million U.S. children under the age of 18 uninsured, with these individuals being disproportionately of racial and ethnic minority status.[18] According to Lieu, Newacheck, and McManus, children in families headed by single mothers, black children, and those living below 150 percent of the poverty index were much more likely to be in poor or fair health than children in two-parent families, white children, and those in more affluent families.[19] Poverty clearly has a strong effect on child health, and poverty, as has been mentioned earlier, is largely correlated with race and ethnicity.

Pointing out that minority youth face unequal opportunities, options, and access to health resources, Guthrie and Low[20] draw from a review of racial and ethnic disparities in the health care of adolescents by Elster, Jarosik, VanGeest, and Fleming.[21] The review, which included sixty-five published studies, suggests that racial and ethnic disparities in health care for adolescents, as with adults, persist after accounting for access to health care and socioeconomic status because of the inherent prejudice in the health care system. Guthrie and Low go on to add that since adolescence is a period of transformation, it is an ideal time not only to identify and address, but also to prevent potential health disparities commonly found in this group.[22] In addition, they add, adolescents should not be considered downward extensions of the adult population with similar needs and experiences. This trickle-down approach fails to recognize the unique health needs and worldviews that adolescents tend to form and must learn to negotiate.[23] Several other studies corroborate the fact that race and ethnicity significantly influence youth health and account for a major part of health disparities that exist among youth in America. Study data, collected by Shi and Stevens (2005) at two points—in 1996 and 2000—demonstrates that before and after controlling for health insurance coverage, poverty status, health status, and several other factors associated with access to care, these disparities in access to care persisted between 1996 and 2000. This is a pointer to the fact that despite some policy efforts to reduce health disparities based on race and ethnicity, such gaps continue to persist not only among adults but also among the youth of the United States.

Racial differences in health, according to Shi and Stevens, reflect the impact of the social environment and the cumulative effect of adversity across multiple domains. One such domain—in today's digital world—is access to technology, particularly the Internet, which has a proven track record of being an important contributor to the good health and well-being of the population, particularly the youth. Thus, comprehensive efforts to improve the health of racial minority youth and reduce racial disparities in health will require consistent focus on the uses and power of digital learning among today's youth. Systematic efforts would be needed to create learning opportunities that build the confidence of minority youth in using online health platforms, and provide training about ways to use online health resources meaningfully. These efforts would need to be culturally sensitive in order to be able to appeal to minority youth. Culture-centered technology platforms might provide spaces of dialogue with minority youth and create conduits for listening to their voices. Finally, given the material disparity in the health care system, digital media provide a space for minority youth to engage in activism that addresses the social structures and seek to transform them.[24]

The Racial Divide: Where *DO* We Stand?

Initially, the exponential growth of available information online was, and to some degree still is, thought to be the ultimate equalizer, by providing individuals and groups access to a variety of information resources that, in turn, would provide access to structural resources. In its simplest form, the argument suggests that information is power, and free information decimates barriers facing the underserved. This notion is evident in documents such as the National Library of Medicine's (NLM) Strategic Plan for Addressing Health Disparities[25] : "improving access to affordable and easy-to-use health-related information . . . can help solve health disparities." On the surface, the argument seems logical: provide free information to all and they will come. However, a more realistic answer to the question "Where do we stand on matters of universal access and the racial and ethnic digital divide in the 21st century, especially in terms of digital media and learning?" is, unfortunately, "even further from where we started." We surely have not failed to provide information; there are more than 70,000 Web sites that contain health information,[26] and the number of health sites is rapidly increasing.[27] However, we are failing to support adoption campaigns with equal amounts of literacy and usability training, particularly with respect to the underserved. This is perhaps a product of the structurally situated nature of online technologies such that online participation patterns reflect offline participation patterns. The underlying structures that constrain the opportunities for ethnic minorities in the offline world also continue to replicate in the online world, when looked at in the context of the overall patterns of usage.

According to the National Telecommunications and Information Administration (NTIA),[28] the *digital divide* can be defined as the gap between people who have and people who do not have access to Internet technology.[29] Patterns of computer and Internet penetration levels show substantive differences between different racial and ethnic groups in the United States, and similar differences are observed in the realm of online health information seeking.[30] Compared to 23 percent of young Asian Americans and 22 percent of white young adults who use the Internet to search for health information, 13 percent of Native Americans, 12 percent of African Americans, and 11 percent of Hispanics in the segment seek out online health information.[31]

Table 1

Percentage of children living in households with computers

Ethnicity	Percentage
African American	56
Native American	58
Latino	58
Asian American	86
White	87

Table 2

Percentage of children living in households with a computer modem

Native American	41
African American	43
Latino	44
Asian American	75
White	80

Noting the ways in which the digital divide plays out in the realm of citizen participation and involvement, Chen and Wellman[32] argue that "ultimately, the digital divide is a matter of who uses the Internet, for what purpose, under what circumstances, and how this use affects socioeconomic cohesion, inclusion, alienation, and prosperity."[33] In other words, disparities in the accessibilities of health care technologies impact the economic outcomes of social groups, and therefore continue to reinforce the broader structural disparities within the population. The Silicon Valley Joint Venture workforce study[34] suggests that, although 99 percent of youth have access to a computer from some location, Hispanics (69 percent) and African Americans (80 percent) are less likely to have access at home than white or Asian students (94 percent). Although strict access (whether or not a student has a computer available at his or her disposal at some location) does not seem to vary based on ethnicity, the quality of this access has been shown to vary in other studies.[35] The California Department of Education found that schools with higher minority concentration have fewer computers per hundred students than schools with lower minority concentration. Racial minorities are less likely to have broadband access at home than their white or Asian counterparts.[36] This is important because broadband users are more likely to engage in online activities in general.[37]

Furthermore, The Children's Partnership report[38] suggests the following patterns of access among children ages 7 through 17. Compared to 36 percent of children who lived in households with personal computers in 1994, 77 percent of children in 2003 lived in households with personal computers. Access among African American, Native American, and Latino children was significantly lower compared to access among white and Asian American children (see Table 1).

Whereas 15 percent of children in the 7–17 age range lived in households with a computer modem in 1994, 68 percent of children in 2003 lived in households with an Internet connection. Ethnic disparities are also evident in the realm of access to the Internet at home, with whites and Asian Americans having greatest access, as compared to lower levels of access among Native Americans, African Americans, and Hispanics (see Table 2).

Table 3
Percentage of children living in households
with broadband connection

Native American	13
Latino	14
African American	14
White	32
Asian American	33

Table 4
Percentage of young adults who searched for
health information

Latino	11
African American	12
Native American	13
White	22
Asian American	23

Compared to 0 percent of children in ages 7–17 that lived in households with a broadband connection, 26 percent of children in 2003 lived in households with a broadband connection. Differential patterns of access are also observed in this realm (see Table 3).

The Children's Partnership Report also documents ethnic differences in the percentage of young adults (ages 18–25) who searched for health information on the Internet (see Table 4).

Fairlie attempts to explain the ethnic disparities of home computer ownership by appealing to other demographic factors such as education and income.[39] In all, demographics accounted for less than 50 percent of the variance in ethnic difference (comparing each racial category versus whites). Published scholarship on the digital divide suggests that ethnic disparities are larger in children than in adults for computer access at home, and slightly larger in children than in adults for Internet access at home.

Consistent with past research, Jackson et al. point out that (a) African American children use the Internet less than white children, (b) younger children use the Internet less to search for information than older children, and (c) girls are more likely to use the Internet for communication, while boys are more likely to use the Internet for information seeking purposes.[40] Controlling for race, the researchers suggest that Internet use predicted GPA obtained after one year of home Internet access. (After the children of low-income families were given free Internet access, the users had significantly higher GPAs than nonusers.) More time online was associated with higher reading comprehension and total reading scores (not so for math scores), and neither GPA nor standardized test scores predicted Internet use. Children in this project used the Internet to search for information more so than to communicate (i.e., e-mail).

The findings of Jackson et al. also demonstrate that income and education cannot explain racial disparities, and that giving people access is not enough to solve the digital divide. Individuals and communities also need to train underserved groups how to use and benefit from Internet connectivity, and motivate them to take advantage of technology access. Jackson et al. provided low-income families with home computers and Internet access.[41] Racial differences in use, with African Americans reporting less overall use than white participants, were present at the first three-month follow-up, and actually increased at the six-month survey. Thus, it seems that, with the dissemination of computers also comes the responsibility to motivate their use, train users in best-practice strategies, offer hardware and software that is user-friendly, provide low-cost and helpful technical support, and offer help in understanding material and assessing information quality. Although investigating the division between the Internet "haves" and "have nots" is important in all context areas, it is especially important in the context of access to and use of health information. Consider this: Among youth with similar insurance coverage and socioeconomic status (SES), black and Hispanic children are between 31 and 42 percent less likely to use inhaler-driven medication for asthma as compared to white children, even though this illness is more prevalent among these populations.[42]

Although the Internet was initially seen as the great conqueror of social disparities, the introduction of the Internet as a tool to aid in disease control and decision making has actually increased this division between the health haves and the health "have nots."[43] Two broad explanations exist for this gap. First, race and ethnicity as social categories are at the root of this disparity. Low socioeconomic status (SES), adverse health behaviors, and lack of health insurance have been identified as the primary pathways through which racial disparities are played out in the realm of health.[44] Therefore, within this framework, race and ethnicity, like any other individual-level difference, should not be considered in isolation but instead should be considered as a part of an individual's overall status.[45] Focusing strictly on demographic characteristics of the individual or specific minority group is similarly flawed. Thus, a second explanation appeals to a psychographic approach[46] that connects macro-level characteristics with individual-level features in the realm of e-health information usage. Online health information seeking among youths[47] seems to mirror general health information seeking offline;[48] both tend to be higher among whites than among minorities. It has been suggested that individual motivation and ability to attend to certain types of information in general, or information on the Internet specifically,[49] and a pattern of decreased medical information seeking overall among certain minority groups,[50] may better explain online health disparities.

The integrative model of online health information seeking we propose in this chapter connects the racial disparities at the population level with the individual-level characteristics that are directly related to the amount and type of health information usage on the Internet owing to broader social structures that undermine most learning opportunities and resources available to minority youth. We suggest that the racial disparities among youth are manifested in the form of individual-level differences in health information orientation and health information efficacy that result from deep-seated structural differences in the learning opportunities available to youth.

Integrative Model of Online Health Information Seeking

The Integrative Model of Online Health Information Seeking (IMOHIS) suggests that macro-level disparities in social structures play out in the realm of individual-level differences in motivation and ability, thus connecting the broader structures in social systems with the micro-level or individual contexts. In other words, the individual-level differences in motivation and ability become the conduits through which the structural inequities reinforce themselves and continue to contribute to health care disparities. Therefore, the racial divide is not only played out through differentials in access to the health care infrastructures within social systems, but are further reinforced and sustained by disparities in access to and

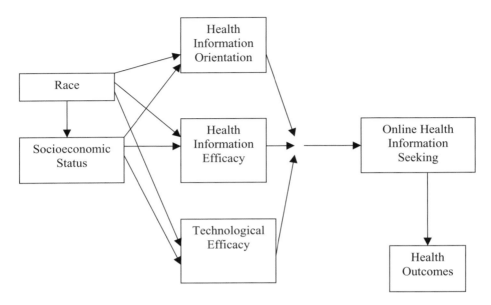

Figure 1
Integrative Model of Online Health Information Seeking (IMOHIS).

usage of communication infrastructures. Figure 1 presents the IMOHIS based on the media effects literature.[51] According to this model, both motivation and ability are key contributors to online health information seeking. The model is particularly relevant for examining youth learning and usage as patterns of access, use, and learning established during youth are reinforced through the life cycle. These patterns also set the stage for future uses of technologies and patterns of health information seeking that are enacted at various life stages of the individual.

The IMOHIS suggests that the underlying social structure determines the intrinsic interest in health that, in turn, results in the search for health information. Health orientation, which reflects the intrinsic consumer interest in issues of health, fundamentally contributes to the consumer motivation to search for health information online. Health-oriented youth are more likely to seek out health information on the Internet compared to their less health-oriented counterparts. This motivation in health-related issues is embedded within the structural context, being shaped and socially constituted through the society within which the youth come to understand and live in the world. For instance, Dutta-Bergman[52] demonstrated that motivation in health-related issues increases with education and income. Existing scholarship also documents a strong relationship between race and health orientation, suggesting that the motivation in health-related issues is greater among certain segments of the population as compared to others. These differences in health orientation are created through the social contexts within which children understand and act on the value of health. In structurally deprived contexts where the day-to-day struggles for survival are played out in the lives of young people, the opportunities for learning about positive health behaviors and health-enhancing resources are fairly limited.[53]

In addition to the motivation for health information seeking, the individual needs to have those structural-level components—like reliable access to the Internet—that foster a sense of self-efficacy (or self-sufficiency) for its use for purposes of health information seeking. The concept of efficacy taps into the individual's belief in his or her ability to engage in constructive behavior. The twin concepts of health information efficacy and technological efficacy capture the perceived ability to seek out health information and use new communication technologies respectively. The greater the efficacy, the stronger the likelihood that individuals will be motivated to engage in health information seeking. Efficacy, once again, is structurally constituted and directly related to a lower level of perceived ability to seek out health information among minorities. Similarly, the perceived ability to use communication technologies to meet felt needs is lower among racial minorities. These perceptual barriers in using technologies and seeking out health information are very much constituted by real differentials in access to communication infrastructures. Finally, the motivation and efficacy components are interlinked, and are themselves defined within the larger structural environment of the American economy.

Health Information Orientation

Health information orientation reflects the underlying motivation the individual feels in regard to health-related topics and, therefore, taps into the degree of personal interest in health information. This degree of interest in a health topic by minority youth is often limited because of the inherent biases built into the system. For instance, existing research on health promotion documents the white-middle-class bias of health-promoting campaigns that reach out to the haves while simultaneously ignoring the have-nots, also known as the underserved segments of the population.[54] The high health information–oriented individual actively monitors his or her environment and scans for relevant health information to ensure that he/she is not at risk of disease or illness. By comparison, the low health information–oriented individual is less likely to participate in health information seeking. Thus, it may be argued that health information orientation would lead to the active search for health-related information, capturing the intrinsic consumer interest in health topics. In the context of the nation's youth, the extent of motivation felt toward health-related topics would influence the ways in which the youth seek out health information, and monitor the environment for health information, as well as the ways in which they learn from the health content that they encounter in both traditional and new media information venues.

Our understanding about health information orientation is that there exist variances in the types of channels through which high and low health information–oriented individuals learn health content. In fact, studies point out that the health information–oriented individual is more likely to learn health information from active and information-heavy communication channels, which is not the same for the individual who is not health information oriented or has a low level of health information orientation. This knowledge about the link between health information orientation and health information seeking is essential to the design, implementation, and evaluation of preventive health interventions. With a large number of youth-targeted interventions focusing on the issue of prevention, it is particularly important to develop communication strategies involving new communication technologies that speak to both levels of health information orientations exhibited by the nation's youth. Also, examination of the relationship between health information orientation and health information seeking provides a theoretical framework for understanding the communication system surrounding high and low health information–oriented individuals, and the ways in which these systems might be structurally improved in order to meet the information needs of individuals, groups, and communities. In addition, by investigating the role of motivation in health information seeking, the IMHIS provides an explanatory pathway for articulating the process underlying the use of the Internet for purposes of health information seeking among the nation's youth. It also offers a mechanism for understanding the ways in which racial disparities influence health outcomes through their impact on information seeking and information processing strategies.

Health information orientation not only influences the amount of health information sought out by the individual, but also influences the information processing strategies he or she adopts. Dual processing theories point out that motivation triggers an individual's intrinsic interest in a particular issue or topic, which leads to active engagement in cognitions, attitudes, and behaviors related to the specific issue/topic.[55] In other words, motivation activates individual engagement in information processing, decision making, and adoption of behavioral choices based on the consideration of arguments presented in health information messages. A high level of motivation increases the attention paid by the individual to relevant information and to the comprehension of such material. It also increases the active information search for issue-based information. Therefore, a health-motivated individual actively participates in health-related issues and actively searches out relevant health information.[56] For America's youth, the extent of health information orientation is likely to influence the degree of attention paid to online health information and the way in which the information is attended.

In the absence of health-enhancing structures within the minority community, young people are less likely to learn about the relevance of health behaviors, to have role models promoting health behaviors, and to value health-promoting behaviors owing to the lack of resources that would support such behaviors. As a consequence, they are more likely to focus on the daily struggles of survival. In this sense, being able to be healthy is more deeply connected with basic survival needs, such as being able to procure adequate food for the day, being able to secure shelter, staying out of the path of violence, and so forth. In terms of racialized social contexts, the structures surrounding the lives of African American and Latino youth provide minimal opportunities for health-enhancing behaviors, and often are embedded within threatening structures of violence, such as police brutality, structural racism, racially driven strike laws, the war on drugs, and so on. Under such circumstances, the opportunities for developing and sustaining health orientation within these underserved communities remain minimal. Therefore, health policies ought to focus on creating sustainable structures within these communities that would promote health orientation among young children and adolescents. Communication initiatives promoting healthy attitudes and behaviors ought to be supplemented with structural changes and allocation of resources that would promote health orientation.

Health Information Efficacy

The concept of health information efficacy is built on the existing research on self-efficacy, which refers to the degree of confidence individuals have in their ability to perform a health behavior, and positively predicts the adoption of preventive behaviors.[57] It is the perceived ability to exert personal control, and in this case, capture the extent of confidence individuals feel in their ability to engage in health information seeking. Self-efficacy influences the likelihood of health information seeking and health information processing.[58] Health information efficacy refers to the intrinsic consumer belief in his or her ability to search for and process health information. Among the nation's youth, health information efficacy varies with the extent to which youth feel empowered to make their own sound health choices, and the extent to which they feel they have access to the basic resources of health that are critical to survival. Efficacy, in these terms, is embedded in social structures, such as when white youth with access receive a variety of educational programs and other advantages that encourage a certain level of comfort with using and evaluating health information. This is in contrast to minority youth who systematically receive lesser opportunities for learning about health information and its uses.

In addition to motivating health information seeking in these minority youth, they need to have access to the Internet, and the ability to use the Internet for pertinent health information processing. Efficacy, then, is shaped by the dispositional orientation of the consumer, his or her experience with the medium (Internet), and his or her demographic characteristics. Of particular relevance are the demographic correlates of access and efficacy, given the technology-related gaps in the population. Individual uses of the Internet for health care purposes influence a variety of outcomes, such as accessibility of care, quality of care, patient satisfaction, physician–patient relationship, and the effectiveness of health care policy. Health information efficacy among the youth varies with race such that African Americans and Latinos perceive lower levels of efficacy as compared to whites. This perception is both created and maintained by the actual limitations encountered by minority youth. As explained above, minority youth are less likely to have computer or Internet access at home, as well as have limited access to broadband connections at school. Moreover, the Web sites devoted to health issues for minorities have been shown to be of poorer quality and are harder to access from search engines such as Google and Yahoo. Lower levels of efficacy are tied to the material absence of tools and resources in the African American and Latino segments of the population. The structural absence of critical resources contributes to the perceptions of barriers where engaging in health information seeking is concerned. These perceptions of barriers however are very tangible and are connected to the material absence of resources in these underserved communities. Furthermore, African American and Latino youth also experience barriers in terms of the knowledge and the know-how with respect to the uses of health information sources, and processing strategies for identifying and using information received from credible sources. This suggests the need for health literacy programs that emphasize training children and youth in strategies for seeking out, deciphering, and evaluating the quality of health information. Such programs may be instituted through classrooms, but also through community-based programs that seek to build health information–processing skills in underserved communities.

Technological Efficacy

Another important element in our research is the concept of technological efficacy, which reflects the extent to which individuals perceive their ability to navigate communication technologies. As a reflector of perceived ability, technological efficacy impacts the extent to which youth are likely to use communication technologies to fulfill their health information needs. Rojas et al. support the argument that dispositions toward technology drive its use.[59] Dispositions come from social, cultural, and economic surroundings and are reinforced (rather than changed) by school and peer environments. The absence of capacity-building infrastructures in minority communities (such as training programs, educational opportunities in schools, support networks promoting technology, and technology-promoting messages) systematically contributes to the low levels of technological efficacy in these underserved communities. Furthermore, in instances in which training programs are available, their racially biased characteristics fail to attract youth from underserved communities. Minorities may not view the Internet as having anything of value to offer, or may not be motivated or able to access information due to other pressures, social climate, et cetera. In fact, the individuals interviewed in the Rojas et al. study[60] reported not accessing the Internet from the libraries where so many have focused attention to alleviate the divide. Similarly, Pinkett[61] argues that "people must be able to see the relevance of technology in order to fully embrace it. At the same time, since access does not imply use, and use does not imply meaningful use, we must also consider the nature of engagement we seek to promote."[62]

Regarding race-related issues, minorities such as African Americans and Latinos are more likely to run into barriers to using new media technologies because of the systematic absence of literacy programs and capacity-building efforts targeting African American and Latino communities. This suggests the need for training programs that equip these underserved communities with skills for using technologies to meet their information-processing needs. In the realm of health, health literacy programs may be combined with technological literacy programs in order to build the overall information efficacy of underserved individuals, groups, and communities. These programs would need to be culturally sensitive in order to respond to the needs of the minority communities. Furthermore, technologically mediated spaces may be developed that are responsive to the characteristics of these cultures as well. Also, a culture-centered approach to technological efficacy would suggest the need to develop technology platforms for the voices of minority youths based on specific technology-based programs that build community capacity to articulate community concerns. This last strategy is evident in the MySistahs project presented later.

Online Health Opportunities: From Information Seeking to Activism

The literature on online health information seeking suggests that searching for health information on the Internet is correlated with a variety of outcomes that are beneficial to individual health.[63] Researchers studying the role of the Internet in the context of health suggest that searching for health information on the Internet equips consumers with the ability to engage in preventive behaviors, empowers them in the context of their ability to navigate physician–patient relationships, empowers active health care consumer participation in the realm of policies that impede health outcomes, and fosters community platforms for social change by presenting possible communicative spaces for engaging the health active segment of the population.

Online Health Information Seeking and Health Disparities
Ultimately, the IMOHIS offers a theoretical framework for understanding population-level health care disparities among youth by suggesting mediating mechanisms through which health information orientation, health information efficacy, and technological efficacy influence online health information seeking. From a policy standpoint, the model also lays out key foundations for addressing health care and communication infrastructures with the goal of reducing the inequities in health care among the nation's youth. The motivation and perceived capacity to navigate health information tends to be lower among the marginalized communities within social systems, thus reinforcing the existing disparities within the social

systems.[64] Health information seeking is a critical component in modern-day consumer decision-making processes and closely tied with a variety of health outcomes,[65] and therefore, the extent to which certain segments of the population seek out health information significantly affects the health outcomes of these segments. In examining issues of inequity in online health information seeking, it is critical to pay attention to issues of access, patterns of usage, and evaluations of quality of online health information. We will argue that all of these components are significantly interrelated with health information orientation and health information efficacy within the population.

Access and Equity

The differential patterns of health care access are a growing area of concern for policy makers, practitioners, and academics working in the health care sector. Increasingly, scholarly articles continue to document the disparities in access to basic health care such that, whereas health care is accessible for some population segments, such care and its benefits are typically inaccessible to the marginalized segments of society.[66] Health care access typically reflects sociodemographic differentials such that higher-SES groups have significantly greater access to health care infrastructures as compared to lower-SES groups. These differential patterns of access in the context of SES are relevant for racial disparities because racial inequities mirror SES disparities. These patterns of inaccessibility to health care services are also replicated on the Internet, such that those with minimal access to health care structures also have minimal access to health information infrastructures, such as health Web sites.[67]

Therefore, African Americans and Hispanics have minimal access to both health information and health care infrastructures as compared to whites. People with preventable health problems and without insurance coverage are least likely to have access to the necessary communication technologies that would serve as repositories of health information.[68] Digital divide studies attest to the significant differences between the higher- and lower-SES groups in the realm of access to the Internet, with the lower-SES groups facing a variety of barriers such as cost, location, illiteracy, physical ability, and capacity.[69] The differential demographic distribution of both health information orientation and health information efficacy between high- and low-SES groups further suggests differential patterns of access to health information resources on the Web. These patterns are also reiterated in the realm of race and ethnicity, and further documented in the context of access among young children and adolescents, because ethnic disparities also provide the contexts for disparities in SES. As documented earlier in this chapter, African American and Hispanic youth have more limited access to health information infrastructures as compared to white and Asian American youth.

We know that research on the knowledge gap documents the fact that public information campaigns typically improve overall outcome levels, and simultaneously increases the gaps between the higher- and lower-SES groups of society.[70] Health information systems on the Internet are likely to contribute to such gaps. Also, the motivation factor serves an important role as a mediating variable because higher-SES groups are typically more health information oriented as compared to lower-SES groups.[71] As a result, higher-SES groups are more likely to seek out health information resources on the Internet, process information from such resources, and adopt healthy behaviors as compared to lower-SES groups.[72] These disparities in SES are also reflective of the structural disparities in the context of race, as certain racial and ethnic groups are more likely to be clustered in the higher-SES segments as compared to other groups. This presupposes the need for public and governmental efforts that are specifically targeted at reducing the gaps between the health "haves" and "have-nots" in society by creating sustainable technological resources for health information access and by developing initiatives for increasing awareness of such resources.[73] Such efforts need to highlight both issues of access and motivation. Eng et al.[74] recommend steps such as providing public and residential access, increasing health and technology literacy, and integrating universal access into health planning. Technology—such as multimedia kiosks, information portals, and Internet-equipped computers—needs to be made available in publicly accessible spaces. One such attempt in bridging the digital divide is the creation of community technology centers (CTCs) that offer public access computer facilities located in low-income neighborhoods.[75] Furthermore, sustainable efforts need to be put into place for developing health information efficacy among the underserved ethnic segments of the population through the development of sustainable communication skills for seeking out and processing health information.

Schools in underserved communities (such as primarily African American, Hispanic, and Native American communities) need to incorporate specifically health-oriented programs that seek to build health information orientation and health information efficacy in the cultural practices of underprivileged groups. Such programs also need to include components of self-motivation and response efficacy to increase the perceived ability of the underprivileged segments in using the Internet for health care purposes. Targeted workshops and training sessions are needed to teach technology literacy skills related to the effective and efficient use of the Internet, and thus build health information efficacy in the everyday lives of the population. For instance, Salovey et al.[76] developed two community technology centers affiliated with two Head Start early childhood education programs in New Haven, Connecticut, one of the three poorest cities in the state of Connecticut. The program trained Head Start staff members to become technology coaches, and offered training programs for Head Start parents as well as other individuals in the neighborhood who desired training. For another option, health Web sites could be deployed for delivering tailored health prevention campaigns that address the needs of the at-risk groups, and deliver communication messages that match the stage of change of the consumer.[77] Such message tailoring might be particularly relevant for the underserved sectors of the population because of the uniqueness of the barriers and the information needs experienced in such segments.

Patterns of Usage

As we have shown, not only do consumers within diverse population sectors differ in their access to communication infrastructures, but they also vary in their patterns of usage of the Internet for various functions.[78] In fact, recent scholarship on the digital divide questions the simplistic notion of the digital divide being conceptualized in terms of basic access or inaccess, and calls for further exploration of the ways in which various segments of the population use the Internet.[79] In other words, we ought to look beyond ownership of computer and Internet connection to explore the ways in which computer access is put to use.

Racial divides are significantly evident in patterns of health information usage, with African Americans being significantly less health information oriented compared to Caucasians and Asian Americans. Internet health information seeking disparities mirror the broader patterns of disparities in the population. This suggests the relevance of investing in capacity building in underserved communities that have low levels of health information orientation and health information efficacy.[80]

In addition to investing in infrastructures in such communities, health communicators and policy makers ought to focus on creating educational resources that foster better patterns of health information orientation and health information efficacy in underserved communities. Specific programs addressing the barriers faced by racial and ethnic minorities need to be put into place; also, efforts need to be targeted toward building efficacy through skills training. For instance, educational programs seeking to provide training in searching, evaluating, and deciphering health information would help address the barriers related to the extent of overload that the underserved groups face. Similarly, culturally sensitive design opportunities need to be created for the developers of online health information to respond to the communities that are in most need for health information.

Quality

The rapid growth in the use of Web sites for consumer health decision making has led to increasing concerns in the expert community about the quality of health information retrieved by patients.[81] This concern is built on the notion that anyone can post health information on the Internet, and in the absence of a qualified gatekeeper, there really isn't a way to monitor the quality of what gets published. In this context, the onus of evaluating online health information and deciphering the quality of the information posted on a certain Web site shifts onto the consumer. Researchers studying quality suggests that the quality of health information retrieved from the Internet influences the value, cost, and effectiveness of care received by the patient.[82]

Criteria for assessing quality in the area of Internet use for health care include source credibility, accuracy, completeness, relevance, and applicability.[83] Also, applying the IMOHIS to our understanding of quality suggests that the ways in which the quality of a health Web site would be evaluated depend on the motivation and ability of the consumer using the Web site. From the perspective of the underlying motivation to search for health information, it may be articulated that highly health information oriented consumers will be more likely to pay attention to systematic quality criteria in evaluating a Web site. In other words, the evaluation of quality is a heterogeneous process that varies with the information seeking functions of the consumer. Whereas certain quality criteria might be particularly relevant for consumer decision making in the domain of particular Internet functions, other quality criteria become critically relevant when the consumer uses the Internet for other functions. For instance, the consumer using the Internet for purchasing medicines might be more likely to evaluate the privacy policy of the Web site as compared with the consumer who is simply surfing the Internet for health information.

Similarly, health information efficacy also influences the quality criteria used by the consumer. Consumers who have high levels of health information efficacy are likely to pay attention to systematic cues that require considerable cognitive effort. Such cues might include the evaluation of the completeness and accuracy of the information on the Web site. On the other hand, individuals who have low levels of health information efficacy are perhaps more likely to apply heuristic quality criteria such as Web site design, the presence of visuals on the Web site, and Web site organization in evaluating the Web site. Given the population-based disparities in the distribution of health information orientation and health information efficacy among the different ethnic groups, there is a greater need for focused efforts on developing initiatives for training the low-health-oriented segments in the evaluation of quality of health information in patient decision making. Sustainable educational programs need to be created that work with the youth on developing quality indicators for evaluating health Web sites and making health care decisions. Finally, engaging with online media also offers an opportunity for challenging the structural disparities through projects of activism involving minority youth.

Health Care Activism: Enacting Agency Online

It is not hard to find digital projects that involve youth in activist enterprises aimed at improving their health. There is the "Truth" project that successfully brands "truth teens" as a socially acceptable, responsible segment of youth who shun the allures of the tobacco industry. Then there are projects like the Youth Action Center,[84] which provides sexual and reproductive health information, important news that affects teens today, and ways for youth to get involved in their communities; Sex Etc.[85] is a Web site organized and run by teens that offers information on sexual health issues for young people; and Teen Wire,[86] a site from Planned Parenthood that provides great information on body basics, how not to have sex if you don't want it, safer sex, and dealing with relationship breakups. It is far more difficult to locate digital media initiatives that are located in the realm of youth who are from underprivileged sectors of society. If this is an indicator of the need to examine such projects as harbingers of youth-driven social change, one project deserves to serve as an exemplar.

In spite of the structural constraints and the disparities in health and technology infrastructures, a growing number of e-health projects involving minority youth demonstrate the opportunity for engaging minority youth and addressing their health disparities online. These projects offer hope as we conceptualize new ways of engaging minority youth in health information seeking and in interrogating the structural injustices in the U.S. health care system. MySistahs[87] has a bold and youthful Web site that makes no bones about proclaiming ownership: "MySistahs is a website created by and for young women of color to provide information and offer support on sexual and reproductive health issues through education and advocacy." This statement, and the banner that covers most of the top half of the Web site's home page, locate the essence of the project—that it addresses health issues of youth of color, and that this Internet project's locus of action lies within the cultural spaces of young women of color. "Who else knows more about us than us" is the catch line that runs across the banner. It also points to education and activism as the prime routes to achieving the objectives of this project. Implicit in these assertions is the notion that participants in this project are aware of their marginalized status in terms of health, and that they realize they can use new media forms like the Internet to influence health and well-being of people like their participant members. Also implicit is the notion that being people of color, and also women of color, does not necessarily mean that they are not capable of harnessing the resources available to them to take care of themselves. The Web site's assertions speak to the contrary—that they can engage with available structural resources to make sense of their needs and frame strategies to take care of these needs. The banner statement, one needs to mention, runs through the entire Web site. The assertions originating on the home page become clearer as one moves on to subsequent pages. For instance, the "About Us" page, where the mission statement is laid out, notes that the project is dedicated to "creating programs and advocating for policies that help young people make informed and responsible decisions about their reproductive and sexual health." It goes on to add that youth are not only part of any problem, but also constitute a part of the solution and should be included in the development of programs and policies that affect their well-being.

The "Features" page has the latest essays on sociocultural issues related to the participant population. The issues range from the influence of mass media on health, to those on activism and "how to make a difference," to self-help guides on how to remain healthy, and to information about young women in hip-hop. This latitude that the "Features" page offers in terms of social and cultural issues essentializes the location of health for underprivileged participants in the realm not of individual behaviors alone, but also within broader sociocultural structures. This is aligned to the arguments that we make in our text that the influence of the Internet on the health of underserved populations should be factored into the creation of communicative structures that locate members of the population at the heart of the discourse. Our argument is echoed in the "Health" page of the Web site. The first paragraph on this page says: "Socioeconomic, cultural, and gender barriers limit the ability of some young women of color to receive information on sexually transmitted infections (STIs), including HIV, access culturally appropriate health care, and reduce sexual risks."

Nested in the Young Women of Color Leadership Council[88] project and under the umbrella of Advocates for Youth,[89] MySistahs' emphasis on building community and its strategy of participant activism is evident too. The "Sistah-to-Sistah" link encourages members of the community to seek the help of peers for support and information—a feature notable in successful health communication initiatives on the ground, like the sex worker–driven Sonagachi HIV/AIDS Intervention Programme (SHIP) in India. Participant-driven health communication empowers members of a marginalized population to participate in the process of sense-making and ensuring better health behaviors for the community. What adds an edge to this call for ground-level activism in MySistahs is the focus on encouraging people to put a face to those names that are already involved as peer educators, thereby encouraging others to join the group.

The "Community" page demonstrates how the project engages in the building of an online community—precious to the operations of an activist organization in a marginalized space. It lists a series of options in this regard: signing up for e-mail newsletters, encouraging political action and organizing by petitioning elected representatives, participating in upcoming events on the ground as well as in the digital space, and searching the database to find local organizations. In this exercise, we see a distinct effort to complement and supplement activist efforts on the Internet with actions on the ground. The resources provided to community members as part of the project cover a range of issues like health, body politics, violence, and lists books, hotlines, and parallel organizations. However, it is worth noting here that most of these links point to projects that have a broader focus. Other than AmbienteJoven, which is a Spanish-language Web site for Latino young men who have sex with men and for Latino/a gay, lesbian, bisexual, transgender, and questioning youth in the United States and Latin America, the other projects appeal to youth in general, and are not focused on youth who are marginalized in terms of health. This is consistent with the argument we made earlier that there is a need for activist projects that involve and focus on health issues of youths in underserved populations.

MySistahs also takes its health activism for the underserved into the realm of politics and public debates related to the framing of health discourse for its user community. The focus is on the fact that policy discourse and maneuvers are as important as ground-level activities to address health disparities based on race, class, gender, and ethnicity. This also foregrounds community-level activism in the digital realm as a critical exercise toward greater equity in health care.

MySistahs' activist emphasis becomes clearer in its "Freedom Corner" section, the purpose of which is to "provide a platform for the creative voices of young women of color." The project staunchly proclaims that it makes central the voices of cultural participants in the framing, design, implementation, and evaluation of programs dedicated to the health of the participants themselves. It is significant to note that this strategy goes against the grain of most health initiatives aimed at underserved populations where the stress in on transmitting messages that are created by people from outside the community. MySistahs is opposed to this logic, and locates its strategies of health and well-being in the agency of its youth members. The testimonials in the "Freedom Corner" provide exemplars of this approach and its validity and effectiveness in addressing health issues among youth of color. Although our example presented here is based ultimately on a single case, it offers new possibilities about ways of engaging minority youth in activist projects that challenge the structural injustices that constrain their lives, and opens up the discursive space to the voices of hitherto marginalized youth instead of the top-down approaches to e-health design based on the agendas of campaign planners.

Conclusion

In conclusion, the integrative model of online health information seeking proposed in this chapter suggests a pathway through which racialized structural disparities presented to the nation's youth are mediated through disparities in individual-level factors such as the motivation and ability to search for health information, and the perceived ability to use communication technologies. From an applied standpoint, the IMOHIS suggests that simply equipping communities, households, and individuals with communication technologies is not enough. Although creating points of access in communities is an important step, it is only a stepping stone toward addressing deeper, structural disparities in online health information usage among the nation's youth. As the research presented in this chapter demonstrates, emphasis needs to be placed on creating sustainable learning opportunities for using digital media technologies, and for seeking out and using health information in underserved communities. Furthermore, efforts of capacity building ought to address the very structures that create and sustain inequitable conditions. Structure-centered approaches to health communication are particularly relevant as such programs directly seek to alter the structures that foster health inequities.[90] Efforts also need to be made to foster learning opportunities in underserved communities. Programs might focus on building health orientation in such communities, and complement such educational programs with structurally supportive components that sustain health orientation in communities. Health and technology literacy programs should be created to teach children the skill sets for using new technologies to fulfill their health needs. Ultimately, this chapter suggests that disparities in technology uses and health information seeking reflect broader structural disparities in society that adversely affect communities of color. These disparities work hand in hand to create, sustain, and reinforce health disparities in underserved communities. Health care activism mobilized online among minority youth offers a space for engaging with these structures and the racialized ills they perpetrate.

Notes

1. The Children's Partnership, *Measuring Digital Opportunity for America's Children: Where We Stand and Where We Go from Here* (Santa Monica, CA: The Children's Partnership, 2005).

2. Amanda Lenhart, Mary Madden, and Paul Hitlin, *Teens and Technology: Youth Are Leading the Transition to a Fully Wired and Mobile Nation* (Washington, DC: Pew Internet & American Life Project, 2005). Retrieved December 15, 2006. http://www.pewinternet.org.

3. Ibid.

4. The Children's Partnership, *Measuring Digital Opportunity*.

5. See http://mysistahs.org. Retrieved January 10, 2007.

6. See U.S. Department of Health and Human Services, *Healthy People 2010*, 2nd ed. (2000). Retrieved September 8, 2006. http://www.healthypeople.gov/Document/tableofcontents.htm#volume1.

7. Barbara J. Guthrie and Lisa Kane Low, Moving beyond the Trickle-down Approach: Addressing the Unique Disparate Health Experiences of Adolescents of Color, *Journal for Specialists in Pediatric Nursing* 11 (2006): 3–13.

8. Claudia Baquet, What Is "Health Disparity"? *Public Health Report* 17 (2002): 426–29.

9. David R. Williams, Race, Socioeconomic Status, and Health: The Added Effects of Racism and Discrimination, *Annals of the New York Academy of Sciences* 896 (1999): 173–88.

10. Institute of Medicine, *Unequal Treatment: Confronting Racial and Ethnic Disparities in Healthcare* (Washington, DC: National Academy Press, 2002).

11. Karen Scott Collins, Dora L. Hughes, Michelle M. Doty, Brett L. Ives, Jennifer N. Edwards, and Katie Tenney, Diverse Communities, Common Concerns: Assessing Health Quality for Minority Americans, in *Commonwealth Fund Health Care Quality Survey* (New York: The Commonwealth Fund, 2002).

12. Nancy Krieger and David R. Williams, Changing to the 2000 Standard Million: Are Declining Racial/Ethnic and Socioeconomic Inequalities in Health Real Progress or Statistical Illusion? *American Journal of Public Health* 91 (2001): 1209–13; Williams, Race, Socioeconomic Status, and Health, 173–88.

13. Sandra A. Black, Laura A. Ray, and Kyriakos S. Markides, The Prevalence and Health Burden of Self-reported Diabetes in Older Mexican Americans: Findings from the Hispanic Established Populations for Epidemiologic Studies of the Elderly, *American Journal of Public Health* 89 (1999): 546–52; Mollyann Brodie, Rebecca E. Flournoy, Drew E. Altman, Robert J. Blendon, John M. Benson, and Marcus D. Rosenbaum, Health Information, the Internet, and the Digital Divide, *Health Affairs* 19 (2000): 255–65; David R. Williams and Chiquita Collins, U.S. Socioeconomic and Racial Differences in Health: Patterns and Explanations, *Annual Review of Sociology* 21 (2001): 349–86.

14. Williams, Race, Socioeconomic Status, and Health.

15. Ibid.

16. Mary Bassett and Nancy Krieger, Social Class and Black-White Differences in Breast Cancer Survival, *American Journal of Public Health* 76 (1986): 1400–03; Robert Feldman and Robinson Fulwood, The Three Leading Causes of Death in African Americans: Barriers to Reducing Excess Disparity and to Improving Health Behaviors, *Journal of Health Care for the Poor and Underserved* 10 (1999): 45–71; James P. Smith and Raynard S. Kington, Race, Socioeconomic Status, and Health in Late Life, in *Racial and Ethnic Differences in the Health of Older Americans*, ed. Linda G. Martin and Beth J. Soldo (Washington, DC: National Academy Press, 1997).

17. Paul W. Newacheck, Sabrina T. Wong, Alison A. Galbraith, and Yun-Yi Hung, Adolescent Health Care Expenditures: A Descriptive Profile, *Health Services Research* 32, no. 6S (2003): 3–11.

18. Agency for Healthcare Research and Quality, *Supporting Research That Improves Health Care for Children and Adolescents*, AHRQ Publication No. 00-P017 (Rockville, MD: Agency for Healthcare Research and Quality, January 2000). Retrieved May 15, 2006. http://www.ahrq.gov/research/childbrf.htm.

19. Tracy A. Lieu, Paul W. Newacheck, and Margaret A. McManus, Race, Ethnicity, and Access to Ambulatory Care among US Adolescents, *American Journal of Public Health* 83 (1993): 960–65.

20. Guthrie and Low, Moving beyond the Trickle-down Approach.

21. Arthur Elster, Julie Jarosik, Jonathan VanGeest, and Missy Fleming, Racial and Ethnic Disparities in Health Care for Adolescents: A Systematic Review of the Literature, *Archives of Pediatric Adolescent Medicine* 157 (2003): 867–74.

22. Guthrie and Low, Moving beyond the Trickle-down Approach.

23. Barbara J. Guthrie, Cleopatra Howard Caldwell, and Andrea G. Hunter, Minority Adolescent Female Health: Strategies for the Next Millennium, in *Health-promoting and Health-compromising Behaviors among Minority Adolescents*, ed. Dawn K. Wilson, James R. Rodrigue, and Wendell C. Taylor (Washington, DC: American Psychological Association, 2000), 153–71.

24. This will be demonstrated through our example of http://www.mysistahs.org.

25. United States National Library of Medicine, *National Library of Medicine Strategic Plan for Addressing Health Disparities 2004-2008* (Bethesda, MD: National Institutes of Health, 2004). Retrieved May 15, 2006. http://www.nlm.nih.gov/pubs/plan/nlm_health_disp_2004_2008.html.

26. Deborah A. Grandinetti, Doctors and the Web: Help Your Patients Surf the Net Safely, *Medical Economics* 63, no. 8 (2000): 28–34.

27. Christine Chan, Maria Bumatay, Weber Shandwick, Suzie Pileggi, and Anthony Loredo, *Health and Finance Sites Capture Fastest-growing Rankings in January* (New York: Nielsen//NetRatings, 2002). Retrieved June 30, 2006. http://www.nielsen-netratings.com/pr/pr020203.pdf.

28. National Telecommunications and Information Administration, *Falling Through the Net: Defining the Digital Divide* (Washington, DC: U.S. Department of Commerce, 2000).

29. David J. Gunkel, Second Thoughts: Toward a Critique of the Digital Divide, *New Media & Society* 5 (2003): 499–522.

30. Stanley J. Czerwinski and Amy D. Abramowitz, Telecommunications: Characteristics and Choices of Internet Users, 2001, Retrieved May 15, 2006. http://www.gao.gov/new.items/d01345.pdf; Joshua Fogel, Steven M. Albert, Freya Schnabel, Beth Ann Ditkoff, and Alfred I. Neugut, Racial/Ethnic Differences and Potential Psychological Benefits in Use of the Internet by Women with Breast Cancer, *Psycho-Oncology* 12 (2003): 107–17; Susannah Fox, *Digital Divisions* (Washington, DC: Pew Internet & American Life Project, 2005).

31. The Children's Partnership, *Measuring Digital Opportunity for America's Children*.

32. Wenhong Chen and Barry Wellman, *Charting and Bridging Digital Divides: Comparing Socio-Economic, Gender, Life Stage, and Rural-Urban Internet Access and Use in Eight Countries* (Sunnyvale, CA: The AMD Global Consumer Advocacy Board, 2003), http://www.amd.com/us-en/assets/content_type/DownloadableAssets/FINAL_REPORT_CHARTING_DIGI_DIVIDES.pdf. Retrieved November 18, 2005.

33. Ibid., 5.

34. Silicon Valley Joint Venture, *Joint Venture's 2002 Workforce Study: Connecting Today's Youth with Tomorrow's Technology Careers* (Santa Clara, CA: Kearney, 2002). Retrieved May 15, 2006. http://www.jointventure.org/PDF/2002workforcestudy.pdf.

35. See also Chen and Wellman, *Charting and Bridging Digital Divides*, 2–4.

36. See, e.g., The Children's Partnership, *Measuring Digital Opportunity for America's Children*.

37. U.S. Department of Commerce, *A Nation Online: Entering the Broadband Age* (Washington, DC: Economics and Statistics Administration and National Telecommunications and Information Administration, 2004). Retrieved November 5, 2005. http://www.ntia.doc.gov/reports/anol/index.html.

38. The Children's Partnership, *Measuring Digital Opportunity for America's Children*.

39. Robert W. Fairlie, Are We Really a Nation Online? Ethnic and Racial Disparities in Access to Technology and Their Consequences, Report for the Leadership Conference on Civil Rights Education Fund, September 2005. Retrieved June 30, 2006. http://www.freepress.net/docs/lccrdigitaldivide.pdf.

40. Linda A. Jackson, Alexander von Eye, Frank A. Biocca, Gretchen Barbatsis, Yong Zhao, and Hiram E. Fitzgerald, Does Home Internet Use Influence the Academic Performance of Low-Income Children? *Developmental Psychology* 42 (2006): 429–35.

41. Linda A. Jackson, Gretchen Barbatsis, Frank A. Biocca, Alexander von Eye, Yong Zhao, and Hiram E. Fitzgerald, Home Internet Use in Low-Income Families: Is Access Enough to Eliminate the Digital Divide? in *Media Access: Social and Psychological Dimensions of New Technology Use*, ed. Erik P. Bucy and John E. Newhagen (Mahwah, NJ: Erlbaum, 2004), 155–84.

42. Tracy A. Lieu, Paula Lozano, Jonathan A. Finkelstein, Felicia W. Chi, Nancy G. Jensvold, Angela M. Capra, Charles P. Quesenberry, Joe V. Selby, and Harold J. Farber, Improving Medication Use Will Reduce Racial/Ethnic Disparities, *Pediatrics* 109 (2002): 857–65; see also Alexander N. Ortega, Peter J. Gergen, David Paltiel, Howard Bauchner, Kathleen D. Belanger, and Brian P. Leaderer, Impact of Site of Care, Race, and Hispanic Ethnicity on Medication Use for Childhood Asthma [electronic version], *Pediatrics* 109, el (2002), retrieved from Medline Database.

43. Mohan Jyoti Dutta-Bergman, Access to the Internet in the Context of Community Participation and Community Satisfaction, *New Media & Society* 17 (2005): 89–109.

44. Black, Ray, and Markides, The Prevalence and Health Burden; Brodie et al., Health Information; and Williams and Collins, US Socioeconomic and Racial Differences in Health.

45. Joy Adamson, Yoav Ben-Shlomo, Nish Chaturvedi, and Jenny Donovan, Ethnicity, Socio-Economic Position and Gender: Do They Affect Reported Health-Care Seeking Behaviour? *Social Science & Medicine* 57 (2003).

46. Mohan Jyoti Dutta-Bergman, A Descriptive Narrative of Healthy Eating: A Social Marketing Approach Using Psychographics, *Health Marketing Quarterly* 20 (2004): 81–101; Mohan Jyoti Dutta-Bergman, Developing a Profile of Consumer Intention to Seek Out Additional Health Information Beyond the Doctor: Demographic, Communicative, and Psychographic Factors, *Health Communication* 17 (2004): 1–16; Mohan Jyoti Dutta-Bergman, Access to the Internet in the Context of Community Participation and Community Satisfaction, *New Media & Society* 17 (2005): 89–109.

47. See, e.g., Joshua Fogel, Internet Use for Cancer Information among Racial/Ethnic Populations and Low Literacy Groups, *Cancer Control* 10, no. 5 (2003): 45–51; and Maria Talosig-Garcia and Sharon W. Davis, Information-seeking Behavior of Minority Breast Cancer Patients: An Exploratory Study, *Journal of Health Communication* 10, Supplement 1 (2005): 53–64.

48. Vicki S. Freimuth, Judith Stein, and Thomas Kean, *Searching for Health Information: The Cancer Information Service Model* (Philadelphia: University of Pennsylvania Press, 1989).

49. Erik P. Bucy and John E. Newhagen, eds., *Media Access: Social and Psychological Dimensions of New Technology Use* (Mahwah, NJ: Erlbaum, 2004).

50. Alicia K. Matthews, Sarah A. Sellergren, Clara Manfredi, and Maryann Williams, Factors Influencing Medical Information Seeking among African American Cancer Patients, *Journal of Health Communication* 7 (2002): 205–19.

51. Mohan Jyoti Dutta-Bergman and Graham D. Bodie, Web Searching for Health: Theoretical Foundations and Connections to Health Related Outcomes, in *Web Searching: Interdisciplinary Perspectives*, eds. Amanda Spink and Michael Zimmer (New York: Springer, in press).

52. Dutta-Bergman, A Descriptive Narrative of Healthy Eating, 81–101.

53. Mohan Jyoti Dutta-Bergman, The Impact of Completeness and Web Use Motivation on the Credibility of e-Health Information, *Journal of Communication* 54 (2004): 253–69.

54. Mohan Jyoti Dutta-Bergman, Developing a Profile of Consumer Intention to Seek Out Additional Health Information Beyond the Doctor,1–16; M. J. Dutta-Bergman, Primary Sources of Health Information: Comparison in the Domain of Health Attitudes, Health Cognitions, and Health Behaviors, *Health Communication* 16 (2004): 273–88; Dutta-Bergman, Access to the Internet.

55. Richard E. Petty and John T. Cacioppo, Communication and Persuasion: Central and Peripheral Routes to Attitude Change (New York: Springer-Verlag, 1986).

56. Mohan Jyoti Dutta-Bergman, Developing a Profile of Consumer Intention to Seek Out Additional Health Information Beyond the Doctor,1–16; Mohan Jyoti Dutta-Bergman, Primary Sources of Health Information, 273–88; Deborah J. MacInnis, Christine Moorman, and Bernard Jaworski, Enhancing and Measuring Consumers' Motivation, Opportunity, and Ability to Process Brand Information from Ads, *Journal of Marketing* 55 (1991): 32–53; Christine Moorman and Erika Matulich, A Model of Consumers' Preventive Health Behaviors: The Role of Health Motivation and Health Ability, *Journal of Consumer Research* 20 (1993): 208–28; C. Whan Park and Banwari Mittal, A Theory of Involvement in Consumer Behavior: Problems and Issues, in *Research in Consumer Behavior*, ed. Jagdish Sheth (Greenwich, CT: JAI, 1985), 201–31.

57. Albert Bandura, Social Cognitive Theory of Mass Communication, in *Media Effects: Advances in Theory and Research*, ed. Jennings Bryant and Dolf Zillman (Mahwah, NJ: Erlbaum, 2002), 121–54.

58. Dutta-Bergman, Media Use Theory.

59. Viviana Rojas, Joseph Straubhaar, Debasmita Roychowdhury, and Ozlem Okur, Communities, Cultural Capital, and the Digital Divide, in *Media Access: Social and Psychological Dimensions of New Technology Use*, ed. Erik P. Bucy and John E. Newhagen (Mahwah, NJ: Erlbaum, 2004), 107–30.

60. Ibid.

61. Randal Pinkett, Bridging the Digital Divide: Sociocultural Constructionism and an Asset-based Approach to Community Technology and Community Building (paper presented at the 81st annual meeting of the American Educational Research Association, 2000, New Orleans, LA). Retrieved January 10, 2007. http://llk.media.mit.edu/papers/aera2000.pdf.

62. Ibid., 1.

63. Monica Murero and Ronald E. Rice, *The Internet and Health Care: Theory, Research, and Practice* (Mahwah, NJ: Erlbaum, 2006).

64. Dutta-Bergman, Media Use Theory.

65. Rebecca J. Cline and K. M. Haynes, Consumer Health Information Seeking on the Internet: The State of the Art, *Health Education Research* 16 (2001): 671–92; and Dutta-Bergman, Media Use Theory.

66. Dutta-Bergman, A Descriptive Narrative.

67. Dutta-Bergman, Media Use Theory.

68. Thomas R. Eng, Andrew Maxfield, Kevin Patrick, Mary Jo Deering, Scott C. Ratzan, and David H. Gustafson, Access to Health Information and Support: A Public Highway or Private Road? *Journal of the American Medical Association* 280 (1998): 1371–75.

69. Ronald Rice, The Internet and Health Communication: A Framework of Experiences, in *The Internet and Health Communication*, ed. R. E. Rice and J. Katz (Thousand Oaks, CA: Sage, 2001), 5–46.

70. Kasisomayajula Viswanath and John R. Finnegan, The Knowledge Gap Hypothesis: Twenty-Five Years Later, in *Communication Yearbook 19*, ed. B. R. Burleson (Thousand Oaks, CA: Sage, 1995).

71. Mohan Jyoti Dutta-Bergman, Health Attitudes, Health Cognitions and Health Behaviors among Internet Health Information Seekers: Population-Based Survey, *Journal of Medical Internet Research* 6, no. e15 (2004). Retrieved November 18, 2005. http://www.jmir.org/2004/2/e15/index.htm; Dutta-Bergman, A Descriptive Narrative; David J. Johnson and Hendrika Meischke, A Comprehensive Model of Cancer-related Information Seeking Applied to Magazines, *Human Communication Research* 19 (1993): 343–67.

72. Dutta-Bergman, Health Attitudes.

73. Freimuth, Stein, and Kean, Searching for Health Information.

74. Eng et al., Access to Health Information.

75. Laura Breeden, Steve Cisler, Vivian Guilfoy, Michael Roberts, and Antonia Stone, *Computer and Communications Use in Low-Income Communities: Models for the Neighborhood Transformation and Family Development Initiative* (Baltimore, MD: Annie E. Casey Foundation, 1998).

76. Peter Salovey, Linda Mowad, Judith Pizarro, Denielle Edlund, and Marta E. Moret, Developing Computer Proficiency among Head Start Parents: An In-Progress Case Study of a New England CIS Digital Divide Project, *Electronic Journal of Communication* 11, no. 3 (2002). Retrieved May 15, 2006. http://www.cios.org/getfile/salovey_v11n3.

77. Barbara K. Rimer and Bernard Glassman, Tailoring Communication for Primary Care Settings, *Methods of Information in Medicine* 37 (1998): 1610–11.

78. Dutta-Bergman, Health Attitudes.

79. Anna Everett, The Revolution Will Be Digitized: Afrocentricity and the Digital Public Sphere, *Social Text 71* 20, no. 7 (2002): 125–146.

80. Dutta-Bergman, Media Use Theory.

81. Mohan Dutta-Bergman, Health Communication on the Web: The Roles of Web Use Motivation and Information Completeness, *Communication Monographs* 70 (2003): 264–274; Mohan Dutta-Bergman, Trusted Online Sources of Health Information: Differences in Demographics, Health Beliefs, and Health-Information Orientation, *Journal of Medical Internet Research* 5, e21, Retrieved June 2, 2004. http://www.jmir.org; Dutta-Bergman, The Impact of Completeness; G. Eysenbach, Consumer Health Informatics, *British Medical Journal* 24 (2000): 1713–1716; Rice, The Internet and Health Communication.

82. Dutta-Bergman, Media Use Theory.

83. Ibid.

84. See http://www.advocatesforyouth.org/youth/index.htm. Retrieved January 10, 2006.

85. See http://www.sxetc.org. Retrieved January 10, 2006.

86. See http://www.teenwire.com. Retrieved January 10, 2006.

87. See http://mysistahs.org. Retrieved January 10, 2006.

88. See http://www.advocatesforyouth.org/about/ywoclc.htm. Retrieved January 10, 2006.

89. See http://www.advocatesforyouth.org/index.htm. Retrieved January 10, 2006.

90. Dutta-Bergman, Primary Sources of Health Information.